MW01599301

SPEECHES THAT SHAPED NEW ZEALAND 1814–1956

HUGH TEMPLETON
IAN TEMPLETON & JOSH EASBY

Hurricane Press
books that blow you away

First published in 2014 by Hurricane Press Ltd
PO Box 568, Cambridge 3450, New Zealand
www.hurricane–press.co.nz

Cover photograph: Portait of Tamati Waka Nene by Gottfried Lindauer, from The Bridgeman Art Library. Image provided by Getty Images.

Cover design: Pieta Brenton.

National Library of New Zealand Cataloguing–in–Publication Data

Speeches that shaped New Zealand : 1814–1956 / by
Hugh Templeton, Ian Templeton & Josh Easby.
Includes bibliographical references.
ISBN 978–0–9876636–0–3
1. Speeches, addresses, etc. 2. New Zealand—History.
I. Templeton, Hugh, 1929– II. Templeton, Ian, 1929–
III. Easby, Josh, 1954–
NZ825.008—dc 23

Printed in China through Asia Pacific Offset Limited.

Foreword

All things living are in search of a better world.
— Philosopher Karl Popper (1902–1994)

The most significant events in history can often be explained in the words of a single speech. We learn much about Britain's bulldog spirit in World War Two from Winston Churchill's 'we shall fight on the beaches' rallying cry in June 1940.

The struggle for racial equality in the United States is etched into our collective consciousness by the stirring words of Dr Martin Luther King's 'I have a dream' speech from 1963.

We've been inspired by John F. Kennedy's 1961 inaugural speech in which he asked Americans to 'ask not what your country can do for you — ask what you can do for your country.'

Our young learn about these and other great speeches as they study the history of the world. But what of the role of oratory in New Zealand's own history, and development as a nation?

Sadly, speeches have rarely been used as landmarks in the telling of our own nation's story.

It's not that such speeches do not exist, nor do we imply any reluctance in the classroom or lecture hall to discuss them. Until now, there hasn't been a single published collection of New Zealand speeches that covers lengthy periods of our history.

3

We have set out to address that, bringing together key speeches that add colour and essence to the shaping of our nation. You'll be able to experience moments in history through the words of those at the forefront of critical events.

In compiling this collection of speeches, we faced some difficult choices. Often, the speaker had made many speeches — so which should we choose? Would we include or exclude based on the significance of the person and the event, or on the quality of their oratory? In the end, we selected the speeches we thought would best help understanding of a period in our history. Some are short and stirring. Others are longer but filled with important content. All played their part in the way we are today.

We chose to end this first collection in 1956, as that marked the period when the British Empire came to an end and New Zealand learned to stand alone as a nation. The story of the speeches that shaped our future post–1956 will be kept for another volume.

As curators of these speeches, we have taken some liberties on your behalf. Where the speech was particularly long, or dealt with multiple subjects, we have abridged it. In a few cases, when we have been unable to find the word–for–word transcript of a speech, we have converted indirect speech (from reports of the day) into direct speech. These instances are explained in the text. With honorifics and titles, we have generally referred to the speaker by their status at the time of their speech.

Our research for this book has taken considerable time and effort but would have been impossible without the work of many historians, scholars and transcribers who discovered speeches ahead of us. We owe a debt of gratitude to those who work for our libraries, long–established newspapers and other media, who continue to ensure we have access to our past. We also acknowledge the fine work by those involved in archiving projects, such as the Papers Past project at the National Library.

Despite our endeavours, we know others will find significant speeches we have missed. Where possible, we'll add them to future revisions of our work and we urge you to contact our publisher if you believe you've found such a speech.

— *Hugh Templeton, Ian Templeton & Josh Easby*

The Speeches

Author's Note

When reading the speeches in this volume, it may be helpful for your to understand some of the decisions made during the editing process.

As much as possible, we have tried to convey the spirit of the original speech, as well as its contents. To do this, we have resisted the temptation to edit the language of the day to what is generally more acceptable today.

A good example is the pluralisation of Maori. When most of these speeches were made, and reported, it was common to refer to 'Maoris'. We have deliberately not corrected these to Maori which is now the accepted plural.

In other instances, speakers have used phrases popular in the day and we discovered different spellings over time (an example is 'by and by', and 'bye and by'). Rather than force conformity, we again decided that language and spelling changes with time and we should try to reflect the words used and reported at the time.

Space restrictions forced us to abridge some speeches. In some instances, we could not find a verbatim report of the entire speech so took the liberty of converting indirect reporting to direct speech. Where we have done this, we have said so in the prelude to the speech.

For one speech — the subject of our opening chapter — we could find no verbatim record of the words used by the Reverend Samuel Marsden so Hugh Templeton used his knowledge of the period to construct what he believes is a fair representation of Marsden's sermonising.

— *Hugh Templeton, Ian Templeton & Josh Easby*

In the Eye of the Needle

Reverend Samuel Marsden

December 25, 1814

The Reverend Samuel Marsden was an English–born Anglican cleric who lived in Australia from 1794 until his death. After becoming the senior Anglican minister in New South Wales in 1800, Marsden sought to lead a group from the Church Missionary Society to New Zealand, aiming to introduce the country to Christianity.

In 1814, Marsden sailed his schooner, the *Active*, to the Bay of Islands, accompanied by chiefs from the Ngapuhi iwi including Ruatara and the war leader Hongi Hika who helped pioneer the use of the musket by Maori warriors. Historians speculate that the ship carried muskets to New Zealand and its arrival fuelled the musket trade into the North.

Marsden laid claim to conducting the first Christian service in New Zealand.

On Christmas Day 1814, Marsden took the healing evangelist's lead text of *Glad Tidings* for his sermon at the Bay of Islands. The Church had been one of the key players in the formation of the British State.

So Marsden's sermon heralded the future State of New Zealand. It gave the cleric the privilege of making the first significant speech in English in New Zealand. We might claim his sermon as the start point of a new state yet to be born. St Luke's text itself provides modern New Zealanders with

Reverend Samuel Marsden (1764–1838)

a high minded foundation for Imperial Britain's reluctant acquisition in 1840 of sovereignty.

The importance of Marsden's sermon lies in its start point.

In the absence of any text, the editors have taken the liberty of drafting a brief sermon representative of those of the day and consistent with what a politique priest might have delivered to those early residents of the Bay of Islands.

'Behold I bring you glad tidings of great Joy'
— St Luke

Your great chiefs have led me here carrying glad tidings, bearing Good News.
I have been sent here with your Chiefs to bring you that Good News.
My Good News is news of the greatest of all chiefs whom I serve.

My service is to the Son of God:
The Son of the Creator of Earth and Sea and Sky,
The Creator of all things living.

Your Chiefs have led us here across the sea on our ship.
Long ago a Star led wise men across the Desert to a Village like yours in a Holy Land.
You have your wise men.
Those wise men of long ago had heard that a great leader was to be born.
That great leader was to bring —
~ great joy and peace to the world,
~great comfort to men and women.

So they traveled a long distance as we have ...
Like us they brought gifts to present to the new Chief ...
They talked to the chiefs of the Land ...
They presented the newborn chief with gifts!

So we will ... to your Chiefs ... Gifts —
~Axes and Nails, Blankets and Muskets,
~But above all the Book of God — the Bible

These gifts are a sign of a holy commitment ...
A commitment to bring you the Good News.
The Good News of the Holy One,
Of the Son of the Maker of Heaven and Earth ...

Here ... to you ... in this beautiful land.

This is the promise my authority ...
My authority as a Chief — of our God and of his Son — lets me make.
You too are children of our Almighty God, Father and Son.

This is why I have come here to these shores, to your land.
This is why I will send my shepherds to teach and baptise you.

This is the good news I bring you of a richer life, of a fuller life, of a life of joy and peace, of Life Everlasting.

Did Marsden, the Good Shepherd, arrive with muskets in the hold of the *Active*? That would have made him more of a Pharisee than a Good Shepherd, a temporal rather than a spiritual Priest. Whether or not he was the initial arms dealer for the ruinous Musket Wars, Marsden died a rich man. Chief Ruatara's interest in encouraging Marsden to visit New Zealand appears to have been in securing muskets, but the voyage did let Marsden establish a bridgehead for the Church. It was the first of seven visits Marsden made to New Zealand — including one in 1819 which introduced wine to the country through the planting of 100 vines at Kerikeri — and his influence cannot be underestimated.

History would hold few more pungent ironies than muskets underwriting his fine Lucian text. The saving grace would lie with the CMS missionaries who in 1840 ensured that the Treaty of Waitangi helped secure a partnership of two peoples in the one nation being born.

Lawless and Degraded

Francis Baring

June 19, 1838

In 1837, a group of influential politicians in London formed a plan to convince their Government to allow them to colonise New Zealand through the formation of a body called the New Zealand Association.

Accounts of its formation suggest the driving influence was Edward Gibbon Wakefield who was following up the suggestions of the third Baron of Ashburton, Francis Baring, who was the MP for Thetford in the House of Commons. Baring agreed to be the association's leader and its members included Lord Durham, Sir William Molesworth MP and Sir William Hutt MP.

Lord Durham said the participants in the association would 'neither run any pecuniary risk, nor reap any pecuniary advantage from the undertaking.' Despite those assurances, their plan sparked immediate opposition, most openly from church missionaries. Dandeson Coates, of the Church Missionary Society, told the group 'though he had no doubt of their respectability and the purity of their motives, he was opposed to the colonisation of New Zealand in any shape, and was determined to thwart them by all the means in his power.' Behind the scenes, a pamphlet headed 'Confidential' was circulated to government ministers, including the Colonial Minister, claiming the association's members were motivated by monetary gain.

The association, which had at first thought it had the support of the House, was forced to appeal to Parliament, unsure whether it would see the passing of a bill 'for the Provisional Government of British Settlements in the Islands of New Zealand.'

On June 19, 1838, it fell to Baring to move the second reading of the bill.

It is now nearly two years since a number of gentlemen, encouraged by the increasing interest which the public took in the matter, and by the knowledge of circumstances which had come under their observation, formed themselves into an association for the purpose of establishing a British colony in New Zealand. They had assembled a large mass of oral and documentary evidence upon the subject.

They had sought the evidence of all those whose opinion was worth consulting, either from local knowledge or from connection in any way with the distant countries into which they were anxious to introduce our religion, our customs, and our laws; and the result they arrived at was, that it was not only expedient as far as the interest of their own country is concerned that their intention should be persisted in, but that they owed it to the natives as a correction of the evils which their communication with us had already entailed upon them.

They found that these islands which, according to the principles followed by other countries, had been acquired by the British Crown by those forms of taking possession which have ever been allowed to constitute a claim against other civilised nations, were situated in a temperate latitude, with a soil of remarkable fertility, a climate perfectly suited to the constitutions of English emigrants, and productions not only of great value commercially, but of especial importance as rendering us independent of other countries for some of the most important of their productions.

They found that their position rendered them of so much importance to our growing settlements in Australia, that the possession of them by any foreign power would endanger the stability of our empire in that part

14

of the world; and above all, their researches led them to the conviction that there had arisen, from the settlement on the islands of a lawless and degraded population, an obstacle to any moral improvement in the natives, which was every year assuming a more serious aspect, and which a very short delay might make it impossible to remove.

They trusted to this latter circumstance for the obtaining the sanction of the missionary body; and they confided in the anxiety for the material welfare of the country which government is supposed to entertain, for the ensuring their support to a plan in the success of which they conceived that the stability of our dominions in those seas was involved. They accordingly brought in a bill.

To this bill there arose an opposition from a quarter whence we least expected it. It commenced by a series of pamphlets circulated in the dark by the secretary of the Christian Missionary Society, in which our motives were impugned, and the existence questioned of all those feelings by which honourable men should be influenced.

It was announced that we were recurring to the old pretence of civilisation and advancement of religion, while there was upon the face of our plan sufficient indication of a design to repeat at the expense of the natives that oppression, and those excesses of arbitrary power, which at all times, and in all other countries, had marked the progress of the European invader, and even degraded the name of civilisation: that the sovereignty of the native tribes, which was inherent in them, and, if it wanted confirmation, had been assured by a formal recognition by the British resident, was to be called in question: that we were an association of jobbers, whose only object was trading in land, — which all their accounts represented as impossible to be obtained; and that we should be the means of impeding the great work of religion, and civilisation, which, under the superintendence of the missionary body, was rapidly and unfailingly going on.

We could not but suppose that when our motives were explained, and the object of our bill fully made known, this opposition founded, as we then supposed it to be, solely upon motives of sympathy for the natives, and alarm on the part of those who had constituted themselves their natural guardians, would give way before a calm examination of the provisions of the bill. We were conscious of having given every protection in our power to the tribes — of having fenced and guarded their interest with a minuteness of jealous care which in some measure complicated our bill, and encumbered it with provisions which constituted almost the only difficulty of execution.

But when we found every overture rejected, we did begin to suspect the existence of some motives beyond those which Mr Coates had thought expedient to avow. Sir, those suspicions have been more than confirmed.

Upon a close and searching inquiry, we became convinced that it was less from a desire to expose our motives than to conceal their own; not so much a desire to protect the New Zealander from excess of power on our part, as to maintain the influence which, from motives which appear rather less than spiritual, they had been engaged in founding, that they had raised an opposition which in its tone and language is little in accordance, with those doctrines of justice and charity which, they so loudly profess.

Sir, some curious facts have come out in the course of this inquiry. The difficulty of obtaining land has been 'solved by the missionaries themselves.'

Baring then produced examples of land purchases by members of the Church Missionary Society which, he claimed, had been bought on their own account and were being farmed by the buyers.

Is it to be supposed that the worldly circumstances have no influence over the state of things spiritual? Do we not know that the churches are more deserted, that the schools are less earnestly supported?

I might make statements upon this subject with less hazard than Mr Coates incurred when he collected imputations against the motives of the association with which I am connected; and I say so with less hesitation, for I should not want facts or testimony to support them. But, Sir, is there nothing to alter Mr Coates's views, in the evidence as to the state of the country, which is contained in the dispatches lately received from Mr Busby, the British resident, and Captain Hobson, who was sent by

16

the Governor of New South Wales on a special mission to report on the spot?

His well–known connection with some of the persons employed in the Colonial Office leads me to suppose it to be difficult that he should not have been cognisant of some of those dispatches even before he made his first statement; but I will allow him, for the sake of his character for sincerity, the benefit of ignorance on this occasion.

But what is the state of society which has grown up under the mild government of the mission? Are not wars, murders, and every possible excess rife in all parts of the island? Have they succeeded in putting an end to the system of slavery which everywhere exists; have they ventured to attempt it; are they in a position to counteract the gangrenous influences of the society of runaway sailors and escaped convicts, which is daily augmenting in a frightful proportion; can they oppose any barrier to the vicious example against which their precepts must struggle in vain, or set any bounds to the profligacy and excesses which are introducing disease and premature mortality into all the districts with which they are in contact?

Are we not aware, Sir, that all the great religious reformers among barbarous nations have established their creeds by connecting its precepts with the material prosperity of those whom they wished to influence; and, in some cases, by making articles of faith many of those regulations rendered necessary by the habits, prejudices, and even the climate of the country to which they are adapted, and which with our purer religion and more rational morality we should leave to be provided for by human institutions?

Can they suppose that these poor savages will not connect the evil doings of these supposed adherents of the new religion with the tenets of their religion, and that in many cases the example will not be more powerful than the precept? I am not blind to the sacrifices and exertions of the missionary body; no one is more ready to acknowledge them. Whatever good is achieved in these islands, they will have been the primary cause of; and the best proof I can give of good feeling towards them, is my readiness to separate them from the person who has constituted himself their organ here, to attribute to them purer motives and a more disinterested zeal.

But the time has come when their exertions can no longer singly avail; and we had hoped that in the plan we had produced they would have found the best co-operation with their labours, and the surest corrective of the evils against which, unaided, they cannot struggle, in the example of a moral and well-ordered community.

Baring then described negotiations that had taken place with the government over the previous year. He indicated support for the project had been offered, then thwarted, until the government had insisted on a condition he knew could not be complied with — namely, turning the association into a joint–stock company. Baring said the principle on which it was proposed to colonise New Zealand could not be successfully achieved by a trading company whose first objective must be the buying and selling of land to make profit.

Having made this statement of what passed between her Majesty's government and the association, I am led to inquire what remedy or what palliative will this government of expedients be induced to adopt? I can hardly think that the native congress, recommended by Mr Busby, with the adoption of collateral measures, such as the establishments of courts, etc. — none of which can be admitted without assuming the sovereignty they affect to disclaim — can be in their contemplation.

They must know that no number of Europeans are likely to submit to a legislative assembly at Waimate; and that by the time the missionaries have made the first step in their constitutional education, half the population will have disappeared, and the white invader will have increased twenty–fold. If they mean to plant factories, at the bottom of every bay where Europeans resort, I would ask them to estimate the probable consequence of small communities: without commerce, without combined labour, arts, institutions, and religion, being grouped round twenty isolated points in the two islands

Let them look to Swan River and the expense — I believe nearly 30,000 (pounds) — which that settlement of fifteen hundred persons entails upon the country; to the chances of collisions with the natives, which weak and ill-ordered communities only serve to invite; to the

18

irregular purchase and disposal of lands; and to the thousand evils consequent upon, their dissemination. It may be objected to us, that the same difficulties will attend our enterprise; and that small communities would spring up which we could not control.

Our answer is simple. Such communities would not be established. In the formation of a great European society, we should have all the advantages of high wages, increasing value of property and, above all, protection to those who joined it. Commerce would centre at the point where supply and consumption are most certain; and there would be no inducement to anyone to resign the certain advantages of a civilised and growing community, to seek a dangerous and precarious livelihood where there could be no security of obtaining the commonest necessaries of life.

Sir, I appeal to the House against the decision of her Majesty's ministers, with a full hope that we shall not appeal in vain in favour of a project fraught with advantages so important and so certain to the empire at large.

The bill itself included clauses which would bestow the association's appointed commissioners with the power to deal with Maori chiefs who were theoretically the sovereign power in New Zealand. Under the bill, the association would become the only body with the right to form settlements, negotiate treaties with the Maori and to acquire sovereign rights for the Crown over large areas in which Maori lived. In an apparent sop to the missionaries, Maori living in those areas would be given the same rights as settlers.

By the time, Baring tried to convince his fellow MPs to support the bill, Wakefield and Lord Durham had left England for Canada. His speech forced Lord Howick, one of those named as having encouraged and then opposed the scheme on behalf of the government, to defend himself against the charge he had misled the association.

In his journal, Lord Howick recorded that Baring's speech was followed by a lengthy debate in which all members of the government were united.

'We in the end threw out the most monstrous proposition I ever knew made to the House by a vote of 92 to 30,' he wrote.

The defeat in the House led to the dissolution of the Association but some of its members, including Wakefield and Baring, formed the New Zealand Colonisation Company. By the spring of 1839, that company had raised sufficient funds to launch an expedition to buy land in New Zealand and ready for the first wave of emigrants.

While Baring's role in this critical stage of New Zealand's history is often passed over, the residents of Ashburton live in the town named after the third Baron of Ashburton.

Birth of a Nation

Tamati Waka Nene

February 5, 1840

The birth of nation, history teaches, is a not unusual occurrence. In 1840 New Zealand came into being in as messy a way as any natural birth. There were pauses and shifts and then, out of the blue, a sudden decision to get it done with.

Over three days of summer, Northern Maori chiefs and British Naval Captain William Hobson, who had won a reputation for his dealing with Maori in 1837, signed up to the Treaty of Waitangi.

Claudia Orange tells the story in her 1987 book *The Treaty of Waitangi*.[1] Captain Hobson, having 'asserted Crown authority over British subjects turned to treat with the Maori.' On February 3 or 4, Britain's appointed diplomat in New Zealand, James Busby, 'submitted his draft to Hobson'. On February 4, missionary Henry Williams rendered the English draft into the Maori language.

February 5 was a glorious summer day. In a gala atmosphere, on a green lawn buzzing with cicadas, Hobson held a levee. It was a memorable scene[2]. Hobson spoke and Williams read the Maori text. For some five

1 *The Treaty of Waitangi (Allen & Unwin), by Claudia Orange, 1987. Also available, The Treaty of Waitangi, 2nd edition (Bridget Williams Books), 2011.*
2 *A brilliant first hand account — 'The Authentic and Genuine History of the Signing of the Treaty of Waitangi February 5 and 6, 1840, by (the polymathic) W. Colenso, FRS' — remains a basic text for*

Tamati Waka Nene (1785–1871)

hours the chiefs debated the Treaty proposal.

Their focus was the land and 'the erosion of authority by sharing power with the British Government ... this country is ours ... we are the Governor ... we the chiefs of this our father's land.'

The tide of opposition was running against Hobson. He was losing the debate. Then the chief Hone Heke[3] spoke.

Maori were uncertain of the future and inexperienced, like children they

---

the history and interpretation of the Treaty of Waitangi.
3 Freda Rankin Kawharu. 'Ngapua, Hone Heke — Biography', from the Dictionary of New Zealand Biography. Te Ara — the Encyclopedia of New Zealand.

22

had to rely on the direction of their missionaries, their 'fathers'. But it was the next speaker who turned the tide.

Tamati Waka Nene[4] tutoyed his fellow chiefs. In the English précis[5] this master orator slashed off the blinkers of the blind.

Imagine the great chief of the glorious Hokianga, whence Kupe had sailed home, moving to and fro, fronting each dissident group. These were the realities.

> *Some of you tell Hobson to go!*
> *But that's not going to solve our difficulties.*
> *We have already sold so much of our land in the north. We have no way of controlling the Europeans who have settled on it.*
> *I'm amazed to hear you telling him to go!*
> *Why didn't you tell the traders and grog-sellers to go years ago?*
> *There are too many Europeans here now.*
> *And there are children that unite both our races.*

Waka Nene then turned to the glum Governor, who may not have been too well anyway (Hobson was soon to be felled by a stroke and die in 1842) to state the imperative. A brutish, tribal society, of ceaseless conflict, required a civil society under a sovereign law.

Just three sentences made the case.

> *Don't be too concerned with what these others are saying.*
> *We need you as a father ... a judge ... a peacemaker ... and as a Governor.*
> *You must preserve our customs, and never permit our lands to be taken from us.*[6]

Then, like any good duelist, Waka Nene, had his elder brother Patuone second his case. After much discussion overnight, on February 6, and much to his surprise, Hobson found himself called from his ship to sign

4 *Angela Ballara. 'Nene, Tamati Waka — Biography', from the Dictionary of New Zealand Biography. Te Ara — the Encyclopedia of New Zealand.*
5 *Published by The Listener, February 2011.*
6 *Published by The Listener, February 2011.*

the Treaty. In the flurry and without any further explanation he proclaimed at each signature 'We are now one people.' And he should have added 'of two races.'

Like the Squire after a village cricket match, Captain Hobson, having again proven the 'discretion and sound judgement' of which his superiors spoke, retired with a Captain of the other side, Patuone, to the *Herald* to dine.

As with cricket, first played at the Bay of Islands, when the *Beagle* was there with Darwin in 1837, the gathering at Waitangi left ample room for future match–ups.

In those tests we have to accept the lack of any absolute truth about the Treaty, save the establishment of British sovereignty[7]. That left Parliament the task of maintaining the Treaty's core liberal values of liberty and equality while absorbing any reactionary Maori nationalism into an emerging multi–cultural nation.

---

7 *Hon. Peter Tapsell, a Minister of the Crown in the Lange administration, and later Speaker of Parliament, held that Maori gave away sovereignty — absolute power — over New Zealand to the Crown, page 67 'Maori Sovereignty, the Maori Perspective', Hineani Melbourne (Hodder Moa Beckett, 1995).*

In Search of Self–rule

John Robert Godley

November 15, 1850

One of the ablest founding fathers of New Zealand was an Anglo Irish Oxford graduate and lawyer, John Robert Godley.[8] His experience in America, Canada and Ireland, and proposals for colonisation, brought him to the attention of Gibbon Wakefield and to the leading role in founding the Canterbury settlement in 1950.

His most important decision in his short, vigorous administration — to extend pastoral leases — allowed the break out from the narrow boundaries of the Christchurch settlement. On governance, his was one of the most authoritative voices calling for settler control of their affairs. In this, he clashed with Governor Grey. Settlers, he proclaimed, deserved not just representative but responsible government.

This case he made to a Settlers' Constitutional Association meeting discussing Grey's proposed Constitution Bill in Wellington on November 15, 1850. Godley may have had the reputation for being a dry speaker, but he made his point emphatically:

I would rather be governed by a Nero on the spot than a board of Angels in London.

8 Gerald Hensley. 'Godley, John Robert — Biography', from the Dictionary of New Zealand Biography. Te Ara — the Encyclopedia of New Zealand.

25

So he helped lay the ground for his original mentor, Wakefield, later to carry the cause of responsible government. Godley's speech to the Wellington meeting:[9]

Sir, although incapable of addressing you for more than a very few minutes, I cannot resist the temptation of this opportunity to express my sentiments on the important question now offered for your consideration. And in doing so, I am above all things anxious to impress upon you the recollection, that the words and actions of this meeting will inevitably form the subject of careful attention and criticism at home, that, if they be wise and worthy, they will support and strengthen the hands of those who are struggling for your rights in Parliament to an extent which can hardly be over stated, whereas, if you betray either feebleness or irresolution on the one hand, or want of calmness, temper, and moderation on the other, you may be very certain that your errors will be promptly taken advantage of, and that in answer to your claims and prayers you will have the old sneer at the unfitness for self–government which you show in your efforts to attain it.

The business before you today is to pronounce your opinion on the Bill which Sir George Grey offers for your acceptance: now, before you do so, and in order that you may do so with justice and effect, I want you to ask yourselves what this great political object is that you have been striving after, for many long and anxious years, and of which this measure professes to be the realisation.

There are some who will tell you that it is 'representative institutions,' for it is the fashion to say that all colonial reformers want 'representative institutions.' If this be so, then I admit that the Bill ought to satisfy you, for it certainly gives you, in a measure, and after a sort, representative institutions.

But I deny that representative institutions are what we have striven and prayed for; we have representative institutions enough already, and can make as many more as we like; this meeting is a representative institution, as soon as we have elected a chairman; but the next question is, what we can do with them when we have them. There is no magic in

---

9 *Nelson Examiner and New Zealand Chronicle, December 7, 1850.*

John Robert Godley (1814–1861)

the word 'representative'; no people was ever redeemed or regenerated by the mere election of delegates.

No, Sir, the object which the colonists of New Zealand have given their energies to obtain, and which they will obtain, if they be true to themselves, is something very different from the mere form of a constitution; it is the substance which all such forms are but methods of exercising; in a word, it is political power; the power of virtually administering their own affairs, appointing their own officers, disposing of their own revenues, and governing their own country.

Compared with this object, all questions which concern the allocation of power among different classes of colonists, fade into utter insignificance, whatever importance they may assume at the proper time and proper place.

Such questions will be settled among ourselves, when we shall have got the power of governing ourselves. Do not weaken your collective influence by disputing about them now. The contest in which we are now engaged, and which requires our undivided energies to conduct it successfully, is with the central authority of Downing Street, whether exercised through the medium of Governors, or of Nominees, or of Colonial Office instructions.

Let us finish that before we begin to quarrel, as of course we shall quarrel like other people, among ourselves, as soon as we have got substantial power to quarrel about. But never forget that the end we aim at is the power of self-government; representative institutions are merely the most convenient and desirable means of exercising it. To give us representative institutions without full powers is worse than a mockery and a delusion: it is a careful and deliberate provision for keeping the machine of government at a perpetual deadlock; or if that be avoided through the weakness of the Assembly, for constituting a political debating club of the worst kind, and investing it with the dignity and the claims of a National Legislature.

I have insisted thus strongly upon this preliminary point, because it is clear to me that, if it were not for this juggle and word-play about representative institutions, nobody could have seriously proposed that you should accept such a measure as this of Sir George Grey's as the charter of your liberties. It is a measure for constituting Provincial debating-clubs; that is all.

The resolution I am about to propose asks you to reject the Bill, because it does not give you the management of your own affairs: this is the ground upon which I trust that you will adopt it Those who come after me will examine, more at length than I have physical power to do, the provisions of the Bill, and will show you its short-comings in detail. I will content myself with stating that it withholds from you the disposal of the greater part of the revenue, and consequently of all practical control over the Executive; that it compels you to conform your legislation to Colonial Office instructions; that it contains that ridiculous and inexplicable provision against making any law repugnant to the law of England; that it makes the pernicious element of nomineeism part and parcel of your Constitution; and that, besides all this, it gives a veto upon all local legislation to a Governor not responsible to yourselves.

If you think that the privilege of electing representatives to do nothing be sufficient to compensate for such defects as these; if your ambition be to enjoy the name of a constitutional country, while the real power of governing you resides 16,000 miles off, then, I say, throw up your hats, and cheer for the Constitution.

But if you think with me, that this Bill will be merely a stumbling block and an obstacle in your way; if you believe as I do, that by accepting and sanctioning it, you will debar yourselves for an indefinite time from getting anything better; that you will compromise every principle that you have been asserting, and make it evident to friends and foes that you have been fighting for names, and not for realities — above all, if you feel convinced, as I do, that if you refuse to be put off with the shadow, you will assuredly get the substance, then I ask you to assert those sentiments and views by an emphatic condemnation of the Bill.

I do not blame Sir George Grey for offering it; I believe that he is bonâ fide anxious to make every possible concession to you, and indeed that he believes he has already done so; but the fact is, that he has not the power of giving you a good Constitution, if he were ever so well disposed; he is fettered by Acts of Parliament and Instructions, which only fresh Acts and fresh Instructions can revoke. He has no power to give up the veto, no power to give you what is called Responsible Government, that is, the virtual administration of your own affairs.

Now, we want no provisional relaxation of arbitrary power, depending on the casual favour of the men who may happen to exercise it; we want the sanction of irrevocable laws for our own rights, and this we can only get from the fountain of law for the British Empire — the Imperial Parliament.

Never forget, that the battle of our Constitution must be fought in London; it is by the influence which we can exercise, or the trouble we can give there alone, that we can hope to obtain our local independence; it is because as yet not one of the Australian colonies has taken a stand which entitles and enables it to be heard in London, that not one of them has got local independence yet. I trust that we shall set a brighter example; I trust that we shall show New Zealand standing pre-eminent and alone among the colonies of England, proclaiming that her people will have nothing to do with counterfeits or half measures; that they will have things in New Zealand called by their proper names — real despotism or real liberty.

For my own part, I would far rather live under the avowed despotism of one able and energetic man, acting on his own responsibility, according to his own pleasure than under such a regimen as it is the fashion in Downing Street to call constitutional and representative; a regimen in which the people exercise no real power, and the Government incurs no effective responsibility; in which the utmost privilege granted to the colonists is that of obstructing the action of their own Government, and in which the right of perpetual agitation is dignified with the name of freedom.

Godley then proposed a resolution:

That the constitutional measure which Sir George Grey is understood to be about to offer to the colonists, and which has been already published by him in the shape of a draft Ordinance, does not deserve their approval or acceptance, inasmuch as it does not confer upon them an effectual control over the management of their own affairs. That the apparent liberality of its provisions with respect to the election and duration of Assemblies, is rendered completely nugatory by the limitations imposed upon their jurisdiction and powers. That while no Constitution can be said to confer real powers of self-government upon a people which does not vest in their representatives the disposal of their own revenue, the Civil List reserved under the proposed measure, which amounts already to nearly one-third of the revenue, and which Sir George Grey has recommended to be increased to nearly one-half, is withdrawn from the jurisdiction of the colonists altogether; and a power is further given to a

30

Nominee Council of taking whatever proportion of the remainder they may think fit for the purposes of the General Government; so that in fact the balance left to the disposal of the Provincial Councils will be little more than nominal. And that, lastly, the institution of a Legislative Council, composed partly of representatives of the people, and partly of nominees of the Crown, is not only incompatible with good government, but appears as if expressly calculated for the purpose of producing discord and mutual obstruction. For the foregoing reasons, therefore, this meeting rejects the measure in question, and pledges itself to resist its introduction by every constitutional means.

A report of the meeting in the *Wellington Independent*[10] said: 'The manner in which Mr Godley expressed himself in moving the first resolution, the emphasis and sincerity with which he declared his sympathy with the Association, and the satisfaction he felt in identifying himself with it, must have carried conviction to every hearer, that his words were not mere words of compliment, but that they came direct from the heart of a staunch and honest supporter of the cause with which his name is identified, the great and sacred cause of self–government.'

The following June, Godley offered to resign his position but was talked into staying until the New Zealand Constitution Act was proclaimed and Canterbury had its own government. He turned down the chance to become the first superintendent of the new provincial government, leaving in December 1852, something he later said he regretted.

Despite having spent only two years in Canterbury, Godley is regarded as the Founder of Canterbury and responsible, at least in part, for the naming of Christchurch ('I hope that my old college is grateful to me,' he said). He died in November 1861.

The people of Christchurch honoured his memory with a bronze statue in Cathedral Square — the first statue portraying a person in New Zealand. The statue fell off its plinth in the February 2011 earthquake, suggesting that even 150 years after his death, Godley remained capable of shaking the thoughts of those around him.

---

10 *Wellington Independent, November 20, 1850.*

Responsible Government

Edward Gibbon Wakefield

1855

In its evolution, two authentic geniuses helped found our new state. Edward Gibbon Wakefield[11][12]and Sir George Grey had vast strengths but many weaknesses. Each with his peculiar gifts and talents, they helped provide what they saw as a stone–age society with the people, structure and institutions of a parliamentary state.

Wakefield, born in London in 1796, was a career politician who was active in the colonisation of South Australia, Canada and New Zealand. As the 1830s drew to a close, Wakefield helped establish the principles of responsible government in the Durham Report, the blueprint for the development of British Colonial Policy.

Fifteen years later, serving his only term in the New Zealand Parliament as the Independent Member for Hutt, he presented the case to the budding Parliament of Governor Grey in Wellington.

Wakefield was putting the Durham Report into practice in the colony of which he was a founder.

In 1840, the British Government had, with much reluctance and little

---

11 *A Sort of Conscience: The Wakefields (Auckland University Press), by Philip Temple, 2002.*
12 *Miles Fairburn. 'Wakefield, Edward Gibbon — Biography', from the Dictionary of New Zealand Biography. Te Ara — the Encyclopedia of New Zealand.*

Edward Gibbon Wakefield (1796–1862)

support, established a new British colony in the South Seas. In the sunlit February of 1840, only a week separated the recreation of an ancient Anglo–French rivalry across the English Channel.

Now, watching Wakefield move in 1855 for responsible parliamentary government, historians can remark on a minor political miracle that a journalist of the day, Maurice Fitzgerald, compiled records of parliamentary sessions before the official introduction of Hansard in 1867. Here is Fitzgerald's record of Wakefield's speech:[13]

---

13 *Fitzgerald's New Zealand Parliamentry Debates, Volume A, pages 27–33.*

My duty today involves the necessity of getting to the bottom of the very principles of government ... to expound and explain to the House something about which some know absolutely nothing — to teach as a lecturer some unknown branch of political science by unfolding its mysteries.

What is meant by responsible government? I answer government according to the principles and usages of the British constitution ...

What is representation for? Why are we assembled here? We have not been brought here for the purpose of making speeches to each other ... we are here to reflect the well understood wishes of the people, to reflect their wants, to give effect to their settled desires. Whenever representation works properly it occasions a popular influence in all the processes of government, legislative as well as executive ... if there was government without regard to the wishes of the representative body, it was not government according to any constitutional law, but an exercise of mere despotism.

He then dealt with the United States system of republican government before moving onto the British system and the development of responsible government out of civil war and a 'stranger King' adopting the system of ministerial responsibility.

From that day to this the system has worked without interruption and with the most beneficial consequences. The Sovereign chooses a certain number of persons to give him advice with respect to every use of his high authority. They are commonly ... persons holding seats in the legislative houses. When the advice given by them is unpalatable to the people as represented in the House of Commons, the bad advisers retire from office, to make room for those who enjoy the popular confidence.

Thus the Sovereign escapes all responsibility and escapes all risk of suspension or disturbance. The advisers, the ministers, alone are responsible for everything ... Such is the operation of responsibility under the monarchical form of government ... where all responsibility rests upon persons over whom the people, though their elected representatives can exercise a sufficient and unceasing influence.

But now comes the question of the application to colonies of this plan of indirect responsibility. Not very long ago it was the fashion in England ... to say that the British constitution is all very well for the people at home, who understand it, but is totally unfit for the purpose of colonial government. Instead of controverting that doctrine I will state a fact. It is that now in every one of the colonies of England which enjoys a House of Representatives without nominees, and which is occupied ... by people of British race, the British constitution, including ministerial responsibility, is in full force.

He listed the Canadian provinces, mentioned Jamaica was to establish responsible government and referred to his doubts despite the 'active part he had played in giving effect to responsible government' whether Jamaica was ready for that.

Sir, if HM's Government think the Jamaica negro's fit for self-government, surely the Governor in this colony must think that the colonists of New Zealand are not less fit.

Let us imagine, however ... that we are less worthy of the proper consequences of representation than the recent slaves of Jamaica ... what will ensue. Inevitably the working of the constitution must come to a deadlock. With how much responsibility will we be satisfied?

Not with what we have now, which is absolutely nil. We shall never be otherwise than perfectly dissatisfied until we have somebody here answering for the government. I shall be content if one or two persons, having seats in this House shall be charged to explain and carry through the policy of the government in this House, and to conduct the business of the government when the session shall be over; but of course with the understanding that their tenure of office as his Excellency's advisers shall depend on our approbation of their policy and conduct.

To such persons, so presented to us I should tender all possible support ... help strengthen such a government ... and work with them for the future in gradually establishing complete and permanent ministerial responsibility.

Sir, we have all heard that difficulties, insuperable difficulties oppose themselves to the adoption of (this) policy that the proposed change may be good to make, but cannot be made, that in order to the establishment of ministerial government there must be two hostile parties tearing each other to pieces.

I can see no such necessity ... the absence of party has nothing to do with the matter. In due time, no doubt, rival parties will grow out of events. There may even soon be a Conservative party and a Movement party such as all free countries exhibit ...

But instead of regretting that there are not two hostile parties we may surely rejoice at observing the general and earnest desire of this House to make the constitution work as well as possible.

But I am far from saying there is no difficulty to overcome ... if for instance we were unable to respond the call. His Excellency, by convening us when it was not absolutely necessary, has evinced his sense of the creditable manner in which the people have performed their duty as electors; he has shown that he is not without confidence in us ... that it is a good House ... and capable of furnishing him with a government.

In the background is another set of objectors ... this thing cannot be done without an Act of Parliament. When this so called difficulty was mentioned I called to mind what had been done in Canada and by what authority. The Canada Union Act does not contain one word about ministerial responsibility. That Act was framed on the recommendation of Lord Durham's Report.

Lord Durham, when urging the necessity of the adoption of a system of responsible government, expressly declares that an Act of Parliament is not required ...

Of course, South Australia and Victoria have recently passed Acts to provide responsible government. But why? Because in each of these legislatures one third of the House are nominees ... if we had a Governor who had made up his mind to refuse and withhold, it might be necessary for us to pass an Act, but with a Governor disposed to grant us the boon, all talk about the necessity for an Act is absolute nonsense.

The proposal has no foundation in fact; it is only a device of men in trouble, who want to delay ...

This reference prompts me to return to the question of a small reality or a great sham ... It would be (a great sham) if the New Zealand Legislative Council of nominees were mixed with us in this house and pretended to be responsible ministers.

Any arrangement will be a sham unless it distinctly provides that ministers retire from office whenever it shall be fully established that they do not possess the confidence of the representative body.

Wakefield then dealt with the problem of dispossessed office holders and the need for retiring allowances, the ignoring of 'ancient malpractices' and the 'promotion of future good for the country.'

Our business is I think to bring before His Excellency in such form and manner that he must either comply with our wish, or stand in the unenviable position of having consciously disappointed the expectations and frustrated the deliberate wishes of the people's representatives.

Therefore I shall be glad if responsible government be pressed upon him by us, instead of being originated by him.

I conclude that he has the sense to perceive the absolute necessity for this concession, and the courage to disregard the bugaboos of dangers which may be raised up to frighten him from a wise and honourable purpose.

Wakefield then offered himself for 'cross examination on points whereon I have failed to express myself clearly.'

It is right that I should take care not to entrap the House into agreeing to any motion without being aware of its consequences.

I must state, therefore, that, if they should adopt the resolution before them, I shall feel it is to be my duty to propose, as soon as possible, a respectful address to His Excellency, praying that he may be pleased to give effect to the opinion and wish of the House as set forth in the resolution.

I beg leave to move as a resolution, That, amongst the objects this House desires to see accomplished without delay, both as an essential means whereby the central government may rightly exercise a due control over the provincial governments, and as a no less indispensable means of obtaining for the general government the confidence and the attachment of the people, the most important is the establishment of ministerial responsibility in the conduct of the legislative and executive proceedings by the Governor.

Of course, Wakefield was only one captain on the sea of British constitutional progress. But the winds were by 1855 fair for a leader like Wakefield, who had been part of the Durham team in Canada and a founder of the New Zealand Association. He knew the case for responsible government well. Our testing start–up required a leader knowing where the colony was, where it should go, and how to get there.

Wakefield at a key point was just such a leader, even if ironically his success ended in his own failure. Having played a unique role in four countries, Great Britain, Canada, Australia and New Zealand, in his choicest colony he led the case for responsible government. That was still insufficient to achieve the office he craved. He told the Fitzgeralds, Welds and Sewells how to form a government but despite his superior skills, was not included.

Falling ill while politicking in his constituency, he caught rheumatic fever and retired from the House of Representatives in 1855.

For his last seven years before his death in May 1862, Wakefield lived as a recluse on The Terrace in Wellington. Doubtless his enemies enjoyed such confirmation of political careers ending in failure. They certainly left him to die alone.

A Clash of Cultures

Renata Kawepo & Thomas FitzGerald

November 7, 1860

Wakefield had painted New Zealand as a colony of settlement. But where were the settlers to settle? Only the Otago and Canterbury settlements, as George Grey later made plain, acquired land easily. In Wellington, Wanganui, New Plymouth and Auckland, the settlers were bottled up.

Breaking out at New Plymouth led to the Taranaki War (1860–61) and at Auckland, to the Waikato War (1863–70). At one point, the British Army had 10,000 troops in the country in fighting that disgusted the Scots General Cameron and the British authorities. James Belich's histories[14] and television series[15] help us understand wars in which the sovereign power imposed its authority over tribes in an emerging State.

By 1860, Anglo–Irishman Thomas Gore Browne[16], in his sixth year as Governor of New Zealand, was finding himself trapped in contradictory policies in Taranaki. Keeping control of Maori Affairs from Ministers, he sought land for settlement as the emerging Maori King movement determined to hold fast to its land. Governor Browne (and his ministers)

---

14 *The New Zealand Wars, by James Belich (1987), and other writings.*
15 *The New Zealand Wars, by Landmark Productions, screened in five parts in 1998.*
16 *B. J. Dalton. 'Browne, Thomas Robert Gore — Biography', from the Dictionary of New Zealand Biography. Te Ara — the Encyclopedia of New Zealand.*

41

believed willing Maori vendors should be allowed to sell their lands. As he saw it, Maori of whatever degree, as British subjects, should be able to sell their land.

Paramount chiefs stood adamantly on their authority over, and were disdainful of, minor chiefs.

The Sovereign authority of the Governor clashed with the Rangatiratanga of the Maori King Te Whereo and Te Rangitake (Wiremu Kingi), the Kingmaker. A high chief could lay down the law: 'I will not permit the sale.'

The breakdown in understanding, the chasm between sovereign and tribal governance, is nowhere better set out in the debate[17] between the Superintendent of Napier, Thomas Henry FitzGerald, and the Maori leader Renata Kawepo[18] at the Whakairo Pa, Heretaunga, Ahuriri (Napier), on November 7, 1860.

The pair met because Kawepo, and the Hawkes Bay tribes that he influenced, were trying to decide whether they should stay out of the troubles in Taranaki or join the fight against the government. FitzGerald, a 36–year–old surveyor, was the first superintendent of the newly–formed province where Maori outnumbered the 1,200 or so Europeans by two or three to one. Having established that he spoke for the runangas (Native Councils) of the Pa Whakairo, of Tanenuiarangi, Waipureku, of Te Timu, of Pakohai, of the Pakipaki, of Potako, of Te Hauke, of Te Aute, of Waipaoa, of the Waipukurau, of Eparaima, of Porangahau, of Tautane, of the Takapau, of Tikokino, Kawepo addressed FitzGerald:

The cause of this meeting is our grief at the war now going on at Taranaki between the Governor and Wiremu Kingi. We addressed you on a former occasion at this place some months ago, and we then gave it as our opinion that the Governor was in the wrong.

We thought that he would probably listen to the protests of this people, the Maoris, and of some also amongst you Pakehas; instead of which he still continues to lengthen out the war between himself and

17 *The New Zealand Text Collection. http://nzetc.victoria.ac.nz/tm/scholarly/tei–KawRena–t1–g1. html*

18 *Angela Ballara and Patrick Parsons. 'Kawepo, Renata Tama–ki–Hikurangi — Biography', from the Dictionary of New Zealand Biography. Te Ara — the Encyclopedia of New Zealand.*

Wiremu Kingi. He continues to collect troops from all directions, even from England, to exterminate those tribes of ours (ena iwi o matou), for which reason we are thinking of going to Taranaki.

Amongst you Pakehas, one is a Bishop, another a Minister, another a Governor, another a Soldier, another a Settler. But we have all but the one name 'Maori,' whether for building houses; for cultivating food; for making canoes; or, as now, for fighting, since you have commenced it.

We call ourselves the Church of God (i.e. Christians); and the scripture says 'If one part feels pain, all parts suffer.' The Church is a name for all; therefore I say let me also go there (to Taranaki) to my countrymen who are being fed by you with hard food. But I would rather that you should agree to a different mode of disputing — let us, at Taranaki, debate upon and investigate the quarrel between the Governor and Wiremu Kingi; that will be the best plan.

Then if it turn out that Wiremu Kingi is in the wrong, let us all, white men and Maoris, join in obliging him to lay aside his present course of action: and if it appear that Te Teira is in the wrong, let the Governor put a stop to his urging on the war.

We have been trying to find out wherein lies the superiority of your great nation, which has caused your name to go forth as a nation acting on principles of justice, and settling all disputes by legal tribunals (he iwi ata whakahaere i nga tikanga, he iwi whakawa mariri).

We were taught by former Governors that it was wrong to fight, but that everything should be settled by investigation.

But when it came to the present Governor, investigation was laid aside, and hard food was thrown to us. For instance, disputes about small affairs, as a basket of potatoes, a bushel of wheat, or a pig, are settled by the Courts: but the weightier matters — land and human life — are not investigated. Then we thought upon what his (the Governor's) newspaper had told us — that he was a protecting father and the Queen, a protecting mother to us.

But when we look for the result, behold guns, powder and ball are the food with which our father and mother are feeding those children of theirs; and ships are coming here with similar cargoes. Under these circumstances, Mr FitzGerald, I shall go to Taranaki to assist my people

43

who are being fed with hard food; for I am like the callow nestling of the koko (or tui) whose mother has gone to gather food, and when she returns the mouths of her offspring are opened wide to receive their nourishment.

Now, my duty to that mother of mine is ended, unless she will look upon the fault of this Governor who feeds us with guns, powder, and ball, and recall him, and give me a Governor who will feed me with digestible food, with Councils, with Courts of Justice, with love, and with good deeds.

My (the Maori) King proposed at first to the Governor that an investigation should take place into the dispute between him and Wiremu Kingi; that they (the Governor and Potatau) should meet at Waiuku, and there discuss the matter, and have it settled according to law. Instead of this the Governor went on to Taranaki, and opened fire upon Wiremu Kingi; from which we can clearly see that the Governor was in the wrong, because there was no investigation (i.e., because he would not wait for an investigation).

Then it was arranged that the Maori should investigate it; Waikato went to look into the cause of that quarrel, and it was decided that if it should turn out that Wiremu Kingi was wrong, he should be made to give up the land; but if it should turn out that the Governor was wrong, Wiremu Kingi should be supported (me tangi ano a Wiremu Kingi). When Waikato arrived it was found that the Governor was in fault, on which account that tribe is now fighting at Taranaki.

However, it was not necessary to go so far to see the fault of the Governor. I have seen it here, at Hawke's Bay, in the purchases of his servants. The former mode of buying land was that all the people should assemble — the chiefs and commoners, the old men and women, the women and children — in his (the Commissioner's) presence, that the transfer of the land to the Queen should be right. The beginning was the Waipukurau, that was conducted exactly in this way; afterwards Ahuriri, precisely the same: these were the lands that were fairly transferred to the Queen (i marama te rironga ki a te Kuini), and we imagined that practice would continue to be acted upon; but afterwards it went wrong, and this was the cause — the sale by single individuals.

Renata Kawepo (about 1808–1888)

There was the Matau o Maui (Cape Kidnapper Block); there was Aorangi; there was Okawa; there was Turiotekanawa; there was the Umuopua; there was Tautane; there was Aropaoanui; you are to have these lands; but through the faulty purchasing of your servants we fought amongst ourselves; and afterwards those lands were agreed to be given up to you in perpetuity, as a token of our regard for the Governor, whilst we said at the same time, 'Put a stop to this purchasing from individuals'— to which the Land Purchasing Officers assented.

A very short time afterwards the purchasers of the Governor went on again buying land secretly; and then we made up our minds that the Governor wished to provoke a quarrel with us, that he might have a pretext for seizing our lands. For instance, there are Omarutairi, Ngapaeruru, and Parangahau; these lands are lying by in consequence of the fault of the sale by individuals (ko nga whenua tenei e takoto ana i runga i te he o te hoko a te tangata kotahi), and the wishes of the majority being disregarded by the Governor's servants. These lands are still lying by, and we nearly had a quarrel with you about the aforenamed places.

Henceforward, angry feeling, however small may be the source from which it arises, will go on increasing by degrees until it breaks forth, and as for its explosion! — there it is being fought out at Taranaki (akenei nawai i iti te whakatakariri a, me te whanake, me te whanake, totahi ka pakaru ki waho, na, te puehutanga atu! koia tera e riri mai ra i Taranaki). Therefore we have arrived at the conclusion that it is the Governor who is in fault.

Perhaps you will say by and bye that the Natives of this island desire to quarrel with the settlers. No, had we wished for a row, we should have joined in the attempt of Wanganui to kill the Pakeha, and in that of Tipa at Whaingaroa; this was prevented by me, by the runangas of the King, who openly find fault with you to your face.

I will not listen to things said to screen the Governor; but if you will agree to our proposal, and let us all go to Taranaki and there make inquiry into this evil, my ears will listen to that.

Cannot you see how justly your enemies have been acting, whilst you still persist in the war? I will not act like the lickplate (miti pereti) assemblage of the Governor's. I say my say straightforward; but that meeting has done wrong.

My weapon (holding up a patu paraoa, or bone weapon) is from Ngatiraukawa to destroy Wellington, but I prevented it. The intention in sending this patu was, that if, on the King's flag being hoisted, the adherents of the Government and the soldiers made an attack upon the King's people to kill them and take the flag (then a simultaneous rising should take place). Wanganui also has gone wrong—and this was the way of it.

46

A certain man living there took the fencing of some graves, and made a fire of the stakes to heat an oven, and he called the food cooked in this oven by the names of the King and his advisers, Porokoru, Tamihana, Te Wetini, Epiha, Rewi, and of all the Chiefs of Waikato, in order that they might take such offence at it as would induce them to kill the Pakehas of Wanganui. This is the fault of those men who went to the Governor's meeting. That man said (the name of that young fellow was Te Mutumutu) 'Finished, finished, finished, for ever.' The name of another was Pakau, 'Blocked, blocked, blocked, for ever, (pa, pa, pa tonu atu).' The King prevented the consequences of this act, he and all of us his runangas.

There was another man named Tipa, who shaved all the hair off his head and off his dogskin mat, with the intent that when the people of his tribe saw what he had done they should kill the Pakehas of Whaingaroa. The King prevented this, and we also, your opponents who meet you openly face to face. Then there is also a part — the major part — of the Ngatiraukawa tribe, which also finds fault with you openly before your face; just as I, who am speaking at large to you now; but you turn round and rebuke those who speak openly to your face, and you turn aside and put faith in the flattering speeches of the meeting whom you invited up there (to Auckland) to tell you lies.

Now, I shall not unwarrantably interfere (po kanoa). What I tell you has been determined on by the King, viz., that all the towns are to be as Parininihi, and the fighting is to be at Taranaki only, at the place on which the Governor's sword has fallen. But if the Governor should climb up one of these Parininihis, there will be a row — it will be the same as Taranaki.

There is another fault of the Governor; his writing in his newspapers to all the Chiefs of this Island to go in a body to Taranaki, that the murderers may be executed, not reflecting that he had implicated himself in murder, in as much as he has made an intimate friend of Kirikumara.

It is said that Katatore committed a murder; but Katatore's was not a murder, it was done openly. For Katatore said his land should not be sold to the Pakeha, and Rawiri persisted in selling it. Katatore said both to the Pakehas and to Rawiri, 'Let my land alone,' but he still persisted in selling it to the Pakeha. Then Katatore said to Rawiri, 'Very well, since you persist, there is a gun, let us fight for it;' but Rawiri went on cutting the boundary of Katatore's land, and when he would not listen, then the gun was fired; it was not aimed at the man, it was fired in the air and into the ground, with the idea that by frightening them (the sellers) they would stop, but they still persevered, and then Rawiri was fired upon and was killed.

This was not a murder but was openly done. But that of Ihaia's was a murder, although it has been called an avenging of death (he nga ki mate); this was a nga ki mate, the course taken by Arama Karaka, who openly in broad day avenged the death of Rawiri Waiaua. They fought in open day, and at length they made a lasting peace: but this which is called an avenging by Ihaia of Rawiri's death, is but a murder of Ihaia's and the Governor's — a murder of the worst description.

I have also a word to say about Teira; he is said to be a chief, but he is a common man. For I have seen this man, and he is but a man of small standing (low position); William King alone is their great man, known as such by all tribes. His father's name was Reretawhangawhanga, from whom descended Te Rangitake. The name of a chief is always raised to the sky. (Wha kapiki tonu te ingoa ki runga te rangi, to te tino tangat a tona ingou.) For instance mine is Tamakihikurangi, but Te Teira's name is Manuka, nothing but manuka (a kind of scrubby bush). There never was a piece of land hereabouts sold by a common man to the Pakeha; they were all sold by the Chiefs — the tribe consented and the land passed to the Pakeha. Te Moananui, Tareha, Te Hapuku, Puhara, Tawhara, Hineipaketia, Hineirangiia, and various other Chiefs, sold our lands to the Queen.

This is another subject — the interdiction placed by the Governor on guns and powder for us to shoot birds with. This is not a good plan; for my custom with regard to my enemy is, if he have not a weapon I give him one, that we may fight upon equal terms.

Now, are you not ashamed of my defenceless hands? Do you put aside your guns, powder, and ball, and let us fight with our hands; and if you don't like this plan, put a stop to the war — put a stop to it once and for ever.

48

Rather let us go back to the Court house for a battle ground, for what is the use of killing men in a bad cause? — no good can come of that. If war is persisted in, we shall all go to the bad; it cannot be right, because you wish to exterminate the Maori; it cannot be right, because you, the Pakeha nation, are boasting yourselves against us, saying that we are a bad nation, a dark people, but that you are a nation of chiefs.

True, you, the Pakeha, are a nation of chiefs, and we, the Maori, are an inferior race; that is quite true. But leave the consideration of these points to the God who made us both. God made you to be a good and handsome race; and God also made us to be bad and dark; but it is not right that you should taunt us with that. Great numbers of the Pakeha boast themselves in this fashion, but the decision in this matter is in the hands of the Almighty.

If you persist in fighting, it is well — the result is in the hands of God both as regards you and us. This is our wish, that we should all join together in putting down this evil that it may come to an end.

That is all: it ends here.

FitzGerald replied:

My friends, Renata, and all of you, listen. Do not imagine that only your hearts are grieved. We also are in a state of sadness.

Yes, all the Pakehas in this country are sad about this. It is not an agreeable thing for a magistrate to try one of his intimate friends or his brother. But what is to be done in a case of wrong? Is evil to be allowed to prevail? Also with one amongst us a father of children, if one or his children does wrong, a great wrong, rebels against his father, is it right for this father to shut his eyes? Can he possibly help whipping him?

If the father rejects the use of the rod, in a very short time all the children will rebel, and turn round and trample upon him: for this reason the father inflicts chastisement and pain upon his children, that they may obey and be good children, and do honour to their father. This is what the Governor is doing. It is not that either whipping or fighting is a good thing: it is a bad thing; a hard, a bitter, a painful, a sorrowful thing; a thing of great sadness. But he is doing it as one administers a

Thomas FitzGerald (1824–1888)

dose of physic, that by it, though it be bitter, good may accrue.

Who will speak in favour of that manner of life now going on at Taranaki? It is far better with us here at Ahuriri; we live together, eat together, buy and sell together, and sleep in peace; that is much better. Now, as to what you say about the Governor, that he should listen to what you say, and consent to your proposals. The Governor follows his own course, because he is from the Queen. He stands in the place of the Queen: he is above all of us, and he alone is the controller of his own actions. His chief business is to give forth good regulations, by which life and peace and good fellowship may be permanent amongst men.

The goodwill of the Governor towards the Maori has been plainly seen these many years past. Yes, he is very sad about this war, and on account of those of us who have been killed, and he desires to put a stop to the war, and to make peace; but the rebellious heart of man must be first put down, that the peace may be a lasting, not a hollow one.

Now, it is quite right for the people to say to the Governor good and true words, and to make their voices distinctly heard when they have a grievance; but we have no right to find fault with him about the war, because in our opinion his quarrel with W. King is a just one. The Governor is the great man of these islands of New Zealand over Pakehas and Maoris.

Well, he heard of the cause of quarrel between W. King and Te Teira about the land at Waitara, on hearing of which he said that it should be carefully investigated, it was investigated accordingly, and at great length, and it was seen that Te Teira was in the right, but W. King obstinately held out.

Then the Governor went to Taranaki, that he might himself see both parties, and hear what they had to say, thinking that his decision would be respected. (Had W. King been an English gentleman the Governor would not have gone, but have sent his people; but he had great regard for W. King; because the Governor knew W. King was an obstinate man, and the Governor had no wish for bloodshed, on which account he went).

Well, when he got there, they assembled together, and the matter was discussed at great length. The Governor asked W. King in presence of the

Assembly about the piece of land, whether it belonged to Te Teira. W. King did not say that land is not Te Teira's, all he said was, 'I will not suffer it to be sold;' and when he had said this he arose and walked out.

Now, my friends, what I say is true; we of the General Assembly at Auckland have seen the truth of this story; therefore we agree in the propriety of what the Governor has done at Taranaki, even though it is a very sorrowful business. For if the Governor had not acted as he did, he and the Queen would have been trampled upon, aye, and all the laws and all good regulations would all have been destroyed together. He is the chief of the Pakehas and the Maori, and let all obey him; as also say the holy Apostles, 'Let every one submit himself to the higher powers'. And this is another word, 'Let the nations of believers be pliant to receive all regulations, whether from the Almighty or from Governors who have been sent by him to punish the evil doers, and as a reward unto the good.'

Now, my friend Renata, and all of you, listen to me. Do not imagine that it is only we, the Pakehas, who uphold the course adopted by the Governor at Taranaki; there are a great many Maoris who say the same thing: and if there be a few Pakehas who say the Governor is wrong, those are not good Pakehas: they are chattering, growling, grumbling Pakehas, aye, bad Pakehas.

For all that a right–minded man wishes is to uphold and maintain the great regulations and laws, so that peace may prevail upon the earth. As for this matter, it was most carefully investigated when I was in the House of Representatives at Auckland. How careful was the inquiry of that Assembly; its diligent researches, its careful and penetrating questions Nothing could equal it; it was greater than I could tell.

This was our chief employment at that Assembly by which our days were taken up, that we might truly arrive at the root and the truth.

And when it was ended and quite finished, it was decided by us that the Governor was in the right. Aye, and it was also determined by that meeting that no peace could be made with William King till he had laid down his arms and submitted himself to the law.

Let William King do this, and afterwards let him set forth his grievance, and he will be listened to if he is in any degree in the right. This is simple enough; it is evident to the whole world, and cannot be gainsaid, that there can only be one head for the body, one chief authority over us all; one fountain from which all regulations and laws spring, that we may all be under one system, that we may be one united people, as is the case in all properly regulated countries.

For it has been written, 'A kingdom divided against itself cannot stand; and if a city or a house be divided against itself it cannot stand.' Now, you say that the soldiers having gone hence to fight at Taranaki, is a cause of complaint to you; but none of the troops have left this: true, two of the officers have gone to Auckland, but two more have arrived from Wanganui to relieve them. At all events, none of us have anything to say to the troops; they are set apart for that particular purpose, that is, to fight in time of war; for that purpose were they made soldiers, and for that purpose have they come here, that is, to protect those who are living peaceably, and to fight with wrong–doers, with men who trample upon the laws, that is their occupation, and they must obey orders.

If you, my friends, go to Taranaki, it will be a source of grief to us; for we have all lived peaceably together for many years past, and we do not wish that our Maori friends should act thus, for we well know that if ten men should go, that same ten will not return. Better that we should act a sensible part (kia manawanui tatou); do not you cut down the tree that has been so well planted by us and those who are gone.

And now, my friends, Renata and all of you, I and all of us know to what this quarrel at Taranaki tends, and what will be the end of it. But of the precise time at which it will end, and how little or how much fighting must first take place, I can, of course, have no idea. Possibly William King and his foolish friends may be able to drag it on some time longer; it may be in his power to lengthen out this trouble, this sorrow and grief which causes such pain to so many people that may be within his reach. But notwithstanding that he may do this, there can be no mistake about the end; and the end is this — that man must let down his bristles and his pride, and must obey his sovereign the Queen; this is the end; there cannot be any other; sooner or later it must come to this.

But if it be long, this island will be covered with soldiers and fighting men; for the Queen will never suffer her Governor and her laws to be made light of, and trampled under foot; whatever she undertakes must inevitably be brought to a successful termination: for Her Majesty lives, and she has full power to carry out this affair.

It is true that some of the Waikato tribes have joined with William King. Perhaps this is the very tribe that sold its possessions in Taranaki to the Governor, and can therefore have no grounds for supporting William King. Is not this seeking a quarrel with the Governor? Probably this has been done to increase the rent in the garment so wide hat it can never be sown together again: that is to say, they fancy that by fighting and divisions they will establish their Maori King in Waikato as an enemy of the Queen.

Alas! do you not consider, my friends? Alas, cannot you divine the root of this course adapted by Waikato? From whom do you suppose emanate jealousy, and divisions, and rebellion, and the evil heart? Who is the one who soweth seeds of evil in our hearts? Now I know that this proceeding of Waikato is not good; from it can emanate no good thing, but only evil; it is a very great crime that setting up of a pretended King by Waikato: yea, I am persuaded that there is evil in it, as well lor the people of Waikato as for all others who join with them. You will find that out anon. For it cannot be right that there should be two great men as heads over one people.

Neither are the Maoris able to fight against the Queen of England, and prevail against her; it is impossible. This is the desire of the Pakeha, to see the Maori nation advancing and improving even as his own has done. This can be accomplished by the Maori people supporting the Governor. The Maori nation cannot exist or advance divided from the Pakeha. There has never been a nation that, having once become acquainted with the use of money, could afterwards do without it. And where will the Maori get money if there are no Pakehas? My friends; reflect care fully over what I have said to you.

Now, as to what you said about guns and powder. What is the use of a quantity of powder being stored up by anybody? The only possible reason for laying it by in quantity can be for the purpose of fighting. In former times, if a tribe were seen building a pa, the reason was known: and so nowadays, the Government takes alarm when the Maoris are seen buying arms and ammunition in large quantities. For instance, there is very little powder and a very few guns in the hands of the settlers hereabouts; for powder is not a thing that is better for long keeping. A Pakeha sportsman buys a very little powder at a time; but the Maori is always buying, always keeping, and always storing up. My friends, to what purpose?

Now for this saying of yours, 'There was one system of purchase formerly, and a different one afterwards,'— that is, with regard to the blocks of land that have been bought. I have not much to say on this subject, because I answered you upon it at our last meeting here. Yes, indeed, it has been seen that you are yourselves the chief cause of this new system of purchase. It has not arisen with the Governor or with his Land Purchase Staff, but with yourselves. We know this: for you locked up the land. The land was free (rangatira) formerly; aye, free from your forefathers down even to yourselves. But now you have locked it up (kua hereheretia); for you have said, 'No man shall be allowed to sell his piece, even though it be his own individual property.'

Verily, friend Renata, this is really the cause from which sprung the new system of purchase — not from the Governor, but from yourselves. All these customs are like those of the tapu Maori, and of the setting up of claims to land (rahui), which do not suit the present times; for these customs are of the dark ages, but now the sun has shone upon you, and your eyes are opened, so that you can see; and you cannot now go back to these old customs which have passed away.

I have nothing to say in reply to your disparagement (kupu whakaiti) of Te Teira, for his genealogy has been printed and published long since. Is not this word about Manuka a childish word, for there are numbers of Maori chiefs, north and south, with names no better than that of which you make light?

You have acted rightly in putting stop to mischievous attempts, such as those you tell me of, of Tipa and Wanganui. We also follow the same rule of putting down the evil tricks of silly and insane persons.

What you say about likening the settlement to Parininihi is very good. Let that word remain and be observed. We shall see hereafter whether the Governor or a Maori will be the first to scale one of these cliffs.

As to what you say in the latter part of your speech about the jeering remarks of certain Pakehas think no more of that, For you know full well that these things are not said by right–minded and well–disposed Pakehas; and which of us pays any attention to the barking of a cur, to the cry of a gull, to the roaring of the surf? You say quite truly, 'This matter is in the hands of the Almighty.'

And then this other word of yours, let me apply this word to yourself, 'If you persist in fighting, it is well; the end is with God, about you as well as about us. This is our wish, that we should all of us join together in putting down this evil, that it may come to an end.' Yes, my friend, this is a very good sentiment, but let us not apply it to this particular evil only, but to all causes of difference.

Therefore I say to you, to this tribe, lay a firm hold on the regulations of Government that you may see life and length of days, and prosperity increasing without end (kia kite ai koe i te ora rahi, i te ora matotoru, i te ora mau tou, tupu tou).

That is all I have to say at present. Shake hands, the whole tribe of you. Salutations to you. How do you do?

Kawepo died on in April 1888 at Omahu. His tangi was attended by an estimated 6,000 people and he was given a military funeral.

After his two–year spell in Hawkes Bay, FitzGerald briefly represented the County of Hawke electorate in the 2nd New Zealand Parliament and two years later moved to Queensland. There he established sugar cane plantations and continued his political career. However all did not end well and he was declared bankrupt and was forced to resign from Parliament.

Ake, Ake!

Rewi Maniapoto

April 2, 1864

At the height of the Maori Land Wars, the British Army had an estimated 10,000 troops fighting wars in Taranaki (1860–61) and in the Waikato (1863–64). Though they out–numbered the Maori, and had ample munitions including seige guns, rifles and hand grenades, the rebels fought hard and were united by their leaders.

One such leader was the Ngati Maniapoto chief, Rewi Maniapoto,[19] whose lack of height and slender build belied the spirit with which he could rally the rebel Kingitanga forces.

Rewi had been emphatically defeated in every battle by the commander of the British forces, General Duncan Cameron, a veteran of the Crimean War called to New Zealand by Governor George Grey to invade the Waikato in 1863.

So it was that Rewi found himself preparing for a last stand at Orakau, not far from Kihikihi, where Waikato chiefs had built a pa. Inside were several hundred Maori warriors, women and children. By the third day of the seige, Cameron had amassed a force of 1,800 soldiers and cavalry who surrounded the pa.

---

19 Manuka Henare. 'Maniapoto, Rewi Manga — Biography', from the Dictionary of New Zealand Biography. Te Ara — the Encyclopedia of New Zealand.

On that morning, of April 2, 1864, two old men tried to break out and were killed. One was Te Waro, the warrior who had predicted disaster after chiefs forbade him from cutting out the heart of the first British soldier killed.

Cameron was impressed by the rebels' courage and instructed officer William G. Mair, who could speak Maori, to offer the defenders the chance to surrender.

The Maori were short on ammunition and had run out of drinking water. They could barely swallow the potatoes that Rewi urged them to cook and eat to maintain their energy for the fight ahead.

Buglers signalled for a cease fire and the British waved the flag of truce. When all firing had ceased, Mair and a companion approached to within a few metres of the pa's ramparts. The Maori crowded to hear what Mair had to say. Later, in a letter to a relative, Mair told of what he saw:[20] 'I cannot forget the dust–stained faces, bloodshot eyes, and shaggy heads. The muzzles of their guns rested on the edge of the ditch in front of them.' Among the nearest Maori were Hauraki Tonganui and Te Huia Raureti.

Many reports have since recorded versions of who said what during the ensuing encounter and what follows is a composite of them[21].

Mair: 'E hoa ma, whakarongo! Ko te kupu tenei a te Tienara: ka nui tona miharo ki to koutou maia, kati me mutu te riri, puta mai kia matou, kia ara o koutou tinana.' ('Friends listen! This is the word of the General. Great is his admiration of your bravery. Stop! Let the fighting cease; come out to us that your bodies may be saved.')

Tonganui: 'E hoa, ka whawhai tonu ahau ki a koe, ake ake! Hoki koutou katoa ki Kihikihi, ka hoki matou ki to matou kainga, me waiho atu Orakau nei.' ('Friend, I shall fight against you for ever, for ever! Let all of you return to Kihikihi, and we will go to our homes and abandon Orakau.')

Meanwhile, Raureti rushed to pass on Mair's message to Rewi who was at the northern end of the pa, with the council of chiefs. They discussed Cameron's offer, deciding to reject it.

---

20 *The New Zealand Wars: A History of the Maori Campaigns and the Pioneering Period: Volume I (1845–64), by James Cowan. Available at the New Zealand Electronic Text Collection.*
21 *Reports from Papers Past archive, National Library of New Zealand.*

Rewi Maniapoto (about 1808–1888)

Rewi: 'Kaore e mau te rongo — ake, ake!' ('Peace shall never be made — never, never!')

Raureti passed Rewi's message to Tonganui who repeated them to Mair. Upon hearing them, people in the pa took up the shout: 'Kaore e mau te rongo — ake, ake!' ('Peace shall never be made — never, never!')

By then, Rewi had emerged and stood in the trench a few metres behind Raureti and Tonganui.

Mair: 'E pai ana tena mo koutou tangata, engari kahore e tika kia mate nga wahine me nga tamariki. Tukuna mai era.' ('That is well for you men, but is not right that the women and children should die. Let them come out.')

Somebody, thought to be the old Taupo chief Te Paerata asked: 'Na te aha koe e mohio he wahine kei konei?' ('How did you know there were women and children here?')

Mair: 'I rongo ahau ki te tangi tupapaku i te po.' ('I heard the lamentations for the dead in the night.')

Before Rewi could consider Mair's offer to release the women and children, Ahumai Te Paerata, daughter of the Taupo chief, stood and called out: 'Ki te mate nga tane, me mate ano nga wahine me nga tamariki.' ('If the men die, the women and children must die also.')

Realising the talking was done, Mair said: 'E pai ana, kua mutu te kupu.' ('It is well; the word is ended.')

In mid–afternoon, the pa was shelled at close range. The warriors attempted a mass breakout, leaving about 50 behind who were killed or captured. About half of the escapees were wounded and 160 of the rebels were killed. Of the government troops, 17 died and 52 were wounded in the fighting.

Rewi was one of those who escaped and years later, returning to the sacred soil of Orakau pa, he told of what happened.

'When we rushed out of the pa, I prayed to God. The words of my prayer were, "E Ihowa, tohungia ahau, kaua e whakaekea tenei hara ki runga i a au." ("O Lord, save me, and visit not this sin upon me.") Just then I stumbled and fell down, which made me very dark in my heart, for it was an evil omen. I rose and started on again, but had only gone a short distance when I stumbled and fell once more. When I rose the second time I recited this prayer—

Wetea mai te whiwhi,
Wetea mai te hara,
Wetea mai te tawhito,
Wetea kia mataratara,
Tawhito te rangi, ta taea.

With these words, Rewi asked his Maori gods to remove from him all sins or transgressions of he or his male relatives might have been guilty.

'Then I slapped my thighs, and I cried out—

Tupe runga, tupe raro, tupe haha,
Kei kona koe tu mai ai,
Ki konei au rere ake ai,
Rere huruhuru, rere a newa a te rangi.

The karakia (war prayer) was often used by Maori after a battle when the victors were chasing defeated warriors. Rewi aimed the words at his pursuers, praying they would stop and let him escape.

The line 'Kei kona koe tu mai ai' means 'Remain there where you are. I will flee on from here, fly like a bird, rising high towards the heavens.'

After the battle at Orakau, Rewi moved to the King Country and the British forces gave up trying to capture him. Over the next two decades, he became helpful in building relations between Maori and Pakeha. In 1879, the Native Minister, John Sheehan, invited Rewi to Auckland where he received a hero's welcome. The government returned his tribal land at Kihikihi and he was given a house and pension. His wish was to be buried with Governor Grey, who he considered a friend, but his remains instead lie at the foot of a public monument erected in his honour in 1894 at Kihikihi.

Rewi's legacy is making what is arguably the most stirring short speech made in New Zealand.

'Kaore e mau te rongo — ake, ake!' ('Peace shall never be made — never, never!')

Ake, Ake stands as a trumpet call for all time for New Zealanders.

The Seat of Government

Thomas MacFarlane

December 9, 1864

After almost a quarter of a century as New Zealand's capital city, Aucklanders became enraged at plans to shift the base of political power to Wellington. As the Maori Wars had dragged on, the Aucklanders stood accused of not having pulled their weight in the efforts to subdue the Maori.

By late 1864, it became apparent that those in the Middle Island, as it was known, would soon have Wellington as the country's power base.

On December 9, more than 3,000 Aucklanders gathered outside their courthouse for a public meeting called by a committee of local businessmen and politicians. The crowd comprised a substantial proportion of Auckland's population, which had been officially recorded as 12,423 that year. It was estimated that at least half the local population was Irish, many of them ex–soldiers.

The meeting was sanctioned by the province's Superintendent, Robert Graham, who had represented northern electorates in the New Zealand Parliament before taking the Auckland post in 1862.

Rain delayed the start of the meeting for two hours but by 2pm, the weather had improved, except for the odd shower, and the proposed speakers were introduced.

The committee that called the meeting chose local businessman Thomas MacFarlane to put their case that if Wellington insisted on removing the seat of Government from Auckland, then Auckland should consider separating itself from the colony and look to run its own affairs. MacFarlane, a Scot, had emigrated to New Zealand in 1860 to take over the affairs of his brother's companies, after his sudden death, and he had quickly become involved in local politics, joining the Auckland City Board of Commissioners in 1863.

MacFarlane was introduced by Superintendent Graham, who had been elected chairman for the meeting. Though newspaper reports[22] had minor variations of what MacFarlane said, the following is a composite of his speech:

Fellow colonists, we are met today in circumstances of unparalleled importance to the colony. The General Assembly has passed resolutions which virtually ignore Auckland as an integral part of this colony. Hitherto, we have been recognised in the Government of this colony, but now we are not so; and we are convened today to consider what ought to be done in the very peculiar position in which we now find ourselves.

Hitherto the various sections of the colony have acted pretty harmoniously; but now the whole colony south of Auckland have decided to leave us to our fate. Having got the ship in which we were sailing together among the breakers, they elect a new captain; they pitch a portion — one third of the crew — overboard; to find their way to shore as best they may, while they are conveying the ship to a safer harbour.

Sir, we accept the fate assigned to us. We were willing to have sailed together a little longer — till a haven of rest and peace had been obtained; but the men of the South have decided otherwise, and we abide the consequences. They have said that all south of Auckland shall be one colony, and that Auckland proper shall be left out.

Cries from the crowd of 'never, never, never.'

---

22 *The content of MacFarlane's speech is from newspaper reports in the Papers Past archive at the National Library of New Zealand.*

Gentlemen, we accept the alternative.

The crowd: 'Hear, hear.'

We are prepared and ready to separate from them, and I think the time will yet come when they will ask to be restored, and again form an united colony. But we venture to think that when the history of this period of the colony shall come to be written their proceedings will have neither generosity, magnanimity, nor patriotism attached to them.

On the contrary, we think that the charge of selfishness which has been unsparingly preferred against us, will be justly chargeable against them, with this addition — moral cowardice, if not political suicide.

Sir, these men have adopted their course of proceeding towards us advisedly, and after being fully warned of the consequences likely to ensue.

Our representatives in the House have spoken out nobly, and have pointed to the disastrous consequences of their measure on the natives and on this province. They have asked them to pause in their mad career; but warning was unheeded, and request denied.

A tyrant majority, in conformity with previous compact, formed in utter ignorance of the real state of matters here, have decided against us; and we are forced into a position where we must choose whether the native affairs of this province shall be governed by men who have agreed to withdraw the seat of action now, and the troops by and bye, after they evacuate the posts of security which it has cost so much blood and treasure and trouble to erect; and to leave us to the tender mercies of the savage — by men who have already manifested so much ignorance of the native character and native affairs, and so little interest in the white men of this province.

Whether such men shall govern us on native affairs, or whether we shall revert again to despotism — to become the slaves of a tyrant.

Don't mistake. Don't say Sir George (Grey) is a despot, or that we would become slaves by placing ourselves under his sway, so far as concerns native matters. But our Southern friends taunt us with a desire to return to this state and I wish to show in what estimation, we hold their conduct, by answering that taunt in this way.

I hate despotism in every shape and form. I hate it with a true and an abiding hatred; but if I am forced to choose whether I will be governed by one or by 35 tyrants, I prefer the former.

Cheers from the crowd.

Despots are not always tyrants; sometimes, just, generous, brave; but a combination of these is never either the one or other. I accept the alternative forced upon us and I trust that this meeting will endorse the sentiment, in order that the colony, mother country, and the world may see the consequences of the outrageous proceedings of our would-be rulers.

It is the boast of our country that Britons never will be slaves, and the men of Auckland will yet prove that they value free institutions, they know how to use them for their country's good. If our friends are sincere in their sneers and taunts at Auckland men and Auckland cupidity, let them join with us in asking separation, and the thing will be done. They will then have a seat of Government of their own, and all the spoils of the office to distribute amongst their own relations and by which they must become rich as we have done.

We shall bear them no grudge, and shall hope that they will be more successful on managing their colonial affairs than they have been in managing their provincial matters.

Having made these preliminary remarks, I shall now come to the resolution entrusted to me: 'That this meeting takes this occasion of expressing its loyalty and devotion to the Crown, its deep gratitude for the generous assistance rendered by the mother country to this colony, and its cordial appreciation of the gallant services performed by her Majesty's land and naval forces in New Zealand.'

Devotion to Queen and country is a principle engraven on the heart of every Briton — a principle which much misgovernment and many acts of despotism will not efface. Our Queen is no despot. Her benignant sway, and the deep interest she takes in the welfare of her subjects, wherever situated, have secured her a warm place in the affections of her people, and nowhere is her Majesty's character more highly appreciated and respected than here.

If we are even roughly treated at home it will not be chargeable to our Queen, and whatever we do here we shall, I am sure, do nothing to interfere with our loyalty and devotion to her Majesty. And in our own intercourse with her representative in this colony, we must ever keep in our view that Sir George Grey is the representative of our beloved Queen, and as such entitled to all due honour and respect.

I am no toady of Sir George Grey. I am here to claim the right and privilege of criticising his public acts, and to differ from him where I think he is wrong. But I must do so in a loyal spirit and with the deference due to his position. I think Sir George Grey has done many things that we disapprove of, and I think that if his Excellency had acted in accordance with the advice of his responsible Ministers, the war would ... now have been at an end. But it cannot be doubted that he is acting under instructions from home, of which we are ignorant.

No man would assume his present position without positive instructions to that effect; and therefore, I say, we ought to be very cautious in blaming him till we know the instructions under which he is acting. We know he takes warm interest in the colony, and especially this province. He is, moreover, disposed to befriend us, and has the power to be most useful to us; and most certainly our native affairs shall be much safer in his keeping than in that of the oligarchy of the South. In every respect, then, it must be our duty, as it is our privilege, to give to his Excellency, as the representative of our Queen, that respect to which his position entitles him. We are the more bound to follow this course by what we know of the despatches from home, and doubtless we shall know more of this by and bye.

These home Ministers are apparently against us at present, but we believe they are so in consequence of deficient or erroneous information, and that the moment they are in possession of the state of matters here, our wrongs shall be redressed and our wants supplied. The really generous assistance rendered us in our hour of need is evidence sufficient of this; and the fact that even now, while they are lecturing us at no allowance, more troops are on their way to this colony, is the best corroboration we can have of their continued interest in this colony. No British Ministry durst do anything else.

Let us be sure of this: and, in judging of the proceedings of the Home Legislature, we ought to keep in view our most peculiar position in this colony and their want of full information on the native question; and if the wise men of the South who have so much time 'while tending their fleecy flocks' have been unable to comprehend our position, we ought to make some allowances for the Colonial Office at home.

Not only was a sufficient number of troops forwarded to us, but these troops were sent under the command of one of the most experienced generals, and naval forces under experienced officers were also sent. And though these services have not achieved any great or brilliant successes in a military point of view, yet they have accomplished deeds of daring that will live in history, and they have otherwise been of incalculable benefit to this province. They would have been ten times more so if the General had had the entire control of the troops.

Sir, the General was fighting his hands tied behind his back, and durst not follow up an advantage when he had it. His troops were the same as those that fought and conquered in the Crimea, in India and China, and they would have been equally successful here if equally untrammelled. We regret deeply that so many brave men have fallen in so inglorious a warfare, and on that very account our obligations to the troops ought to be all the greater. And here let me say one word regarding our colonial forces. We have been taunted with making no sacrifices in this war, with relying on Imperial troops, and doing nothing ourselves excepting looking after the commissariat contracts.

Sir, I emphatically deny these charges — charges also made in utter ignorance of the circumstances of the case. Why, sir, the truth is, that the men of this province, old and young, married and unmarried, responded to the call of the Government, and did all that was required of them, and some of them much more.

Especially was this the case in the money–making town of Auckland. Why, sir, you know that some establishments were at the closing point for want of assistants, and even the banks were obliged to carry on their business with about one–third of their staff. Many young men had to give up good situations, which they never got again. The married men, perhaps, suffered most. Many of them had businesses and contracts requiring their personal superintendence, but their premises had to be closed, or left to the care of wives not accustomed to the work. Others gave up business altogether for a time.

It is true that the local forces were not often required to face the enemy; but when they had, they did their duty well, if not often. The fault of this was not theirs, as they would infinitely have preferred to be at the Front to being in the quarters assigned them. But if there were not many that fell in the rifle pits, there were a goodly number who from exposure and unaccustomed hardships contracted diseases of which they have since died. One I know sent out two sons in the prime of life, and thought healthy, who are now in their graves; and hundreds of instances occurred where parties suffered severe hardships.

I speak not of our settlers who were driven from their homes. Their hardships would be spoken on by others. I allude only to our local forces, because I know these things from my own knowledge; and I do so in no spirit of boasting, not for informing you who either suffered more or less. Yourselves were eye witnesses of what I speak of; but I mention these things with the view of informing our friends at home that the charges so assiduously and recklessly charged against us are utterly groundless.

I have just one word more and I am done. We are now placed in circumstances requiring the united action of every man in this province. We must, therefore, forget our own local politics and petty squabbles, and agree on a platform, comprehending all the men amongst us capable of public duties. By this means alone can we show ourselves deserving of free institutions.

Nations, as well as individuals, achieve happiness through suffering. We are now in the furnace, and if we are true to ourselves to our destiny — manifest more love for country than for self — we shall come out of it purified, refined — better men, better citizens; and we shall transmit to our children a name and a country worth fighting for.

Despite MacFarlane's impassioned plea, the shift of power went ahead and Aucklanders quickly set aside their talk of separation.

After Wellington became the country's capital in 1865, Auckland suffered a sudden fall in population as military regiments were withdrawn and affluent families, in particular, headed south. Many businesses failed and bankruptcies soared.

Clearly deciding that if you cannot beat them, you might as well join them, MacFarlane entered national politics in 1867, representing the Northern Division in Parliament. In May 1885, he died from injuries received when knocked down by a train at Auckland Railway Station.

Graham continued to represent the Franklin electorate until his resignation from Parliament in 1868. While that ended his own role in national politics, his name returned to the House when two of his great grandsons entered Parliament (National cabinet minister Sir Douglas Graham, 1984 to 1999, and Green Party MP Kennedy Graham, elected in 2008).

The Trunk of an Elephant

Julius Vogel

June 28, 1870

Something seemed to come over 19th–century Britons like Charles Darwin, George Grey, Samuel Butler and Cecil Rhodes when they crossed into the southern hemisphere. Having traversed the globe, they appeared to develop strong vision for the new worlds before them.

Another such visionary was Julius Vogel[23], who arrived in New Zealand in 1861 as a young man who had studied chemistry and metallurgy in London and had spent almost eight years working as a journalist and editor in Victoria where he had been drawn by the gold rush. When news broke of the gold rush in Otago, Vogel left Australia and recommenced his newspaper career, helping found the *Otago Daily Times*, and entering local and then national politics.

By 1869, Vogel had built a reputation for political aggression, advocating the separation of the North and South Islands (views that led to his sacking as editor of the *ODT*). He was a robust debater in the chamber, where he represented the Goldfields (Otago) electorate. When William Fox successfully led a coup to topple Premier Edward Stafford in mid–1869, he appointed his supporter Vogel as Colonial Treasurer, Postmaster–

---

23 *Raewyn Dalziel. 'Vogel, Julius — Biography', from the Dictionary of New Zealand Biography. Te Ara — the Encyclopedia of New Zealand.*

71

General and Commissioner of Customs. The three roles potentially gave Vogel control over the country's finances which had so far suffered from an absence of national thinking — all the provinces were more used to squabbling over their own money and cared little for any bigger picture. Vogel's own fierce parochialism, for which he was known, made it all the more surprising when the 35–year–old finance minister stepped up to present his first Financial Statement, a document we would today call a Budget, on June 28, 1870.

Vogel was not the best of speakers, struggling to cope with partial deafness, and he toiled for more than three hours to read his 6,000 word statement to the House. It called for the country to put aside parochialism and to unite behind a bold plan to stimulate immigration to New Zealand, and to borrow money needed to buy land from Maori and to build roads, railways and bridges.

Here's an abridged transcript of his visionary speech[24]:

Last year we had in this Assembly many evidences that the colonising spirit was reawakening. During the recess, from all parts of the country, those evidences have been repeated, in the anxious desires expressed for a renewal of immigration and of public works. I now ask you to recognise that the time has arrived when we must set ourselves afresh to the task of actively promoting the settlement of the country. I am about to state the proposals which the Government, after mature consideration, have decided to submit to you.

I wish the task were in abler hands, for it is an onerous one. I will, very briefly, trouble you with the principles which are at the base of these proposals. They are, firstly, that both islands should aid in the colonising work both be placed in a condition to contribute to the general requirements; both share in the results obtained. Secondly that it is inexpedient to embarrass colonising operations with unnecessary political changes and that, therefore, it will be wise to adhere as closely as possible to the political institutions with the working of which we are familiar. Thirdly, that the conditions and circumstances of different parts of the colony vary widely, though there is throughout the colony the same

---

24 *New Zealand Parliamentary Debates (Hansard), June 28, 1870.*

necessity for colonising operations. I think that a recognition of these principles will be apparent in the proposals I am about to describe.

We recognise that the great wants of the colony are — public works, in the shape of roads and railways and immigration. I do not pretend to decide which is the more important, because the two are, or ought to be, inseparably united. I will first refer to public works. One island, we are aware, is tolerably well provided with ordinary roads, but is deficient in railways. The other island is deficient in both railways and roads, and wants, moreover, the special means for constructing them, in the nature of a public estate. We have to consider the best means of supplying those wants, and also how far those means should be made accordant with the conditions which have grown up as between the two islands.

The Middle Island will not consent to colonise the North Island at the expense of neglecting its own colonisation. Whatever it consents to, as for the North Island, it will expect and require to be done as for itself. The North Island, unsettled, can do but little. The North Island, settled, will support a fully equal share of population, and meet a fully equal amount of the general liability. We propose that, in a part or parts of the North Island, the colony shall be at the cost of constructing a trunk road, to place it or them in communication with the rest of the Island.

The expense of this we estimate to be £400,000, requiring an expenditure of about £100,000 per annum for four years. But if the colony finds the money for these works, it is fair that it should contribute an equal amount to analogous works in the Middle Island. We propose that it should be so — that an equal amount should be placed to the credit of the Middle Island, to be spent on railways, each province to be entitled to share upon the basis of its receipts from the consolidated revenue. Such a sum will not, of course, be sufficient for the construction of railways, but it will be a valuable contribution towards their cost, and, as between the two rounds, the arrangement will be absolutely fair.

The opening of a road through the North Island will promote its real, and probably rapid settlement and this brings us to the consideration of whether, in common prudence, we should not, when we improve the value of the North Island estate, endeavour to procure a portion of that estate to share in the profit of that improvement.

Whilst we do not seek to disable private purchasers, we do seek, in the interest of both races, that the Government shall not be precluded from acquiring land. We propose that land for a public estate shall be purchased from time to time at its fair value that such estate shall be subject to the land laws in force in the province or provinces within which it is situated that the cost shall be a charge against the provinces respectively, to be recouped in such manner as shall be agreed upon with the Provincial Government when the land is handed over and that the land itself, or its proceeds, shall be exclusively devoted to immigration and railway purposes.

We propose that, for the purchase of these lands, £200,000 shall be available. I may add that the Government intend to ask for power, under similar conditions for recouping the outstanding liability for treasury bills on their account, to hand over to the provinces from time to time such portions of the confiscated lands as may be relinquished without fear of evil results following. The condition of such relinquishment would be that the proceeds in excess of the repayments of liabilities should be set aside for railway and immigration purposes.

We are now to suppose the two islands with a landed estate, and therefore possessed of some means for promoting settlement with the inducement to encourage settlement which the consequent improvement in the value of the estate will afford. The position of the islands is the position of the provinces they comprise. We are to suppose that within those provinces there will exist such a desire for public works in the shape of railways, and for immigration as will be suitable to their several conditions.

We propose that the Government shall be armed with power to conclude arrangement for the construction of certain railways within the different provinces, as desired by their respective Governments. By certain railways, I mean that the Legislature should indicate the direction of the railways for which it is proposed to allow the General Government to contract and I think that, speaking generally, railways should in each island, be designed and constructed as parts of a trunk line. According to the nature of present traffic should be the immediate character of the respective railways. I hope the provinces will recollect that the colonial rate of interest on money is large, and that it is extravagant to lock up more capital than is necessary.

In America, I am told, there are what are called 'revenue railways,' that is to say, railways constructed in the manner precisely suited to the traffic, and out of the traffic returns those railways are, from time to time, improved, in accordance with the traffic demands. The constructors are satisfied with a moderate speed, and, as an example of the system, they are satisfied to do without expensive stations — indeed, without what we should call stations. Here and there, perhaps, a shed is erected for watering the engines but for the rest, flags put out on the line of route indicate that the use of the railway is required for passengers or goods. Interesting statements have lately been published concerning a Welsh railway, constructed partly out of revenue, and which is said to be very successful.

Now, as to the mode of paying for these railways. It is essential, in order that we shall not proceed too fast and undertake more than our means will justify, that we should fix a very effectual limit to the liabilities to be incurred. Speaking broadly, I contend that during the next ten years the colony will run no risk if it commits itself to an expenditure, or a proportionate liability for guarantee of interest, of ten millions for railways, and for the other purposes comprised in these proposals. This would mean an expenditure, at the rate of present population, of £40 a head or for interest at five and a half per cent, of about £2 per head per annum supposing the whole amount was expended, or an average on the ten years of, say, £1. This supposes that the cost is all to be paid in cash, and that there are to be no returns to reduce cost or interest. If the railways are inexpensively constructed and worked, I contend that a considerable portion of them will soon be self–supporting, that is to say, will yield sufficient, beyond working expenses, to cover either interest or guarantee, according to the principle adopted for raising the money for their construction.

But there is another source from which to anticipate a reduction in the money cost — the land should be made to bear a considerable portion of the burden. We propose that authority should be given to contract for the railways by borrowing money, by guaranteeing a minimum rate of profit or interest, by payments in land, by subsidies, or by a union of any two or more of these plans. I am inclined to think that, judiciously combined, they will enable us to obtain our railways to the greatest advantage. The contractors may want some money, but they should be glad to receive some land to yield them a profit consequent upon the effects of the railway and similarly, if the routes be judiciously selected, the contractors should be glad to keep the railways with the security of a minimum guarantee. I will not dwell further on this part of the subject, because I am sure honourable members will see that almost every agreement must possess its own special features.

I now come to the question from what source the payments, if any, are to be made. We may at once concede that the colony is to be primarily liable; but the question is, should the colony find the money finally, or should the charge be made a local one I do not submit an arbitrary rule on the subject. Two courses suggest themselves — first, that any money paid should be charged at once to the provinces or second, that if the colony makes the payments, it should, on contracting the liability, take possession of land of commensurate value.

Against the first, it may be urged that a province might be unable to meet its liability that the colony would have to pay it; and that the local charge would be merely one of account. I answer this objection by suggesting that in making any agreement the Government would not be bound solely by the wish of the province. They would have to be satisfied that the work was one which it was prudent to undertake, and that the means of the province justified if.

I have already endeavoured to show that, spread over a term of years, the liability would not be enormous and looking at the vast benefit each province would enjoy, it seems to me that special taxation, to be resorted to if necessary, would not be a hardship. In some cases the Government might take as a collateral security the results of a special tax, or a mortgage over particular properties, such as railways in course of progress, or over rents and tolls.

If the provinces are to be made liable, each work would have to be constructed in accordance with their wishes, the General Government approving. There would, in fact, be at once constituted a mixed tribunal of the General and Local Governments. There is much to be said in favour of the second plan — that of the colony taking land as security but, on the other hand, there may be urged against such a plan, that it would involve, in each case, a duplication, so to speak, of Provincial Government.

I have already said it is desirable to avoid as much as possible mixing up organic political changes with the great colonising question. I would not shrink from declaring that if the existence of the present institutions of the country are inconsistent with the promotion of public works and immigration, and a choice must be made, I would infinitely prefer the total remodelling of those institutions to abandoning that stimulating aid which, as I believe, the condition of the colony absolute demands.

But violent political changes are much to be deprecated, and in the present case they would not answer the end in view. You might sweep away the provinces and provincial institutions by legislation, but you could not destroy those feelings of separate and distinct interests which have grown up with the settlement of the provinces. In the course of time, as the separate interests become blended, the distinctive sentiment will subside but time and the progress of settlement and intercommunication must work their undemonstrative yet inevitable effects.

To attempt to anticipate their action would be to induce an exciting political struggle hi the determination of which public attention would be so much absorbed as to lead to the neglect of the great colonising question. We say that we attach far more importance to the progress of colonisation than to the maintenance of any particular form of government; but we say, also, that we see that colonisation can be best promoted by using, as far as they are capable of being used, those institutions which already exist, making only such changes from time to time as circumstances demand.

Therefore, we do not pretend to determine that either of the plans I have referred to must be adopted to the exclusion of the other. In the cases where railway can be carried out by the provinces, we are of opinion that it is desirable the provinces should be charged directly and immediately as already explained but we are not willing to exclude the colony from undertaking the primary liability, and in some cases, as proposed by the second plan, we think it should accept, as a satisfaction of the liability, a fair equivalent in landed estate.

Let the railways go on, we say, and from time to time the internal policy in reference to them can be adjusted. Supposing them to be commenced under Provincial and General Government auspices combined, there will be nothing to prevent their being, should it ever be found necessary, consolidated into one entity.

In justice to the provinces, and to my own opinions, I must say that I think, in relation to provincial institutions, we are apt to mistake cause for effect. I admit that the provincial divisions of the colony make it a work of enormous difficulty to come down with any proposal for a comprehensive scheme of colonisation. But to suppose that those divisions are consequent upon the political institutions of the provinces is, as I have said, to confound cause with effect.

Provincialism, as it is called, is consequent upon, and not the cause of, the manner in which the country was settled. It was an ambitious effort to attempt to settle the colony from so many points; but the effort was made, the work was effected, and its consequences survive: you have to deal with a number of different communities. Provincialism represents not only their different ideas and the different circumstances in which they are placed, but it represents also their strong protests against an indiscriminate, precipitate, and arbitrary fusion. If we were dealing with colonies having each only one metropolitan centre, we should propose to apply a new colonising scheme gradually commencing from one point. But to do so in New Zealand would involve gross injustice not because of the political organisation of the provinces, but because those provinces contain different communities, composed of men who have built up the provincial edifice on the clear understanding that something in the nature of proprietary rights attached to it.

We may undervalue local distinctions, but why should the inhabitants of one province submit to a lengthened period of depression, whilst the means they partly contribute are devoted to consolidating the prosperity of another province?

It is very well to talk about narrow views, but one body of settlers is entitled to just as much consideration as another. If the settlers in any province understood they were occupying an outlying district which would only be entitled to attention after more favoured districts had been served, we might then deal with this colony as we would with another: but it is quite otherwise.

Each provincial community has been taught to believe itself on a par with its neighbours, and a colonising scheme, to aid which the credit of the whole colony was pledged, would be looked upon as a gross injustice if it did not provide for due consideration to every province. That is why we must pledge ourselves to a large scheme if we wish to do justice to all. Interprovincial barriers will in time be removed, but the removal should be effected through the agency of prosperity, not of adversity.

What we as colonial legislators require to be assured upon is this. Supposing that, from various centres of population and of settlement, we allow with the approval and assistance of the Colonial Government, to give life to a number of railway enterprises, all (within each island) designed for an ultimate junction, is there reason to fear that the combined operations will prove too much for the colony?

So long as we know that, if necessary, the colony may take the whole thing into its hands, we are safe in adopting that eventuality — in considering what may be the possible consequences. We want to know what may be the worst, the most burdensome, effects of the adoption of a railway policy.

I am going to put before you a conjectural sketch of what might be the position, supposing the colony sooner or later took the whole matter into its charge, or that it remained partly a colonial and partly a provincial matter. It does not signify that, in the meanwhile, the whole large result is built up little by little by the action of the General and Provincial governing bodies conjointly nor does it signify whether the joint action continues, or in course of time becomes wholly or in part suspended. I want to trace aggregate results.

I suppose that some 1,500 or 1,600 miles of railway will require to be constructed, and this can be effected at a cost of £7,500,000, together with two and half millions acres of land, and that in addition about £1,000,000 will be required to carry out the other proposals I am making.

Julius Vogel (1835–1899)

I leave on one side the cost of immigration, because as I have before remarked, that expenditure will be essentially and immediately reproductive. Suppose that this money is expended at the rate of £850,000 a year for ten years. It matters not, for the purpose of our inquiry, whether the money is procured by direct borrowing, by the security of a guarantee, or by the aid of payments in land, in excess of the two and a half millions of acres, which I have assumed to be part of the construction money.

Vogel laid out a table of proposed expenditure, and explained his thinking on how it would be paid for. He painstakingly went through the assumed costs — it would cost £5,000 to build each mile of railway line, for instance — and he avoided making any promise that his plan would not require an increase in taxation.

My conviction is in a contrary direction but, looking to the worst, what I wish to maintain is, that the fear of a mild and moderate future addition to the taxation should not be placed in competition with the great effects which will follow the construction of railways, through the employment they will afford, the immigration that will accompany their progress, the facilities they will render for bringing produce to market, and the aid they will lend to the general settlement of the country.

It is fortunate that the time for a general election is approaching. The Assembly may prefer that the country should be consulted on the whole plan. Ministers could not object to such a course but if the Assembly, as now constituted, is willing to deal with the question, Ministers do not shrink from the responsibility of pressing it, for they are of opinion that the state of the colony is such that the sooner measures of progress are matured the better will it be for the colonists.

Before I turn to the subject of immigration, I may mention that, in connection with public works, the Government propose that power shall be given to enable the Government to aid the provinces, to a limited extent, to afford assistance to the construction of works for supplying the goldfields with water.

I have already said that the subject of immigration and public works are most intimately allied. Because I deal with them separately, honourable members must not suppose that we overlook the probability that the construction of railways will itself be a large and comprehensive means for promoting immigration.

I might detain you for hours in discussing the question of immigration in its various aspects. It is essentially one of the greatest questions of the day — a question of transferring to lands sparsely populated, portions of the excessive populations of old countries.

We ought, in dealing with this question, to recollect that it is regarded from opposite points by the country parting with, and that which is receiving the population. In the one case, the desire is natural to part with the worst, in the other to obtain the best portion of the population. A class of persons may be introduced to the colony than which even the convict element would be scarcely more detrimental.

I allude to the refuse population of large towns and cities, composed of beings hopelessly diseased in body and mind, deficient in all capacity for useful labour, vagrant and idle alike by habit and inclination, paupers by profession, and glorying in being so.

You could not subject those beings to the discipline to which convicts might be subjected they would be not only themselves burdens to the State, but they would be fruitful sources of corruption to others. It is painful to have to make reflections of this kind but it is due to the colonists that they should be assured that the Government have their attention directed to the possible pernicious use to which the agitation at home for emigration may lead.

We do not hesitate to declare that if, as has been proposed, the Imperial Government enter upon the task of directly exporting a portion of the idle masses, the Colonial Parliaments will have to jealously watch the class of persons sent out, and, if needs be, by legislation to prevent the colonies from being converted into receptacles for the worst form of refuse population.

The Imperial Government are willing to expend money on emigration in conjunction with the colonies, then, to make the movement satisfactory, the colonies must absolutely have the charge of selection. We put on one side the contingency of Imperial aid, and ask the House to concur with us in determining that the colony must take into its own charge the conduct of immigration. I will show you presently that, in assuming that charge, it is part of our proposal to remember that provinces and provincial institutions exist.

The colony requires immigration of several different descriptions, and it will be the care of the Government, if power by legislation is given to them, to enter into agreements in relation to different parts of the colony, in accordance, as far as possible, with the views of the local authorities and with local requirements.

In placing immigration on this footing, I am not dealing with it in vague terms because it is part of the principle I desire to establish that the only limit to profitable immigration is that set by a want of local preparedness to receive the emigrants.

From whatever point of view you regard it — whether from the highest social or the narrowest pecuniary view, immigration is a profit to the State, if the immigrants can settle down and support themselves. If many thousands of immigrants, introduced at once, could earn a livelihood in the colony, I would not hesitate to ask you to vote the money to pay for their passages.

Long before the money would have to be paid, supposing it to be borrowed, the immigrants would recoup the amount by contribution to the revenue. But it would be cruel to bring out immigrants if you do not see the way to their finding the means of self-support. As every immigrant who becomes a settler will be a profit, so every immigrant who leaves the colony, or is unable to procure a livelihood in it, will be a loss.

We therefore say that we will introduce immigrants only to those parts of the colony which are prepared to receive them. What the nature of the preparation may be it would be impossible now to define. It might be land for settlement it might be employment of an ordinary nature, or on public works it might be that facilities for establishing manufactories, or aiding special or co-operative settlements, were offered.

All that I can do by way of definition is to say that the Government will be prepared to assist immigration in every way possible, whether by direct grants, or by indirect agreements with powerful associations, so long as it is evident that the provinces desire and are prepared for the immigration. What we shall ask will be, a guarantee that the desire and preparation exist — the proof that the province is willing to contribute towards the cost.

Whatever the cost, we propose that the General and Provincial Governments shall share it, and we shall be quite willing that the provinces should appoint agents to select suitable immigrants. The more immigration agents there are the better, so long as they are properly qualified persons.

I believe a great many immigrants may be introduced free, or at a small cost, in connection with public works, or land grants, or special or co-operative settlements. In any of those cases the provinces, though not actually paying money, will otherwise give good evidence of their desire to encourage immigration. Be it large or small, the cost will be divided. The provincial share will be recovered by a stoppage of 30s a head, for the requisite time, to cover the actual half cost, with interest added. The provinces will in other words, only have to relinquish, for a time, the poll receipts on the new arrivals, as I will explain directly. In no case will they have to make actual payment.

If I have with sufficient clearness shown our opinion of the thoroughly reproductive nature of immigration, judiciously managed, honourable members will understand why, in no spirit of hostility to the Imperial country, we say that the whole thing must be in the hands of the colony — the selection of the immigrants, the decision of how many are wanted, the preparation to receive them.

What cultivation is to the farmer, what sheep-breeding to the runholder, what an increase of clients to professional men, are immigrants, if they become settlers, to the State. We cannot too strongly insist upon this, and so lead ourselves up to the recollection that the conditions of an under-populated country widely vary from those of a country suffering from the evils of an excessive population. If we also remembered that there is a broad distinction of circumstance and of the treatment required between a country which is able to produce more than sufficient animal and vegetable food for its population, and one which is unable to feed its population, and has constantly before it the necessity of choosing between the production of animal or vegetable food, we should have less than I think we have at present of that servile imitation which tends to impede the search after the legislation which the colony requires.

I cannot close this branch of the subject without adverting to the effect which the promotion of railways and immigration must certainly have on the native question.

The employment of large numbers of well–paid natives on public works, to which, in their present temper, they will resort with avidity the opening up of the country, and its occupation by settlers, which will result from the construction of roads; coupled with the balancing of the numbers of the two races by a large European immigration — will do more to put an end to hostilities and to confirm peaceful relations, than an army of ten thousand men.

Vogel finished his statement to what the newspapers described as 'faint applause'. One report said he had failed to elicit any 'genuine applause' and his words had prompted laughter.[25] The *Evening Post* suggested: 'Mr Vogel had better keep away from Otago for the present, if he wishes for a quiet life.'[26]

Regardless, after two weeks of debate, the plan was accepted by the House (with only two dissenting votes) and with reductions to the amounts of money to be committed to immigration (£1,000,000 instead of £1,500,000) and railways (reduced to £2,000,000).

In moving the second reading of the Immigration and Public Works Bill[27], Vogel said:

I say that this Bill in adaptability is like the trunk of an elephant — capable of picking up a pin, or of knocking down the strongest man; it may be used for constructing half dozen yards of railway or it may be used for constructing many hundred miles.

Urging his fellow members to put aside self–interest, he said:

---

25 *Evening Post, June 29, 1870.*
26 *Evening Post, July 12, 1870.*
27 *New Zealand Parliamentary Debates (Hansard), July 28, 1870.*

Those who can at all appreciate the enormous amount of care which has been given to this Bill; and those who can realise the great objects which the Government most sincerely and heartily desire to carry out, will understand what I mean when I say, during the last few days of this Parliament, let us think of the people, not of ourselves, not of parties! Let us forget all differences, and give to the country the future which this Bill promises!

Vogel's position as the driver of his country's growth plan made his political role secure even when Stafford regained power from Fox, though Stafford's second stint as Premier lasted only a month. In April 1873, with the support of the provincialist–minded politicians, Vogel became the eighth Premier of New Zealand. He retained the role until 1876 when provincial government was dismantled, bowing to the decision–making of central government. Newly–knighted, Sir Julius became agent–general for New Zealand in London but returned to his adopted home to re–enter Parliament in 1884. After quitting politics in 1887, he moved back to England where he died in 1899.

No matter what else he achieved, Vogel was clearly visionary in many respects. Not content with foreseeing the country's need for infrastructure, he worked for reconciliation with Maori and was an early supporter of gender equality, introducing the first Women's Suffrage Bill to Parliament (although suffrage was not adopted until 1893).

His visionary ways were epitomised by one of his quirkiest achievements — that of writing what is thought to be New Zealand's first science fiction novel. Called *Anno Domini 2000 — A Woman's Destiny*, it predicted a utopian world where women would hold many positions of power by the year 2000. Of course, by then, New Zealand was about to enter a period where its leading constitutional positions — Governor–General, Prime Minister, Speaker of the House and Chief Justice — were all held by women.

'Millions Yet Unborn'

Sir George Grey

March 8, 1878

Sir George Grey, with Edward Gibbon Wakefield, was a political genius of the British Empire as it developed to its apogee in the 19th century. Both played vital roles in the evolution of the New Zealand state, its Parliament and constitution.

The radical liberal Grey was, in the phrase of his recent assessor, 'a sphinx with an answer.'[28]

His career as an army officer began at Sandhurst and traversed Ireland, West Australia, New Zealand, South Australia, the Cape province and then New Zealand again. Here, he served twice as Governor, fighting two wars, first to assert Crown sovereignty and then to promote British settlement and Native assimilation in a Parliamentary state for which he wrote the first constitution.

Wakefield then drove for immediate responsible government.

Grey was a great, if not a good man. Falling out with British ministers, and failing to secure a seat at Westminster, Grey took to the New Zealand

---

28 *Bernard Cadogan, Oxford D.Phil Thesis: Constituting the settler colony and reconstituting the indigene—the native administration and constitutionalism of Sir George Grey KCB during his two New Zealand Governorships (1945–53, 1961–68) until the outbreak of the Waikato War in 1868.*

Biography of Sir George Grey with publishers at time of publication.

87

political stage. As a radical liberal, he pressed his concept of a small holding property owning democracy. On the stump and in the House — though failing to master the Parliamentary machine he had helped create — he attained a rare eloquence. Opponents hated him, some like Fox were scathingly critical.

Grey was not a likable man. Yet his vision of a greater New Zealand of 'millions yet unborn', the greyhounds of the Liberal era 1891–1912 put in place small land holdings, women's suffrage on top of male suffrage, labour laws, old age pensions and Empire in the Pacific.

In March 1878 — 30 years to the month after the arrival of the Otago settlers — Grey visited Dunedin and, according to his biographer, showed 'his genius in understanding the structures, the connections, the magic of power.'[29]

Five generations later, his Dunedin speech, given at the Princess Theatre on March 8, ignites any imaginative mind. The theatre was packed, upstairs and downstairs, with 1,500 men and women, many of whom were forced to stand as every seat was taken.

If Grey 'was the most intelligent man who has led government in New Zealand,'[30] this was perhaps the most eloquent speech ever made in New Zealand.

The Premier's Address:[31]

It is with feelings of very great pleasure I have the opportunity afforded me of addressing the citizens of Dunedin.

What renders this so peculiarly agreeable is this, that many years ago — so many years ago that those now approaching middle age who are here were not then born, and those who have attained middle age could have been but children — I formed a belief that this portion of the country would constitute a very great country, and that its inhabitants would be distinguished in many respects. At that time there was a great doubt

---

29 Bernard Cadogan, Oxford D.Phil Thesis: *Constituting the settler colony and reconstituting the indigene—the native administration and constitutionalism of Sir George Grey KCB during his two New Zealand Governorships (1945–53, 1961–68) until the outbreak of the Waikato War in 1868. Biography of Sir George Grey with publishers at time of publication.*
30 Bernard Cadogan, again.
31 Recorded in the Otago Daily Times, March 13, 1878

whether the Middle Island should be settled by a European population for many years. It was contended that the soil was not adapted to the inhabitants of Great Britain ... and that altogether it was desirable to turn the tide of European population solely into the Northern Island of New Zealand.

Many objections to that course presented themselves to my mind. One was this, that I believed impossible to pour suddenly into the Northern Island a large European population without creating such alarm in the native mind that contests must have taken place throughout every portion of that Island; and that the European race could only have become its conquerors by having almost to exterminate the race of Native inhabitants. Such a series of events must have delayed the colonisation of that island for many years.

On the other hand, in the Middle Island there were hardly any Native inhabitants, and ... those Europeans who did enter it, would enter it unencumbered by any Maori population, by any Native questions, or war; would establish themselves here without acts of cruelty, without acts of injustice, and from the first moment they planted foot on this island would have a field before them for developing all their energies ...

These were strong arguments for placing a large European population in the Middle Island, and I thought ultimately when this island had become tolerably peopled the inhabitants would spread off gradually, and as gradually occupy the North Island without alarming the Native population.

I believed that when the North Island was being gradually settled such friendly relations might spring up between the two races that insensibly the lesser population might be adopted into and absorbed in the larger population.

But another circumstance weighed in my mind. I knew that it was proposed that this part of New Zealand should be occupied by a hardy race, a race whose religious institutions necessarily inclined them to freedom, because they are the freest in the world — and I thought that here a great opportunity would be presented of trying what could be done in a new colony by conferring upon the inhabitants of that colony the most absolute freedom of self-government that the world had perhaps ever seen.

Cheers from the crowd.

I therefore for a great number of years most sedulously devoted myself to the task of drawing the form of a constitution which would give to freedom the utmost limits that freedom could desire to attain, and I trusted that here, separated from any central government by a great distance — here separated from any interference with institutions of perfect self–government, a love of liberty might grow up which nothing afterwards could efface.

Devoting myself to that task, I used my influence with leading statesmen at Home, and with the British Parliament, to pass an act by which a constitution of the kind I spoke of was conferred upon the inhabitants of the province of Otago, and I devoutly hoped, and still rest unshaken in that hope, that in a population trained under institutions of that kind would also be trained sturdy defenders of the liberties of this country ... who would never relinquish the freedom handed down to them by the Queen and the British Parliament ... (and) that they would to the last always struggle for the perfect freedom of their institutions.

Cheers.

To that assemblage which I hoped to raise up, I am addressing myself. I am realizing the dream of my comparative youth. I am now appealing to them — no standing before them, telling them what I think should be done to render the future secure to New Zealand ...

You are all aware that institutions of the kind I speak of were conferred upon the country. You are all aware they led to no disasters of any kind. You had no quarrels with the provinces coterminous with yourselves — nothing resembling the Customs Duties which separate Victoria from NSW. No disaster occurred.

The development of its resources were unparalleled. Colonisation took place, and happiness, contentment and prosperity were enjoyed by its population in a manner never yet surpassed in any newly founded community.

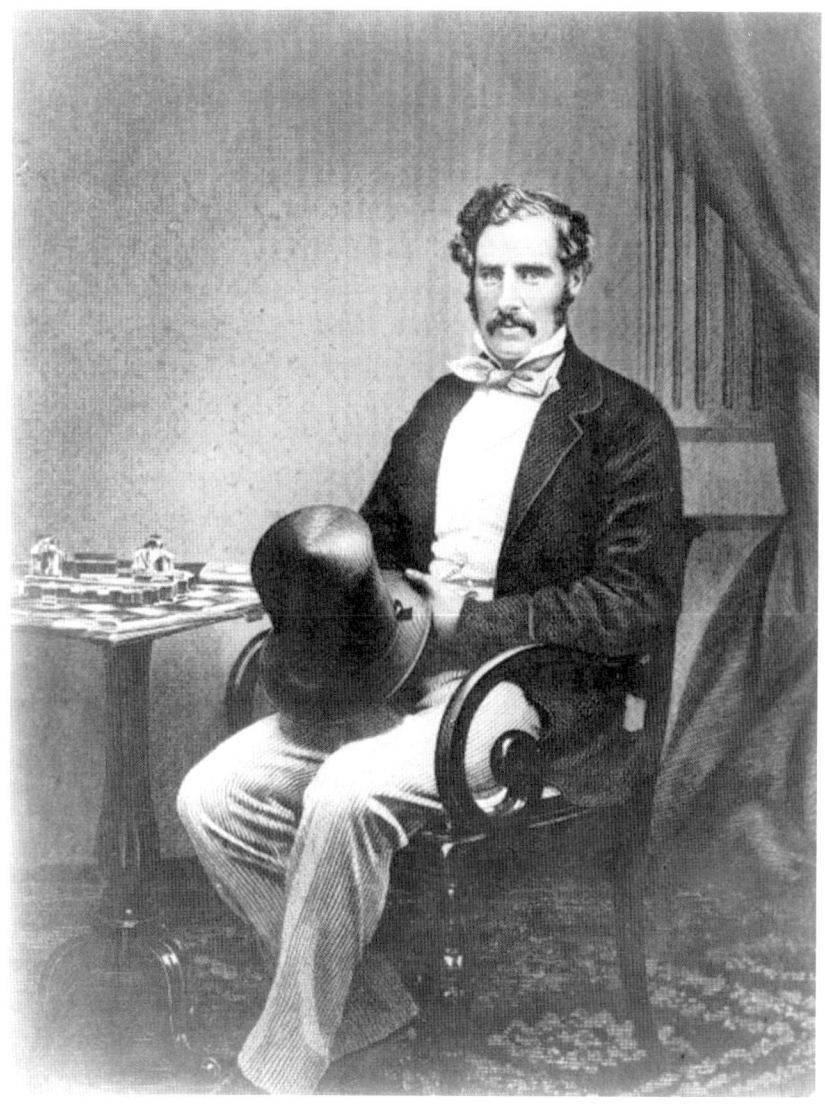

Sir George Grey(1812–1898)

Cheers.

Nevertheless these institutions have been swept away. Are the new institutions such as become free men?

A voice from the audience — 'Yes!'

Are the new institutions such as will conduce to happiness and prosperity?

Let us calmly consider the whole of this question. First ... the franchise was most liberal. That (universal) franchise was conferred upon you ... every man possessing the franchise would have one vote and no more. Now the law says one man is to have one vote, some none at all, and some to have four or five ... I say that a violation of the constitution more open than that could never possibly have taken place.

Those who think with me in Parliament are anxious ... That every male adult should have a vote in that district to return its representative (cheers) — and that no man should have more than one vote (renewed applause) ... The greatest statesman in England (Mr Gladstone) is claiming the same right ... (Mr Gladstone) believes the welfare of his fellow men depends upon every male of his fellow countrymen having a vote.

Cheers.

Now I argue in this way. If a man loves his wife — if he loves his children ... if he so far neglects his children (on their behalf) he is a man devoid of all self respects interests, if he does not struggle to get the right of having a voice.

(Then) if you do not allow every individual to assent to the laws under which he lives under which he lives through his representative, or at least to have a voice in dissenting from them, if you compel them to live under laws imposed upon him in which he has no voice whatever, I tell you that you must educate the people badly ... that the person who is shut out from civil rights is inferior.

Now, all these reasons satisfy me that you have the best chance of educating a free population, the best chance of educating ... a moral population, the best chance of creating happy homes, the best chance of raising eminent statesmen, and of giving to all a free and fair race in the battle of life if you provide by legislation that ... every adult male ... shall have a vote in returning representatives for that district.

Applause.

No honest man ought to deprive his fellow citizens of a vote for a representative. The Queen herself assented to in the constitution which is part of the land ... a right of which you have been deprived by your own legislators, but which the British Parliament never intended you to lose.

Cheers.

We must revert to that rule of the constitution.

And again on that subject I have Mr Gladstone's absolute declaration that he agrees thoroughly with these views, and will do his utmost to get them altered in England. Therefore I ask you to join me in claiming the representation which your sovereign gave you, and which, in asking for, you prove yourself a loyal population.

As I told you the old constitution has been shattered to pieces and a new constitution set up which satisfies nobody. Let the whole male population deliberately choose a commission to frame a constitution for them, and let them determine the constitution under which they will live. And see that a fair system of taxation is established ...

Prolonged applause.

Now in asking you to see that a system of that kind is carried out, people will tell you I am a radical. I have heard myself called a chartist. But reflect upon this, what I ask you to do is done in England.

Therefore I say again let us in the next session of Parliament acquit ourselves upon this subject like men and do our best to get a reform made in this great and pressing question of taxation.

I think men are pretty much the same ... Where you place power in the hands of the wealthy, they will naturally legislate for their own good ... they think it is good to set a great landed aristocracy.

No country can thrive without it; it is good any should we not be that landed aristocracy. I feel such a constituency as I speak to now will always endeavour to have a fair land law, and a very different one from any you have had in this country ...

Somehow it leaked out I advised the Governor to disallow a land law. I was said to be a democrat (but) if I believed I could save the rights of the people of New Zealand, after the Crown to save the rights of one subject had disallowed the law. I was quite justified in order to save the rights of the whole of the inhabitants of New Zealand to try to get the law disallowed to ...

Cheers.

... the act which was accomplished last session of prolonging these licences for ten years was a fraud upon the entire population of New Zealand —

From the crowd: 'Hear, hear' and laughter.

I say this that if you do not attend to the question of the franchise you will achieve nothing ... unless you get the power into your own hands abuses will spring up almost instantly again. Now remember this: here we are all placed in a position such as the world had hardly ever seen ... a country of extraordinary fertility, minerals, forests, fish, the climate the most healthy possible.

It is our duty to be a nation in which wealth is tolerably well distributed. The poor shall not be trodden down by the rich, that enormous property must not be in single hands.

We must strive to build up a really great and free nation in which whoever he is, should take an active part in the affairs of the country and try to become one of the statesmen of New Zealand —

Loud applause.

Just think for a moment what position a statesman is in. Go forth and do the almost unlimited good which we enable you to do, with power to make laws, power to remove abuses, power to reward merit, power to promote education, and power to the lasting good. Is that not a career towards the achievement of which everyone should strive?

Loud applause.

Every one of you has to take part in this transaction. Every one of you must aid in building up what I believe will be one of the great nations the world has ever seen.

I fancy I sometimes see passing along the beach what are vast populations, now say half a million, then in a few years two or three millions, then in a few years countless millions, all passing on, all founded by you, the present inhabitants of New Zealand, all depending upon the lands you have made, depending upon the institutions you have established.

And then I look carefully to see as I gaze at these populations passing by, what is their aspect. Is it one of general comfort, general happiness, general contentment? Are these countless millions which I see ... leading a happier life than the men hitherto were? Am I to see a mean, wretched squalid population, some million or two strutting with pomp and power, and perhaps 38 million starving, scarcely fed, scarcely clothed?

Which are the populations to pass before us?

Well the hopes I indulge in are these: I imagine I see banners in their hands and upon them the names of families that I have known in New Zealand, and I hear loud shouts and loud acclamations of joy and an encouragement as these banners wave. I believe — I believe that such will be the future of New Zealand —

Loud cheering.

Let us strive to found such a nation such as never been ...

We have power to do it. Who will prove recreant to such a trust.

Who will prove ungrateful to such a course? I believe the people of New Zealand never will.

At a grand party Auckland gave Grey on his departure from New Zealand in 1884, 4,000 turned out. There perhaps he passed the mantle of statesman to another populist politician, Dick Seddon, thrusting him onto the political stage.

'Iron Joined to Clay'

Te Whiti–o–Rangomai

February 1878

At its end, the mass land confiscation of the 1860s and 1870s saw the brief appearance of one of the greatest New Zealanders of the 19th century. In fertile Taranaki, a Maori warrior who had fought in the Waikato war, became a prophet of non–violence.

Having eschewed violence in 1864, Te Whiti–o–Rangomai[32] went to live in Parihaka in 1868, a coastal settlement 55km south west of New Plymouth. By 1870, it had become the largest Maori village in the country. Te Whiti ordained a lifestyle of peaceful co–existence and raised the white feather of the albatross as the symbol of that peace. The village had become a haven for the dispossessed, and on the 18th day of every month, Maori and Pakeha leaders were invited there to discuss the land grabbing and to air grievances.

In 1879, Te Whiti, with his fellow chief Tohu, stood fast against the perfidy of the State and a range of ministers, judges and officials sworn to uphold the rights of the people. He urged his people to obstruct the surveyors who were pegging out land for confiscation. Men were sent from the village to plough confiscated land and at Te Whiti's urgings, they

---

32 Danny Keenan. 'Te Whiti–o–Rangomai III, Erueti — Biography', from the Dictionary of New Zealand Biography. Te Ara — the Encyclopedia of New Zealand.

97

offered no resistance when arrested. In June that year, Te Whiti told his ploughmen:

Go, put your hands to the plough. Look not back. If any come with guns and swords, be not afraid. If they smite you, smite not in return. If they rend you, be not discouraged. Another will take up the good work. If evil thoughts fill the minds of the settlers, and they flee from their farms to the town as in the war of old, enter not you into their houses, touch not their goods nor their cattle. My eye is over all.

In 1880, the people of Parihaka put up barricades across roads and pulled survey pegs. Parliament passed a law, enabling protestors to be arrested and held indefinitely without trial.

Te Whiti addressed his people:[33]

Things that are planted cannot be disturbed till they are ripe. There is only one to direct everything on this earth — to direct the judges, the controllers, and the directors, people in power and are titiau (to run one side of a boat, and throw it out of its balance). They must bow to me. Things are on the tip of my tongue this day, but the conclusion is with the Master of the world (Ariki o te ao).

Power has been sent upon the earth ... and if the lifters up of guns are anxious to raise them, they cannot do so. Go where you will, there is someone before you. There is only one to rule things on this earth — only one; old things have swept away, and new things are about to come to pass. The former mode of judging and directing the things of this earth has been done away with.

The seed of Te Whiti is spreading. I am telling you this that you may know, and not be led blindly by the Government. Things have so bounded us that one could scarcely move, but men have not been allowed to carry out their works The Master will not allow the doings of great and wicked men to be accomplished. Evil cannot be upheld. What I am speaking to you now is not what is said to be, but I am telling everything to your faces, so that you may know the doings of this generation.

---

33 *Reported by the New Zealand Herald, February 21, 1880.*

The wise men are as if they were drunk; the soldiers, their guns will not go off. The Master of the world has said to the surveyors, the Master will not allow you to complete; all works, great or small, cannot be accomplished. The Master has so ordered. We are approaching the end. The day has arrived. This should not make us afraid. Be of good heart. These things were all prophesised, and it was said that before the coming of the Master troubles should arise.

The other year these things were told to you here (Parihaka), and I said you should see and hear for yourselves that I am the true one. It would be good for the sword to glisten in the eyes of men. The Government has thousands — Tohu is only one but this does not make him afraid. All these things were foretold. It was not said before that this day would bring trouble. The Master of the world will settle everything this day. Trouble, war, and everything will meet. The Master will submerge everything. Bitterness of the heart with everything will be completed by Him.

The workers of the world are not known this day, but things that were prophesised are about to come to pass. What if the Government takes the land? What next? Who shall fight? The Master has taken the world this day. The natives who have gone over to the Government will bow down to Him (the Master). The strangers (Pakehas) have everything this day — land and people — but at the last everything shall be yours. It rests with me to disturb the earth — with me also to quicken.

Things of brass, silver, iron, and clay that were joined together cannot hold. They are like the natives who have joined the Government — iron joined to clay. The rain comes and moistens; the sun then shines on it, and it fall to pieces. So also will the natives fall from the Government!

I am telling you these things openly, so that you may all hear, not like the Government, who keep everything to themselves. I am speaking to Europeans and Maori, so that you may all hear. Everything that has been done this day, taking lands and surveying, has to be finished by the Maker. The Government have nothing but their guns this day, but they do not know where they (the guns) will reach, but the morning and the evening will replace the people on the land. It will not be carried out as the Government wish. Tohu says: 'The Government have a thousand, he only one; the thousand have guns, the one nothing.'

Te Whiti–o–Rangomai (c1830–1907)

We can only look on and laugh. This is the year you were told of on the former 18th, the year in which all would be clear. I would not hide anything, and I go to my loving friend and confide in him, but I speak to everybody only as everyone may hear. Tho hiahia (yearnings) of men of wisdom, men of war, will not be accomplished. Although Tohu says the Government have a thousand who wish to lift up the guns, no evil will be allowed by the Maker.

Even though the bayonets of the soldiers blind your eyes with their brightness, do not flinch. Surveyors who wish to survey the land cannot do so without the consent of the Master. I have not much to say this day. Everything is going on the straight road, and in the one direction. If it were to branch off or turn aside, then I should speak.

A month later, in another address, Te Whiti instructed his people:

Though some, in darkness of heart, seeing their land ravished, might wish to take arms and kill the aggressors, I say it must not be! Let not the Pakehas think to succeed by reason of their guns.

By late 1881, it was obvious the Government was going to act to try to quash the protests. Preparing his people for what lay ahead, Te Whiti issued an order — not of battle, but the feather of peace. He told them:

The ark by which we are to be saved today is stouteartedness. Flight is death. Let this sink into the ears of all. Even the children. There is nothing about fighting today, but the glorification of God, and peace on the land. Many generations wished to see this day; but we, a blind, small and despised people, have been chosen and glorified this day ...

The canoe by which we are to be saved is forbearance. It has been prepared by Tohu during months and years, and is now launched, and will bear us safely through all tempests. It will save us all ...

What matter to us what happens; we have our ark as Noah of old. I now say, come into the ark.

Now is the glory of peace upon the land. Let us wait for the end; there is nothing else for us. Let us abide calmly upon the land ...

If any man thinks of his gun or his horse, and goes to fetch it, he will die by it ... place your trust in forbearance and peace ... let the booted feet come when they like, the land shall remain firm for ever.

I stand for peace. Though the lions rage, still I am for peace. I will go into captivity ... the Pakehas are indeed robbers ... oh, hard-hearted people! I am here to be taken. Take me for the sins of the island. Why hesitate? Am I not here? Though I be killed, I yet shall live; though dead

I shall live in the peace, which will be the accomplishment of my aim. The future is mine, when asked as to the author of peace, shall say —Te Whiti— and I will bless them.

On November 5, at dawn, more than 1,500 armed troops surrounded and entered the village, prepared to put down any resistance. Instead, they were greeted by hundreds of children who skipped, sang and offered them food. More than 2,000 residents sat peacefully at the marae, quietly awaiting their fate.

The troops evicted 1,600 residents from the village, dispersing them through Taranaki without food or shelter.

Te Whiti and Tohu were arrested and taken to the South Island where they were refused trials and held for five years.

Te Whiti's campaign of passive resistance did little to stop the confiscation of land, nor the destruction of Parihaka, and the illegal imprisonment of many of his people.

But it is a sublime story of applied Christianity. The now well–told narrative[34] rests on the words of the noblest orator in our history, an orator of such passion and power, of such magnetism, as to lead a whole community to martyrdom and desolation.

Te Whiti's story contained a wider significance for the future. Mahatma Ghandi seized on his doctrine of passive resistance in leading India to independence. After Ghandi, through Maui Pomare, a child at Parihaka, he fuelled the Mau of Samoa.

Martin Luther King picked up the doctrine of non–resistance for the civil rights movement in America. And some 100 years after Parihaka, Te Whiti's white feather helped shame Parliament into redressing the not–so–ancient iniquities of the Land wars.

Our first Maori Governor General, Paul Reeves, in honour of his tribal lines, took the white feather as his crest. Te Whiti's white feather, like John Brown's body, marches on in our Aotearoa New Zealand.

Of the many admirable men in public life of the time, Robert Stout (was it because he was a Shetlander?) appears to have spoken up against the

---

34 *The Parihaka Story (1954) and Ask That Mountain (1975), both by Dick Scott, and the paintings of Hotere, Smither and McCahon awakening New Zealanders a century later to the Parihaka saga.*

102

War. Honoured names like Bryce[35], Chute, Dillon Bell, Fox, Hursthouse, Prendergast and Rolleston stand convicted at the bar of history as hard–hearted people who betrayed the rule of law. Only the radical orator of the British Parliament, Charles Bradlaugh noted that the Parliament of New Zealand had been responsible for the imprisonment of British subjects, without trial, and in many cases, leading to death.

To any living New Zealander, their most moving memorials are the cliff caves in Dunedin where the Parihaka prisoners sheltered in bad weather. Faintly, they convey a sense of the crime of our fledgling state against a tiny 'despised tribe, but a tribe led by our greatest orator'.[36]

35 Admired as 'the people's Bryce' for his championing of the rights of humbler settlers.
36 The Parihaka Story (1954) and Ask That Mountain (1975), both by Dick Scott.

The Shadow of the Queen

King Tawhiao

August 20, 1884

King Tawhiao, the second Maori King, reigned for 34 years during one of the most turbulent periods of Maori history. As the leader of the Waikato tribes, he had seen more than 14,000 Imperial troops invade his territory in 1863 and seize about a million acres (4,000 sq km) in contravention of the Treaty of Waitangi.

Tawhiao and his people moved south to the area now known as King Country where he waited for the opportunity to redress his grievance. For 20 years, he urged his people to wait for a peaceful resolution, reminding them that war always had its price.

In 1884, the King saw his chance to get the justice he had been denied in New Zealand. He came up with a plan to sail to England to petition Queen Victoria, to plead with her to put things right.

Accounts of his journey were reported in many newspapers, now available online through the Papers Past Archive of the National Library of New Zealand.

When asked about his journey, he told a reporter: 'I am going to see the Queen of England, to have the Treaty of Waitangi honoured.' He intended to present the Queen with a petition asking for a separate Maori parliament, a special commissioner to act as an intermediary between

King Tawhiao (unknown–1894)

Pakeha and Maori parliaments, and for an independent commission to investigate land confiscations.[37]

Tawhiao sailed with his cousin Putara Te Tuhi (son of the chief Maisha), Topia Turoa (a Wanganui chief), Hori Ropia (a Wellington chief) and Major Te Wheoro, an MP and respected Maori elder. They took with them an interpreter, George Skidmore.

37 R. T. Mahuta. 'Tawhiao, Tukaroto Matutaera Potatau Te Wherowhero — Biography', from the Dictionary of New Zealand Biography. Te Ara — the Encyclopedia of New Zealand.

After the long journey to Britain, no one was there to greet them on behalf of either the Queen or the English Government when the *Sorata* berthed at Plymouth on May 31. Instead, they were left to their own devices, though their arrival had attracted the interest of the press.

Asked why the party had travelled to London, Skidmore told a journalist: 'Oh, you will see it all in the papers, by and bye.'

The King's plans relied significantly on the efforts of John Gorst, who had been a magistrate and the Waikato Civil Commissioner in 1863 when the land war had driven both men from the area. Gorst, who had sympathies with the King movement, had left New Zealand for England where he had become a Tory MP. Gorst was tasked with trying to arrange a meeting between the Queen and the Maori King.

After more than six weeks of fruitless effort, it became obvious the Queen would not see the deputation. Instead, on July 23, the King got to meet the Secretary of State for the Colonies, Lord Derby. Dressed in a smart blue suit and wearing patent leather shoes, the tattooed King tried to put his case but to no avail. His petition proposed a separate Maori parliament, an independent inquiry into the land confiscations and a special commissioner to work as an intermediary between the European and Maori parliaments. Reports of the meeting say Tawhiao acknowledged Queen Victoria's supremacy and defined his own role as uniting the Maori as one people, not for the purposes of separation but to claim the Queen's protection.

Lord Derby said the petition would first need to be referred to the New Zealand government and it was not appropriate for his government to deal with it.

Gorst, the initiator of the meeting, brought Lord Derby's attention to article 71 of the Constitution Act.

According to an account in the *New Zealand Herald*, the following exchange took place:

Lord Derby: 'Do I understand you to say that a clause in the Constitution Act gives the Crown the power, by an order–in–council, to cut off and reserve a district for the Maoris, where they may enjoy practical independence, over the heads of the Colonial Government?'

Mr Gorst: 'Yes … And a long time ago, when this Maori King first sprang up, Sir George Grey seriously considered whether he should recommend the proclamation of a Native district apart from the colonists, where the Maoris could have exercised their own power, and I believe if this had been done there would never have been a Waikato war.'

The meeting ended, with Lord Derby promising the party he would do his best to make the rest of their visit enjoyable.

Over the next month, the visitors were variously entertained at Windsor Castle, Crystal Palace, the Royal Naval dockyards at Plymouth, and shown the scene of the Battle of Hastings.

By August 20, after 81 days in England, the King had achieved little, if nothing, and he and some of his party prepared to leave.

On the eve of their departure, they were given a farewell function, attended by the Lord Mayor of London, representatives of the Colonial Office and a number of invited guests.

The King's party was presented with a gift — a framed portrait of Queen Victoria.

'On receipt of the portrait, the chiefs composed and sang a song, expressing their regret at only having seen the "shadow of the Queen", and not her very person,' it was delicately reported by the *New Zealand Herald*.

The report described the parting of the King and the Lord Mayor as 'very tender and expressive.' It gave a verbatim account of their exchange:

Lord Mayor:

May it please your Majesty — it gives me pleasure to see you here this afternoon. I hope that the result of your visit to England will be of much use; and this it will create an interest in the affairs of New Zealand among the people here. I hope what you have seen in England will be of interest to you, and that you will look back with pleasure hereafter to your visit here. I have no doubt that Lord Derby has been very much interested in the statements which you have made to him, and he is very anxious to use what influence he can with the Government of New Zealand to promote the just and righteous objects which have brought you to this country.

King Tawhiao:

My Lord Mayor — salutations. Here I am, speaking in your presence, in your dwelling, in the midst of your own people, where you are living under the dominion of justice, with the Houses of Parliament living under the same rule. The thing which has brought us here I have very much at heart. It was through my constant effort that we came here.

We had been here only one month when New Zealand and all our lands were lost to us, and now we have been here two months–and–a–half, and we have heard the words that we are to return, and Te Wheoro is to remain. I am not at all condemning this. I think it is quite a proper arrangement.

All the things have been brought together under one head, and the whole thing has been laid down at your feet. We have left nothing whatever unsaid.

It is quite right that you should look after the affairs of New Zealand, and that Te Wheoro should remain to keep you enlightened in these matters.

We have come to this country, and our coming here has been a cause of life again to New Zealand. Therefore we have said these words that the very Queen herself should cherish and embrace us to give us life again.

Though you look at me and see that my face is dark, yet my heart is like the pounamu — clear and transparent — and there is no warfare in my heart.

Here I am returning to my country. I freely open my heart to you, knowing that our affairs will be carried on here.

This is the greatest word of all — love, love. It is love which has caused us to be called to the houses of ladies and gentlemen.

The King briefly paid tribute to John Hilton, the Secretary of the United Kingdom Alliance, a temperance group that sought the prohibition of alcohol, who had recruited he and the other chiefs to the Order of Good Templars, which also advocated temperance.

I will carry back to my own people the work of a Good Templar.
Remain you here to make things clear and bright and let your light be

diffused abroad. Great is your love; great is your kindness; great is your uprightness; great is your charity; and we thank you for cherishing us.

We have come here to bid you all farewell, leaving one of our number while we go away and return to our own country. Dwell here in your place. May God help you!

After tea and coffee, the King prepared to leave. He grasped the Lord Mayor's hand and said: 'I shall ever keep you in remembrance, God bless you.'

The next day, the *New Zealand Herald*'s special correspondent witnessed the King and the other chiefs leaning over the side of the steamship *Potosi* as it drew away from its berth at Gravesend, heading for the other side of the world.

The reporter said the parting of the King and Major Te Wheoro, who was to remain in England as his emissary, was emotional — 'the usually stolid Major was well nigh overcome.'

Tawhiao and his cousin Putara waved their handkerchiefs from the ship's railings, tears in their eyes, while Te Wheoro sat in the tender returning him to shore, smoking his pipe, 'evidently full of thought, and almost mastered by his feelings.'

The King had tried to seek justice, using the power of oratory and the personal approach. Now, the outcome depended on whether his words would be relayed back to New Zealand and make any difference.

The New Zealand Premier, Robert Stout, received the advice from the Colonial Office and responded by refusing to discuss any events preceding 1865, when the imperial government was responsible. He denied any breach of the Waitangi Treaty had happened since.[38]

The King continued to represent his people, advocating a peaceful resolution to their grievances, and he refused various honours offered to him by the New Zealand Government, including a seat in the Legislative Council and an annual pension of £1,000, for fear it would jeopardise his standing with his people. He died on August 26, 1894 — almost 10 years to the day after his departure from England.

---

38 R. T. Mahuta. 'Tawhiao, Tukaroto Matutaera Potatau Te Wherowhero — Biography', from the *Dictionary of New Zealand Biography*. Te Ara — the Encyclopedia of New Zealand.

'The Sin of Sweated Labour'

Rutherford Waddell

November 7, 1888

George Grey sowed the seeds of radical liberalism in New Zealand. A prophetic Ulster–born preacher in Dunedin watered the plants. Rutherford Waddell, after late training as a Presbyterian Minister and rejection as a missionary, had come in 1877 to Christchurch. In the 1880s, he became a leader in a Dunedin deeply influenced by George Grey and his radical liberalism. At the influential St Andrews Church Rutherford Waddell preached an active Christianity that provided impetus to the radical liberal movement.

In the astonishing social and economic development of a fledgling nation, Rutherford Waddell involved himself in establishing bibles in schools, planned Sunday schools, the Presbyterian Deaconess order, *The Outlook*, the outstanding church journal of its day, and church savings banks and free libraries, the Temperance movement, probation before prison, technical education and a burgeoning conservation movement.

In one prophetic sermon, Rutherford Waddell changed society.[39]

In October 1888, *'The Sins of Sweated Labour'* shook the establishment. But it brought results in the Royal Commission of 1890 on which he

---

39 *The Sermon That Moved A Nation', from Great Tales from New Zealand History (Penguin Books), by Gordon McLauchlan.*

111

sat. That Commission seeded the radical liberal legislation of the 1890s. Related particularly to the work place, notably the hours and conditions of work, its radical arbitration system underwrote social harmony in New Zealand for 80 years.

Waddell was a leader in thought and action. His motto might well have been 'what are we going to do about it?' Having preached the sermon (of which we can find no record) he took the debate to the Presbyterian synod in Dunedin on November 7.

We have taken the liberty of turning the full report in the *Otago Daily Times* of November 8, 1888, of his prophetic call to action, into direct speech.

That the attention of the synod having been called to the existence of … the 'sweating system' in Dunedin and elsewhere in the colony, and as it appears that the wages paid for many classes of work are miserably inadequate, this synod records its protest against this social injustice. It urges the members of the church to lend their aid to every legitimate means to mitigate the evils of excessive competition, enjoins its ministers to give special prominence in their teachings to the sins of covetousness, which is the worst of all such evils, and also to proclaim more emphatically the laws of Christ as laws of social and commercial, not less than religious life.

This is a matter of some importance. Since I called attention to the subject from the pulpit, it has found its way into the columns of the newspapers, and is now discussed in every city in the colony.

What is called the 'sweating system' does exist in this new country and in our new cities. People here are earning wages which if not lower, are at least as low, as those which have been condemned as sweated wages at Home.

I myself know of cases in Dunedin where wages are being earned totally inadequate to keep body and soul together. The situation is worse in Wellington. In Auckland the wages are perhaps the lowest in any city in the Australasian colonies.

These facts tell a terrible tale of the state of life that must be endured by those struggling for existence under such conditions.

The Rev. Rutherford Waddell (1849–1932) at the pulpit, St Andrews, Dunedin.

I am not going to single out any class for blame. All classes of the community are to blame. But Christians especially must take the greatest blame on ourselves. As Christians we are in a position to teach the laws of Christ. If the laws of Christ are learned, no such state of affairs would exist.

What then is the duty of the Church? The duty of the Church is to take more interest in social questions and in the social welfare of the people. The Church is only preaching half the Gospel when it preaches the moral uplifting of the community. We have to consider the physical condition of those for whose spiritual welfare we are concerned. We must carry this two-fold Gospel. We must deal with the thought why the working classes do not go to Church on Sunday.

Is it because some say the capitalists pray for them on Sunday and prey on them for the rest of the week?

Is it because when women and other workers are receiving just a bare allowance for their support they see the well-to-do not curtailing their expenditure? It is natural that bitter feelings are aroused.

So what can the Church do? We can protest and do what we can to mitigate the evil.

Sweated wages are caused by excessive competition, by the enormous rage to get cheap things. That is the effect of the lust of gain.

You see, getting good bargains is much the same as gambling. Gambling is getting something without giving any return for it, and that is neither more nor less than robbery. Getting good bargains is getting things without any equivalent for them, and that is practically robbery. Cheap things are produced at the cost of the life, prosperity and happiness of working men and women. It is our duty to speak against the sin of cheapness. The rage for cheapness must be mitigated.

But how may we aid the cause of the masses? Might the direction lie in profit sharing and co-operation? The Church might do immense good by aiding the movement of profit sharing and co-operation, by aiding the movement to co-operation that has set in all over the world.

It is our duty to take hold of this tendency because it is the Church alone which holds those principles which make co-operation practicable. There can be no brotherhood of men without the Fatherhood of God.

To attempt to found co-operation on any other principles is useless.

This is the point. We have to hold up the laws of Christ as the laws of commercial and social as well as religious life. There are men who are good, with good designs and purposes. Yet somehow they hold that the laws of Christ do not apply to commercial life.

The test in this respect of course is how many obey the law of charity.

Let me be clear. I do not care what the law of political economy teaches. If the laws of political economy are different from the laws of Christ, they must be brought into conflict, and the laws of Christ must prevail. The Christian life must be lived, as a Christian life, on every day of the week, and in all places of business.

Am I to be told that this is all very ideal and dreamy? Of course it is. Christ's laws were all ideal and dreamy until people endured great sacrifice to make them real. There is just as much room now for heroism, and even for martyrdom, as there has ever been in the past. It is our duty as Ministers to bring our people up to the laws of Christ, not to bring the laws down to the people.

Seldom can any speaker have done so much for the social and economic progress of our nation. His clarion call for social justice ranks among the most influential speeches ever made in New Zealand.

It was the synod speech rather than the sermon which led to the Royal Commission and initiated a radical social reform of enormous influence and importance for the country.

Votes for Women

Kate Sheppard

August 21, 1890

In the late 1880s, while Rutherford Waddell was calling for equity in the work place, Kate Sheppard[40] led the movement for equity at the ballot box. Effective social reform, as the Temperance movement sought, required the involvement of women.

Kate Sheppard's case, though the campaign for the vote took four taut years, was simple. Why should not every adult person (except the criminal and the lunatic) have the right to vote?

In the late 1880s this highly intelligent, well–educated, eloquent, Scots–born Christian socialist drove forward a cause advocated by the likes of Alfred Saunders, William Fox and Mrs Muller, the wife of the Resident Magistrate in Nelson (encouraged by John Stuart Mill) at the birth of the colony. Not until 1877 did Dr Wallis, MP, in tune with Grey's 'millions yet unborn' oration, move, seconded in the House by William Fox, for the granting of political rights to women.

By 1879 John Ballance was committed to the cause, but not until 1887 did Julius Vogel, with his support and that of Robert Stout, put down the Female Franchise Bill.

---

40 *Tessa K. Malcolm. 'Sheppard, Katherine Wilson — Biography', from the Dictionary of New Zealand Biography. Te Ara — the Encyclopedia of New Zealand.*

117

When Vogel's Bill was dropped after its second reading, the cause passed to a remarkable politician at the heart of the New Zealand Women's Christian Temperance Union (WCTU) movement. This had emerged in the 1880s, drawing on the experience of American women in the turbulent 1850s in their battle against the drink trade and slavery. Kate Sheppard, as head of the WCTU Franchise Department, and a logical thinker and bold speaker, laid out the issue in two simple propositions:

'The claim that to vote is unwomanly is an absurdity.'

'Depriving women of the vote is false to the concept of democracy.'

In 1889, talking in Wellington to that rising power in the land, the WCTU, she summed up the issue in two biting paragraphs.

In one way the subject of the franchise is very like that of temperance. Both seem almost to be exhausted, threshed out so to speak, until nothing or next to nothing remains to be said.

When we are told the franchise would make women unseemly; that she would neglect her home duties on account of it; that it would cause dissension between husband and wife; that giving the women the franchise would only be giving dual votes to married men; that because she cannot fight she should not vote; that because of motherhood she has not time to vote; that it should demoralise women to associate with men at polling booths; that women are already represented by their fathers, brothers, or sons; that women do not want the vote. When we hear these objections, we feel somehow as if that way of thinking had gone out of date a long time ago, and that the speaker or writer could not have thought much on the matter, or they would not give expression to such opinions.

Legislation for Woman Suffrage then required, as with Reeves' labour laws, a long campaign over several years. We have taken the editorial liberty of converting Kate Sheppard's speech on Woman Suffrage reported by the *Lyttelton Times* of August 21, 1890, to direct speech.

The WCTU has been working for five years with the object of getting the franchise for women. During the last few years a great change has

Kate Sheppard (1847–1934)

come over public opinion on this question.

Numbers of men and women, who once considered it unwomanly, and immodest, for a woman ever to think on political matters, or anything else beyond her home, have come to see the fallacy of such ideas. Supporters of the proposal wish it to be understood that we have great objection to setting one sex against the other. This is not just from motives of policy. It is because we believe we can work best when working together, each contributing his or her individuality and sex characteristic to the common good.

As a rule women are more keenly interested in moral and social reforms than men. Take the drink evil as an instance; as women and children are the main sufferers through drink, women will use their influence to do away with this evil.

Woman's real claim to the suffrage is based on the principle that every adult person, who is neither a criminal nor a lunatic, has an inherent right to a voice in the government, and in the making of laws which all are called to obey.

For fifty years the inherent right of women to vote has been acknowledged by leaders of political thought and action like Charles Kingsley, the Rev F.D. Maurice, Richard Cobden and Lord Beaconsfield. Gladstone, Jacob Bright, John Stuart Mill, Professor Fawcett and Lord Salisbury held similar views.

Among women, Miss Thackeray, Harriet Martineau, Mary Howitt, Frances Cobbe, Elizabeth Barratt Browning, Mrs Gaskell, Mary Carpenter, Mrs Sommerville, Florence Nightingale, Lady Dilke and many others have written and spoken claiming the electoral vote for women.

In the States of Wyoming and Washington women have had the franchise — in the former for over 19 years. In the Isle of Man, women have possessed equal political rights with men for nine years, and Sir Henry Holt, the Governor, who at first opposed the change, has testified that the results have been good, and that he would not wish the measure altered. A correspondent from Wyoming says that he does not know of one citizen who would have the measure repealed if he could, and the Governor of the State gave evidence of its success.

In New Zealand 11 years ago, Mr Ballance carried a motion that the word 'male' should be exchanged for 'person' in the Electoral Bill, but an interpretation clause had provided that 'person' should not include 'female'. That clause is there still. The Stout–Vogel Ministry carried the second reading of a Woman's Franchise Bill, but went out shortly afterwards, and until August 5 of this year no government has given any expression on the question.

We should be proud of the fact that New Zealand has been one of the first to offer an opportunity of obtaining university degrees to women. The success of women in the learned professions, and at the universities, has led thoughtful people to see it is right that woman should have the same opportunity of working out her destiny as a man has of working out his. Many of the present laws are the cause of great injustice to women.

Of course, women will need time to become accustomed to the idea of taking part in the franchise but the women who will first exercise votes will be those who care most for the moral welfare of the community. It is said that the majority of women do not demand the franchise, and that we should wait till a majority do so before granting it. But this has never been the history of legislating in extending the suffrage or granting any reform. There is no reason why an exception should be made in this instance.

The right or privilege of voting does not conflict with that of any other person's. The fact that a large portion of our women have shown an indifference on the subject does not afford the slightest argument against the right of all women to the franchise, and the duty of duly exercising it for those who see and feel their need of it.

Kate Sheppard then moved:

That each member of this meeting pledges herself to strive to waken an intelligent interest in the suffrage question.

Ultimately, as she implies in her speech of August 20, 1890, to the WCTU, Kate Sheppard had to take the battle back to Parliament. In putting forward legislation she worked closely with the statesmanlike Sir John Hall, notably in organising a petition signed by one third of the women in the country to confirm the will of the people.

Seddon was opposed, but was eventually overrun by the combination of the Sheppard juggernaut and an elderly statesman.

Their triumph was to put our democracy at the forefront of the world. New Zealand became the first country, even if Parliament took several runs at the fence, in which all women exercised the vote (Australia did not follow suit until 1902, the year after Federation).

On August 24, 1891, Sir John Hall moved the second reading of the Female Suffrage Bill:[41]

... I believe we are on the eve of a great and decisive victory. We come fresh from the elections, with the mandate of the people of New Zealand to put this law on the statute-book ... a measure of great justice ... a measure of great wisdom ... a lasting credit to the New Zealand Parliament ... a lasting blessing to the New Zealand people.

Sir John Hall was disappointed. Despite his eloquent exposition, his Bill failed in the Upper House. It was John Ballance in July 1892 who then successfully put the question of Female Suffrage before the House in a new Electoral Bill that left out, at that point, though he did not preclude it, female membership of the House.

Kate Sheppard, though she went on to create the influential National Council of Women, never sat in Parliament. She was nevertheless, an able and far–sighted politician, and deserves her place in our history as the pioneer for all our women politicians.

---

41 *Female Suffrage Bill New Zealand Parliamentary Debates (Hansard), Volume 73 pages 497–502.*

Settlement of the Land

John McKenzie

1892–1894

The most significant Minister of the Liberal Ministries of the 1890s, in retrospect, was a Highland Scot, John McKenzie.[42] As Minister of Land and Agriculture, and later for four years as Richard Seddon's Deputy Prime Minister, his single–minded focus made him the definitive potter of New Zealand's pastoral economy.

In a strong field, John McKenzie might emerge as the most effective Minister of Land and Agriculture in our history. His monumental legislation, on which he orated with increasing determination over three sessions (as the Upper House had forced Reeves with his Labour laws) were the famous Land for Settlements Acts 1892 to 1894.

After the Upper House (as with Reeves) failed in 1893 to pass his legislation, McKenzie came back with renewed energy and bile, and the mandate, to set out, in cutting speeches, on his 1894 Land Settlement Bill, the rationale for the compulsory purchase of land.[43]

In a surge of energy, the State acquired an enormous tract of 1.3 million acres of land. There was enough for the settlement of some 7,000 farmers.

42 Tom Brooking. 'McKenzie, John — Biography', from the Dictionary of New Zealand Biography. Te Ara — the Encyclopedia of New Zealand.
43 The Nemesis of Dummyism" from Great Tales from New Zealand History (Penguin Books), by Gordon McLauchlan.

John McKenzie (1839–1901)

This extraordinary feat, coupled with his work in agriculture, force–fed the building of our budding political economy as Britain's Antipodean farm.

The irony lies in a Highland Scot of the land clearances, while breaking up the big estates, riding roughshod over the owners of Maori land. Did his vision of a farm–based settler society exclude those he deemed poor farmers? Or did his single–minded focus, on the strategic issue, over commit him to securing land for settlers at Maori expense?

As Minister of Agriculture as well as Lands, McKenzie was responsible for developing vital national institutions in the Department of Agriculture and the State Advances Corporation for the evolution of our unique and prosperous agricultural economy, and a dairy industry, that has gradually come to dominate New Zealand agriculture.

Falling ill and dying suddenly at the height of his influence, John McKenzie was much loved and mourned. Few New Zealand Ministers achieve a monument in their home country, as McKenzie did in North Otago. It's a direct result of his first Land for Settlements Bill in 1892, that sets out the case briefly for State acquisition of land; and that of 1894, where with much resolution, he makes his case for compulsory purchase.

1892:[44]

Sir, I thought that this session I ought to bring in a bill which would give the Government power to make arrangements to take land where the people were prepared, on one side were prepared to sell, and the Government. on the other side, were prepared to purchase ... I do not think that there can be any doubt as to our right to apply the revenue of the colony, if this House agrees, to the purchasing of land for settlement where it is found to be necessary, and where, through our having no Crown land to dispose of, settlement is retarded.. All will, I think, admit that it would a good thing, if land can be got at a reasonable rate, that we should be in a position to buy it ...

Referring to the necessity for obtaining this power to obtain land, I think there can be no doubt upon that point. I know many honourable members are anxious that this Bill should become law, so that we can get land for settlement in small areas ... You must get good land to make small settlements in this way successful. This Bill provides for a Board of Purchasing Commissioners ... They are to advise the Minister ... then the whole transaction will be laid on the table of the House as soon as the House meets.

44 *New Zealand Parliamentary Debates (Hansard) 1892, Volume 77 page 77.*

1894:[45]

... The passing of this Bill is looked forward to by a large number of people throughout the colony of New Zealand — the only hope they have of ever being able to secure to themselves homes in this colony. Every year that passes by, the area of Crown lands of the colony, which we have had in the past to deal with, so as to supply the number of people who come to the country and want to get land to settle upon, is diminishing, while the number of people who are anxious to obtain homes themselves is every year increasing. Therefore if we intend to keep up the supply, and to find land for the settlement of our people, there is no other course open to us than that of getting it this way ...

Here we are in this colony, with a population less than three quarters of a million of people, and we already find a scarcity of land for people to settle upon. We could in this country, with comfort and ease, settle at the very least five millions of people; so that if we have arrived at such a stage ... and yet we already find a scarcity of land to settle them upon, it is evident that we have, to a certain extent, abused our trust in the past. It is true that in most parts of the colony we have still a certain area of Crown lands, and also lands that we are obtaining from the Natives in the North Island ... but there are other parts of the colony where this is not the case, where the Crown lands have already been disposed of, and it is impossible for us to settle any larger number of people without getting hold of land from those who have taken it up, in large areas, in the past.

This refers notably to North Otago, Canterbury, Marlborough and Hawke's Bay ... in these districts large estates prevail ... So far as Canterbury is concerned, I may say that the whole of the Crown lands suitable for small settlement are disposed of, and there is no chance there for the progress of settlement unless we are prepared to obtain land in this way for this purpose ... what would have happened in Canterbury this last year had it not been for the acquisition by the Government of the Cheviot Estate? ... The number of people there before was only some 80, so that 569 people have been provided for already on the estate ...

---

45 New Zealand Parliamentary Debates (Hansard) 1894, Volume 83 page 630.

This shows the necessity of land for settlement in this way, and what can be done in this manner. Here we have provision made by the taking of the Cheviot Estate for 560 people who otherwise ... would be among the unemployed in Christchurch ... a dairy factory has been started there ... The settlers there have 58.000 sheep ... 300 head of cattle, and a large number of horses. Some of the settlers have even sent freezers this year to the freezing works in Christchurch, to be sent Home ...

What has been done in the case of the Cheviot Estate can also be done in hundreds of other cases in the colony, if the House rises to the occasion ... We have ... a large number of people in the colony who are prepared to take up land for settlement in this way if they can get it on reasonable terms. Honourable members may ask me the reason why private people do not cut up their estates ... the Government are able to give better terms to the settlers than any private company or individual can do. In many cases these large estates ... are in the hands of companies and monetary institutions ...

Then we have to meet the fact that every year in this colony a large number of young people grow up on the various farms and settlements ... who are desirous of getting land for settlement ... and we must meet this demand if we are to progress satisfactorily.

Then ... we have to face the evil effects of past legislation and administration ... a large number of these estates have been created in the past by very questionable means ...

We have had gridironing and dummyism ... in Canterbury. We have had bad legislation in Marlborough — legislation passed by a few people (who had a direct interest in the lands ... and who passed laws) to suit their own requirements ... Then we have had evasions of the land laws in Otago, by which a great number of people have been able to buy large estates. And ... in the Hawke's Bay district ... 'Native land jobbery' ...

And through these processes we have had large estates created ... which at the present time force us to take the course we are now taking ...

You will find a number of honourable members tell you in this House that there is no necessity for this Bill; that private individuals ... will cut up their estates themselves, and provide for the requirements of settlement. I believe that cannot possibly be done, and I think that it is absolutely necessary to deal with the large estates in the way I refer to ...

... There are numbers of people who are not prepared to sell their property to the Crown at fair value ... you have a clear reason why the Crown should come to the House and ask for compulsory clauses in the Land for Settlements Act ...

Every morning, when I take up the papers, I find the facts regarding this Bill distorted all over the colony ... the journalists of the colony ... distort facts in connection with this measure to such a degree that I am somewhat astonished ... I do not know what is the reason why they are not honest and just towards this Bill ... Is it that they do not understand it — that they have not sufficient brains to comprehend it? Or is it simply for mischief's sake, and to assist the Conservatives? ...

I went to the country with the full responsibility of this Bill upon my shoulders, and as you are aware, the country returned me, and ... the colony has returned to this House a majority in favour of this Bill ... Honourable Members may recall that the Bill was killed in another place, and it was killed accordingly ... There were 27 members on that side who voted against me, and at the present time 17 of those gentlemen are out of the House ...

Almost all those who supported me on that occasion are now present here to a man, thus showing that the country approved of it ... no measure was more clearly put before the country than this Bill was at the last election ... And I think I may go the length of saying that it would be the duty of the members of the Upper House also to pass it on this occasion, that is, if they are going to take into consideration the views of the people of this colony on this very important question.

I may go a little further and say that the Government is determined that this Bill shall be carried and become the law, so that the people will have an opportunity of getting under it homes for themselves ... I say any Government that may be on these benches, and who have the interests of the country at heart, must take the responsibility of finding the people land for settlement, and must be responsible to the House for their action ...

Good For Our Fellow Men

William Pember Reeves

September 1892

The firebrand of the outstanding Liberal administrations was a smooth–talking editor, and man about town, from Canterbury. William Pember Reeves[46] was an intellectual, a finished politician, and a brilliant orator.

He had the nervous energy coupled with worldly experience to hold his own with his colleagues, put down opponents; and thread his way through the labyrinthine issues of the 1890s, like prohibition and votes for women.

He also had the stamina to take through three tortuous parliamentary sessions the writing and passage of the labour laws that were to underwrite New Zealand's emerging liberal democracy.

Reeves' skill in political manoeuvre shows first in securing a half–day holiday for shop assistants before weaving his way through the Factories and Arbitration and Conciliation Acts that made his name.

It is worth briefly first considering the first Shop Assistants debate in terms of political tactics, before embarking on the second and grander issue.

---

46 *Keith Sinclair. 'Reeves, William Pember — Biography', from the Dictionary of New Zealand Biography. Te Ara — the Encyclopedia of New Zealand.*

129

Addressing the House, Reeves said:[47]

This Bill is not as wide and as good a Bill as it might be. Yet it is as good, and strong, and wide a Bill as I think there is any chance of passing through Parliament ... seeing there was no reasonable prospect of passing the Bill of last year, I brought in one which, at any rate, would effect something in the desired direction.

It is complained that it inflicts hardships and embarrassments upon working people. Well, at any rate, what it will do will be to provide that every shopkeeper shall keep one half-day out of six as a half holiday.

So far from being a tyrannical interference with the freedom of shopkeepers, this is a very small interference indeed. It is not considered to be an interference with any industry in the world to oblige people to cease working one day in seven.

That custom is universally observed, because it is generally admitted to be good, and therefore this provision for a half-day is a mere question of degree. It is good to cease working one day in seven, it is also good to cease working a half-day in the remaining six. Public opinion shows that it is so; and member after member in this House has got up and admitted he believes in the one half holiday in six.

Then why deny to a large and useful section of the community one half holiday out of the six, which is admitted by honourable members to be good, and which they would be sorry to be deprived of themselves because by attacking a Bill like this, they are practically denying to other members of the community this privilege of a weekly half holiday.

In the grand sweep of history it's easy to forget it took Reeves three sessions — and then only after a general election — to secure the passage of his world famous Industrial Conciliation Bill. He is at his best, intense, determined, erudite and witty, in summing up the critical debate in 1892, long before the Bill became law in 1894.

---

47 *Shop Assistants Bill, September 11, 1892, from New Zealand Parliamentary Debates (Hansard), page 136.*

Reeves summed up:[48]

Sir ...

... This is the fourth day on which the Bill has been debated ...

I think there has been an overwhelming consensus of opinion all over the civilised world among the men who have any opinions on this greatest of labour problems that the State should make some effort to alleviate, ameliorate, or possibly put an end to, the evils of industrial war.

Some honourable gentlemen on the other side ... (have) seen nothing but evil motives lurking behind this Bill. The Bill ... has been introduced simply for the purpose of pandering to the mob and gaining a little popularity. Is it the case that ... rulers and statesmen ... have been animated by nothing better than a mere personal desire to pander to the mob?

Because in nearly all civilised countries legislation has been introduced dealing with this question, and going in the direction of preventing strikes. However, we are told that our legislation has been brought in from the low, base and contemptible motive that, because certain people elected us, therefore we are bringing in this Bill to please them.

Now is not that a rather poor method of arguing a great question of this nature? And would it not be a fairer suggestion to say that we were elected ... because it was known that we were in favour of legislation of this kind— that because of our ideas on these great labour problems we were elected to carry them out?

Every Government does introduce measures which are in accord with the views of the majority of those who support it ... One can only disprove the charge (of insincerity) by consistency of political action and public conduct ... when a man of respectable character, elected to support certain measures and to support a certain party ... does preserve a measure of consistency in political life, then he ought to be accepted as possessing common sincerity and honest political motives.

To pass from the question of motives to the question of some of the arguments brought against the measure ...

The honourable member for Ellesmere ... did not condemn it ... but

---

48 *New Zealand Parliamentary Debates (Hansard), Volume 78 pages 180–186.*

somehow or another nearly everything in it has managed to displease him ... after listening to the honourable gentleman, was that, somewhat like the old fowling piece, the Bill only wanted a new stock, a new lock, and a pair of new barrels to be a very fair weapon indeed. The hon. Gentleman found fault with ... three of the most vital principles of the Bill — namely that is based upon unionist lines, that it includes the Railway Commissioners and that it includes the principle of compulsion.

It is stated that because I based this Bill on unionist lines I propose to confine it to the men of the unions of the colony, and therefore I am ... shutting out a lot of men who would like to come in; and secondly I am driving all these men into the unions.

My reason for not extending it to all workmen is a very simple one. There are species of disputes in which public opinion has asked the State to interfere — that is disputes between organised labour and employers; but disputes between unorganised labour and employers have never alarmed the public, have never paralysed industry, half-ruined employers, beggared men, women and children, and desolated homes. The industrial conflicts that have arisen from disputes between unions and employers, however, have done all these evil things, and will do them again.

That these conflicts have alarmed the public, and have done a great deal to shake public confidence in different countries in the world there is no doubt ... unless some machinery, some safety valve is provided for dealing with disputes between masters and men, these strikes are an absolute necessity ... If you wish to put a stop to strikes you must provide this machinery; and that is what this Bill proposes to do ...

A union, after all, is a substantial and responsible body; it has a reputation to keep up; it has to keep control of its members and attach them to it, and not disgust them and drive them out; it must not suck the pecuniary blood from its men; it must not drain their pockets by legal expenses. These are reasons why the unions could not be perpetually dragging their members before the Court of Conciliation, or Board of Arbitration, both of which will cost money ...

It is argued ... that this Bill is to build up and strengthen unions; ... other honourable members are equally emphatic that it is a bill for the

W.P. Reeves (1857–1932)

disruption and ruin of unions. These two points are urged; yet both cannot be true.

Then it is stated that because I have put certain compulsory clauses into the Bill, therefore the Bill is bad and tyrannical — that it is in fact not conciliation, but coercion ... but, Sir, he went too far when he stated that under this Bill awards are to be made compulsory.

I have attempted as said before, to steer a middle course. Awards need not be made compulsory at all. This Act might work for 20 years without an Award being made compulsory; but we have left it to the discretion of the Court of Arbitration whether they will the award force or not. We simply trust the President of the Court, who will be a gentleman of high judicial attainments and standing; we trust the two assessors ... of the employers, and ... of the unions; we trust them with the discriminating power to saying whether they will make their award compulsory or not.

It seems to be taken for granted by the critics on the other side that the gentlemen selected will necessarily be unreasonable and tyrannical ...

Why, Sir, if you are to assume that every Court appointed in the country will be composed of madmen, why appoint Courts of justice and why pass laws?

... Why should you assume that a Court of Arbitration will act in this ridiculous and tyrannical manner? ... If a Court of Arbitration were found so insane as to make an award which an employer could not possibly obey ... The Legislature ... would immediately step in and dispose of the Court, and reform the Law.

The Bill is experimental, and if need be it will be altered ... Of course it is imperfect. Who could imagine that at the first attempt we could solve a problem the perfect solution of which has not been arrived at by the greatest intellects in the civilised world? This is only an honest attempt, and as an honest attempt I commend it to the House ...

The honourable member for Wellington City (Mr Duthie) ... supposing his caricature of my life had been true; what would that have to do with the principles of the Bill? Suppose it were true that after I left school I acted as a cadet on a sheep station; what has that to do with whether the Bill should apply to working men in general, or to unions?

Supposing it were true that after I left the sheep station I studied law, what has that to do with the ... clause relating to the Railway Commissioners? Supposing it were true that after leaving the law I became a professional newspaper editor, what has that to do with compulsory arbitration? Finally ... after giving up journalism I became a Minister of the Crown, what on earth has that to do with ... whether we should establish district Boards of Conciliation?

In regard to the remarks of the honourable member for Manukau ... we need (not) take them into consideration ...(he) is the champion of burlesque ... he burlesques the legislation of this house ... the honourable gentleman is his own most remarkable burlesque — his own most screaming jest. You have only to look at him ... his gesticulations, his tones, and the extraordinary matter of his speeches themselves, to see that in him you have a living burlesque of politics and politicians ... I used to think that Charles Dickens was merely a caricaturist — that he did not draw from life. But when I have seen he honourable gentleman's wild gesticulations and wordy accusations, when I have seen him beating the air with his clenched fist and working his arms, I have said to myself ... Dickens did draw from real life, and no one need leave this Chamber to meet Sergeant Buzfuz to face ...

Now, as to the accusations levelled against the Labour members of this House. They have been called by implication asses ... political agitators, accused of trucking and pandering, of living upon the miseries of the poor, fomenting strife, and setting class against class ... Well, all I can say to the Labour members is this: It is true that the lot of politicians who come not to work for themselves, but to work for those who sent them here, is not the smoothest and pleasantest lot in life.

I often think that those who stand aloof from the stress and fight of politics, who simply look on and attend to their own affairs, have by far the easiest and pleasantest time. But ... we, the liberals who are sent here to work for the masses of the people, to do what we believe to be best for the advancement and raising up of the poorer and less fortunate of our fellow men, have this consolation. If we look back at history, after all, what are a few hard words, a few epithets and insinuations, compared with the sufferings which were endured by reformers who have gone before us?

Why, men have laid down their lives in the effort to do the kind of thing we are trying to do now. Our lot, after all is very easy compared with that of our predecessors; and we have this consolation: that although we cannot have rank, or wealth, or even enduring popularity — because popularity is a fickle thing, it simply lives in the breath of the people — we have this incentive: that we are doing some solid, real good for our fellow men.

When we look at the legislation passed during the past two years, we see what I think is solid real reform. Look at the Factories Act of last session. Look at the report of the Bureau of Industries.

Let us think of the women and children whom the Factories Act has rescued from foul air, filthy surroundings, overwork and ill health ... Think of the overwork, the life of degradation, and the increased wretchedness and misery from which that Act has rescued whole generations of workers to come.

Surely that is consolation enough. If as I think we cannot enjoy popularity, or rank, or wealth, at any rate we can feel that we are doing good to our fellow men.

'I Only Ask for Justice'

Alfred Hanlon

January 25, 1895

Fifty years after Waitangi, New Zealand basked in the creation of a modern liberal state. In 1893 we had led the world — somewhat grudgingly, it is true, until the world's admiration flowed — in admitting women to universities and offering votes to women. Just two years later, in 1895, less grudgingly, we hung a woman for murder.

Minnie Dean is the only woman ever hung in New Zealand.

Dean and her husband Charles had been making a living from looking after young children, caring for up to nine at a time at their Winton home, The Larches. In May 1895, police found the bodies of two infant girls buried in the Deans' garden, as well as the skeleton of an older boy. After police dropped charges against Charles Dean, the 42–year–old Minnie went on trial at Invercargill for the murder of one of the girls, Dorothy Carter, who had died of an overdose of the opiate laudanum, in common use to calm infants. Dean pleaded not guilty, claiming the death had been accidental. She was brilliantly defended by the ablest advocate of the day, Dunedin–born Alfred Hanlon[49] who

---

49 Geoffrey G. Hall. 'Hanlon, Alfred Charles — Hanlon, Alfred Charles', from the Dictionary of New Zealand Biography. Te Ara — the Encyclopedia of New Zealand

Minnie Dean (1844–1895)

became one of our leading orators. An eminent and admired judge, Joshua Strange Williams, also out of Dunedin, determinedly pushed aside Hanlon's exquisitely honed defence of 'reasonable doubt' to put on the Black Cap. Was the prosecutorial direction of Judge Williams to the jury a blot on our moral compass as well as our legal system?

Hanlon had all the passion and flair of the Anglo Irish. The crowds gathered to fill a court room when he appeared, as he did for the Dean trial. He put to the jury that the Crown had not proven beyond reasonable doubt that Mrs Dean 'murdered' this particular child.

The Crown said it would produce the evidence for this murder. The Crown had failed to do so, Hanlon argued. Hanlon's concluding remarks urged the jury to bring in a verdict of not guilty or of manslaughter.

Here's an abridged version of the reported speech by Hanlon to the jury on January 21, 1895:

The duty you are called upon to perform is the most solemn and most important upon which you will be called to perform in your entire life. We have all seen you giving great attention to the evidence. I am sure you will devote to me the same attention to what I have to say; and the construction, I will suggest, you put upon the evidence, in favour of the prisoner

First of all I must emphasise the very great importance of the absolute necessity of your totally erasing from your minds every word you have heard outside before the court hearing. The newspaper has filled columns upon columns with reports of the case and its every little detail. It is absolutely essential that you as the jury should obliterate from your minds every word you have read or heard outside the courthouse. If you do that I have no hesitation in saying that you will come to a just conclusion upon the case.

Your duty, as you know, is to decide the case upon the evidence, and upon the evidence alone. My learned friend has told you that he would prove certain facts, and that these facts must be consistent with the guilt of the prisoner, and absolutely inconsistent with any other theory.

Many of these facts may be consistent with the theory that the prisoner should be found guilty of murder. But my submission — and I make it with every confidence — is that I can prove to you that those facts are consistent with another theory. And if I show you that they are consistent with some other theory, it is your bounden duty to find that they are not consistent with my learned friend's theory, whatever that might be.

My learned friend says that murder be defined, for the present charge, as unlawfully and intentionally taking a life of a human being. He then says that if he proves to you, and you are satisfied that Mrs Dean intentionally caused the death of Dorothy Edith Carter, it will be your duty to convict her of murder.

139

Has my learned friend proved that Mrs Dean intentionally caused the death of the child? My submission is that he has not proved that Mrs Dean killed the child intentionally. Where indeed, is there any evidence to show that Mrs Dean killed the child intentionally?

My learned friend has in fact adduced no evidence to show that she premeditated the killing, nor that she actually did kill the child.

Let us look at the facts of the case.

You have heard that Mrs Dean arranged with Mrs Isitt to take the child Dorothy Edith Carter. Mrs Cox was to meet her at the Bluff and hand the child over. The place of meeting was to be the private boarding house of Mrs Cameron at the Bluff.

Mrs Dean goes there, having given her name beforehand as Mrs Grey. There she meets Mrs Cox who comes on the Manapouri with Dorothy Edith Carter.

There the child is handed over at the Bluff to Mrs Dean under the name of Mrs Grey. Mrs Dean then leaves the hotel and purchases some laudanum. Having got the laudanum she dines at the hotel, takes the train to Invercargill, and from Invercargill, to Gap Road.

At Gap Road she meets Esther Wallace and goes with her to their own house, The Larches, at Winton. She keeps the child there from Tuesday night until Thursday morning.

Mrs Dean then goes to Dipton, taking with her the child and the tin box. She actually takes out a first class ticket to Lumsden, breaks the journey (at Dipton), and stays at Dipton for some considerable time. She then goes on to Lumsden.

On the journey from Dipton to Lumsden the child disappears. When she arrives at Lumsden there is no child with her. She then goes from Lumsden to Gore.

The prosecution claim in further support of their theory that the child's body was found in the Dean's garden in Winton; that a post mortem examination was made; that the organs of the child were sent to Professor Black, who found a quantity of morphia in the organs.

The prosecution also proved that the accused made several false statements.

There in a nutshell, you have the whole ground of the case of Dorothy

Edith Carter. The prosecution has been further allowed — perhaps properly (perhaps not?) — to bring evidence that Mrs Dean got into her possession a child named Eva Hornby, and that that child's body was also found at The Larches.

The prosecution tried to show that Mrs Dean made certain false statements with regard to that child.

Upon these facts the Crown asks you to find Mrs Dean guilty of murder. The prosecution has also given evidence that the remains of another child were found in Mrs Dean's garden, and that certain other children she had received, had also disappeared.

This evidence I submit does not justify the conclusion of guilt you have been asked to reach.

At first sight, counsel for the prosecution puts a strong case against Mrs Dean. But let us consider the facts. The facts, I put to you, are perfectly consistent with another theory. This theory is quite different from the theory of the counsel for the prosecution!

Mrs Dean was continually getting children to nurse. The evidence shows and clearly proves children coming and going from The Larches. It is also clear in a business of this sort it has to be conducted with secrecy.

You saw that Mrs Hornby did not want her identity to be known. She signed herself ABC in replying to Mrs Dean's advertisement. She did not give her own address. She did not want Mrs Dean to know her identity.

What do we see?

We see clearly that an unfortunate girl has an illegitimate child. Outlawed by our social customs, the poor, unfortunate girl has to hide her shame. Otherwise the outside world will stare aghast at her. She has fallen. The child has to be sent down the road if the mother is to hold up her head again.

What rottenness is this in our society? Yet we know this can happen over and over again. You will have heard of poor unfortunate girls making the one mistake of their lives. They then send their little child away. No matter where. It has to be got rid of somehow.

This is what has happened in this case. It was absolutely essential for the woman receiving these illegitimate children to keep secret from inquiry the names of the parents of these unfortunate children.

You cannot then blame a woman because she told a lie.

Of course Mrs Dean has told lies. I do not deny that Mrs Dean told lies. She had ample reason for those lies. She had to shelter the fathers and mothers of those unfortunate children.

That is the reason for the lies. That is the reason you, the jury, must accept in dealing with this case. These falsehoods were told for other people. You do not have to place the construction on the facts my learned friend has put to you.

Mrs Dean did not register the house when she had children there less than two years of age. She was punished for that but even then she did not register the house.

Why? It must strike you at once why she did not get it registered. It was because she did not want the police to make enquiries and give occasion for the fathers and mothers to complain.

After she was fined, from that time forth she never gave the police any information.

Could you blame her? You cannot when she has pledged herself to secrecy in regard to the children. She never afterwards divulged anything about the children.

This you must bear in mind in dealing with this case

Let me deal now with the disappearance of Dorothy Edith Carter.

You heard in evidence that Mrs Dean was anxious to adopt that child.

Hanlon put it to the jury that such a claim was not true.

There was correspondence between Mrs Dean and Mrs Isitt.

The outcome was clear. Mrs Dean received the child from Mrs Cox at Bluff. The Crown asks you to believe that she was then premeditating the murder of the child. My learned friend goes on to suggest that she purchased laudanum at the Bluff in order to murder the child.

That purchase, does not show anything of the kind. The woman had laudanum in the house. She may quite reasonably have bought more laudanum to replenish what she had in the house. You have been told Mrs Dean used laudanum diluted with water for her eye. There is a clear and necessary reason before you for the purchase of laudanum.

You have not heard a word about the bottle of laudanum purchased at the Bluff. The police have certainly not found that bottle. What they found was a bottle containing laudanum and water.

The mere purchasing of a bottle of laudanum at the Bluff creates no more than a theory — that she may have intended to murder the child.

My learned friend has put to you that there can be no other theory. My submission is that she wanted the laudanum for her own complaint. The purchase is consistent with a theory of innocence and if so, you are bound to adopt the theory of innocence!

Hanlon guided the jury to the issue of intent.

Mrs Dean we know went from the Bluff to Invercargill with laudanum in her pocket and a baby in her possession. Only two people knew of her having the baby besides Mrs Cox, who went back to Christchurch.

You have been told when she bought the laudanum she had it in mind to murder that little child.

Why did she not do it then? She had the means. She had the child with here. Only two people had seen her. Only two people could have given any information about her. So she goes up the line from the Bluff to Invercargill with the child in her possession and the laudanum in her pocket?

And my learned friend wants us to believe she had the deliberate intention of murdering the child?

Then why did she not do it?

How can you account for that?

Why did she bring that child home to Winton?

She could have administered the laudanum on the road and thrown the body in a river. That was perfectly possible. But she does not. She goes to Invercargill: Where people who knew her might have seen her. She then goes on to Winton.

My learned friend asked why she got out at Gap Road instead of going straight onto Winton by train. She did not want the police to see that she had a young child with her

143

Not for one moment would I deny that reason. Mrs Dean does not want the police to know what is going on. If they find out, they will bring her up for not registering the child. Of that there was no necessity. She was only going to keep it for a few days.

My learned friend claims Mrs Dean made a confidant of Esther Wallis. The fact is people make confidants of anyone when they are not going to commit murder. Why ever let Esther Wallis see the baby if she wants to dispose of it? How can you possibly consider she premeditated murder? Was she really so stupid? As to keep the child in her possession till they knew of it? And then murder it?

In the face of this proof any theory of intent to murder the child is absolutely absurd.

Then Mrs Dean meets Esther Wallis at the Gap Road. Here it is alleged she intended to murder baby. Here we come to the real crux of the Crown's case! What does Mrs Dean actually do? No, she does not murder the child. Instead she takes the cloak off her own back. She wraps it around the infant. And this is what happens. 'You will catch cold,' says Esther Wallis. And Mrs Dean replies 'Oh, never mind.'

Is that the mind of a woman contemplating murder?

Yet that is what the Crown asks you to believe.

You cannot believe it. You simply cannot believe it.

This is not the action of a woman with the full intention in her mind of murdering a child.

The Crown suggesting that this is the action of a murderess is preposterous.

Mrs Dean carries the little child home and puts it to bed. In the morning she lifts it up, bathes and dresses it. The next day she tends the child in the same way. Is that the action of a murderess?

I put it to you: It is positively and absolutely absurd to say that.

My learned friend then says that the child was taken away on the Thursday morning after being bathed and clothed and fed.

And an empty tin box was taken with it. And, because the box was taken with it, my learned friend asked you to conclude that the box was taken — for no other purpose — than to put in it, the body of the dead child after being murdered.

Let us consider that issue? Why would Mrs Dean treat the child as she had done if she intended in a few hours to take away its life? There would have been no need to do so.

Hanlon said the circumstances were not consistent with the intent to commit murder.

They are consistent with the theory of innocence.

Hanlon said it was perfectly reasonable for Mrs Dean to need the tin box to carry clothes as she had no valise.

When Mrs Dean goes up the line she has a ticket for Lumdsen. On the way she breaks the journey at Dipton. It is on the train she asks the guard to break the journey at Dipton.

Why did she do this? There are two answers.

Mr Ayling, who keeps the hotel at Dipton, says Mrs Dean told him the baby was sick. Perhaps she said more that was not true. But the question is clear: Was that part of it true?

On the issue of the sick baby we have evidence. Miss Duncan, the housemaid at the hotel, notices that the baby is sick. She mentions that to Mrs Dean. 'That is why I broke the journey here,' Mrs Dean replies.

What, if the baby was sick, might we ask, was there to make the baby sick? Might Mrs Dean have given it some laudanum?

Possibly. But that was not so. If Mrs Dean had given the baby laudanum it would not have looked as it did.

Then we are told the child was crying. Now, if it was crying, it would not have been suffering from laudanum poisoning. Laudanum produces drowsiness, and coma.

The evidence suggests the child was sick. The reason given for breaking the journey at Dipton is absolutely correct.

What, let us consider, happened then?

Mrs Dean goes by the evening train to Lumsden. The child disappears. The Crown proves that the child disappears and that later morphia is found in its body

If Mrs Dean gives the child laudanum to allay pain and produce sleep, she is not guilty of murder.

If however she is guilty of negligence in administering the laudanum — to allay pain and produce sleep — then it is possible that she might be convicted of manslaughter.

But if the child was killed by misadventure, Mrs Dean is entitled to be acquitted.

You have the evidence of Mrs Cameron. Mrs Dean gave a child laudanum at The Larches to quieten it, because it was going away.

Esther Wallis too, tells us Mrs Dean gave the child something. Mrs Dean affirmed it was to keep the child quiet.

Now the Crown wants you to believe this evidence of children disappearing in some mysterious way (means) that the children were done away with.

How for a moment can you believe that Mrs Dean would let anyone see her give the children laudanum — if she intended to do away with them? Would she not say she was giving the children a dose of soothing powders?

Mrs Dean told Esther Wallis and Miss Cameron that she was giving the children laudanum, a poisonous drug.

That is not the way people act when they want to commit murder. They try to hide the crime.

Mrs Dean clearly thought the children needed laudanum,

So she gave it to them.

Dr Young has told you laudanum is frequently given to children to stop them from crying.

Mrs Dean clearly thought it no harm to give laudanum to children when they were in pain, or when she wanted them to sleep.

Let us then consider the case that Dorothy Edith Carter died through misadventure or negligence. (You, the jury) cannot for a moment believe that Mrs Dean would let people know what had been done. The child was put into a tin box, and taken home and buried in the garden. Is that the action of a person committing murder upon a little child? Not at all. If Mrs Dean wanted to murder the child, why did she go to Lumsden or Dipton to do it?

The Crown has pointed to little children on former occasions disappearing from The Larches. And that Esther Wallis and Miss Cameron were sent away from the house. What was easier if that was her intent but to have disposed of Dorothy Edith (Carter)? All she had to do was send Esther Wallis and Miss Cameron away.

Why go to the expense of going to Dipton? And going moreover where people could see the child?

Hanlon drew the jury's attention to evidence by Esther Wallis who said Mrs Dean was asked by her husband if the lady who was going to adopt the child had any more children.

In short a woman was going to adopt the child. That was the inference, members of the jury, you must draw.

(Mr) Dean could not ask if a lady had any more children unless something had been said about the child being adopted. That accounts for Mrs Dean's journey to Lumsden. Mrs Dean bringing the child home and burying it in her front garden does not show she had murdered it.

If she had murdered it, why did she bring it home and bury it at her own front door? If she had informed the police there would have been an inquest. The names of the parents would have been revealed. There is the probable reason for burying the child in her own front garden.

You have heard evidence that the body of another child named Eva Hornsby had also been buried in the garden.

The Crown's objective has been to show that the death of Dorothy Edith Carter was not caused by accident. If the Crown case was strong there was no necessity to call such evidence.

Why then did my learned friend call such evidence? ... it was perfectly open to the defence to say that the child had died accidentally. Then his case would have fallen to the ground. If 40 children had been found buried in the garden that would not affect the circumstances of this case. It does not matter whether all those children were buried in the garden. That would not affect the circumstances surrounding the present case.

No matter whether all those children were murdered — you the jury have to try to find a true verdict, according to the evidence, so far as it concerns Dorothy Edith Carter. You are not trying Mrs Dean for the murder of Eva Hornby. You have to confine yourselves, solely and wholly, to the evidence, so far as it concerns Dorothy Edith Carter.

If there is a shadow of a doubt in your minds, as to whether Mrs Dean killed that child, you must give her the benefit of the doubt.

With regard to the other children in the garden, it does not matter how these children came by their deaths, if the child Dorothy Edith Carter was accidentally killed.

There is another point of exceedingly great importance in the trial. This is the question of motive.

My learned friend in his opening said that in nearly all cases of murder a motive for murder should be assigned. Has he proven that there was a motive in the case? He has produced no evidence of motive. You have a duty to look for a motive in a case trying to prove murder by circumstantial evidence.

In this case the evidence is purely circumstantial.

Why indeed should Mrs Dean kill the child? She had got nothing for it.

My learned friend suggests that she had not got the money — but expected to get it. She had simply disposed of the child to save expense, time and trouble.

When you consider what Mrs Dean did in the case of Willie Phelan (his) case does not hold water. The money had not been paid. What security had Mrs Dean that she would get it? None at all. As long as she had the child in her possession she could make sure of getting the money.

This you recall is an illegitimate child. The parents want it taken away from home. If she does not get paid all she has to do is, as she did in the case of Willie Phelan, take the child back. But when she disposes of the child all chance of getting the money is gone.

So what motive can the Crown assign for the murder of the child? There is absolutely no motive.

It was to her interest to keep the child alive, at least until she got the money.

The doctors say (Eva Hornby) died in a state of asphyxia. (Her) stomach was empty, the doctors say also. Mrs Hornsby swears she gave the child some milk the morning she handed it over to Mrs Dean, and a bottle of milk with it.

What then became of that milk? If Mrs Hornsby gave it that milk where did it go, unless the child vomited it? If it did vomit the milk it is possible it may have choked itself in doing so.

Hanlon pulled together his concluding remarks.

Let me put to you a clear alternative explanation for the death of the child. (And you know what it is!) Mrs Dean is a baby farmer. She has to protect the names of the poor unfortunates using her services. This is what Mrs Dean did. You cannot beyond reasonable doubt find her guilty of murder.

You have open to you the finding of not guilty, at worst of manslaughter, by overdosing, with laudanum. This drug is in common use. Mrs Dean herself used it (and many of you do too.) She used it for sick children. That is what will have happened in this case. She was committed to concealing names, and when the child sickened and died, she acted to avoid a coroner's inquest. You cannot beyond reasonable doubt find her guilty of murder. That is what I put to you. That is the justice I seek for my client. I ask no more than even handed justice.

Hanlon's final plea laid the responsibility for justice on each juror.

Members of the jury, it is your duty to take the whole facts of the case into careful consideration, and to give a true verdict, according to the oath you have taken.

I do not ask for sympathy or pity. I am not entitled to ask for that. I only ask for justice. It is justice I am entitled to get.

Such was the histrionic passion and eloquence of Hanlon's dissection of the Crown case, and compilation for the defence, the judge stayed proceedings. He would deliver his summing up to the jury the next day. There he unhesitatingly ruled out Hanlon's defence. Even the press

149

noted the judge's deliberation in countering Hanlon's eloquent pleas for a balanced judgement. The jury should not neglect the (inadmissible) evidence as to other children. The jury should not, between guilt and innocence of murder, choose the middle course of manslaughter.

The judge made his opinion clear:

If you accept the view learned counsel contends — that the death of the child amounts to manslaughter only — you will be responsible for nothing short of a weak kneed compromise.

The jury took an hour to find Minnie Dean guilty. Hanlon had lost the only one of his 16 murder cases to the hangman. Over forty years later he showed no ill will to a partial judge. He too thought Minnie Dean guilty[50].

Dean was sentenced to hang at Invercargill at 8am on August 12, 1895. Press reports say she slept for three hours during the night before her execution and declined breakfast, taking instead a sip of spirits provided by the prison doctor. Her parting words to the doctor were: 'Don't let them keep me in agony, doctor.'

At a few minutes to 8am, with hundreds gathered outside the prison, Dean was marched to the scaffold, last used to hang a man who had poisoned his wife quarter of a century before. The gallows allowed for a drop of 7ft 9in (2.3 metres) and her legs were pinioned.

The Sheriff asked Dean if she had anything she wished to say. Her only statement was:

I am innocent.

To the attending surgeon, she said:

Oh God, don't let me suffer.

The hangman then drew the lever and Dean dropped, dying instantly.

---

50 Random Recollections — Notes on a Lifetime at the Bar. A.C. Hanlon K.C.

The Cause of Humanity

Richard Seddon

October 1898

A century after his death, Richard John Seddon[51] still stands on its forecourt, the colossus of the New Zealand Parliament. Few leaders can claim to have been more popular ending than starting his reign or to have achieved such domination of the political scene.

Traveling anywhere and everywhere the bearded, frock–coated giant, easing in 1893 into the place of the ailing Balance, and urged on initially by his mentor George Grey, emerged as the uncrowned King of the nation. As an orator, he saw a crowd as a large, good humoured, tractable animal ready to be turned around by a speech.[52] He was 'a red–blooded, hearty orator, a man of the people, who knew the mind and heart of the people.' Gradually focusing more and more authority in his office, our longest serving Prime Minister might stand accused of 'turgid verbosity' on the stump.[53] But as Prime Minister he clawed close to Tsardom — but as the greatest of his great debates show, a Tsardom dependent on carrying Parliament.

51 David Hamer. 'Seddon, Richard John — Biography', from the Dictionary of New Zealand Biography. Te Ara — the Encyclopedia of New Zealand.
52 Evening Post, December 30, 1911.
53 William Downie Stewart in speech to the Historical Society, Dunedin, 1936, titled 'Politics in Retrospect', MS 0985–00p/024 Hocken Collections Uare Taoko o Hakena, University of Otago.

Nowhere is this clearer than in the important debates of 1897 and 1898 on Old Age Pensions, the defining legacy of Seddon's long reign. Once on track nothing deflected him from his goal. In an age of revolutionary financial, industrial and social legislation, including votes for women — that defined the modern Liberal democracy Siegfried discovered in New Zealand — Seddon's Old Age Pension Act of 1898 is, as he himself suggests in his third reading speech, his prime legacy. The speech contains more than the odd hint of the Greyhound pedigree Seddon openly acknowledged.

That speech itself came at the end of 90–odd hours in committee, perhaps the longest debate in the history of the New Zealand Parliament, one of the first major measures acting on demographic realities. Seddon had inherited the first generation of longer living, but aging settlers. What is notable is Seddon's own recognition that his 'experimental and improvable' legislation was an imperative for 'God's Own Country' and that it would prove of, lasting benefit. Only those who have led in long debates, in a fraught, combative Parliament, can appreciate the physical and intellectual effort involved, as he indicated in his summing up at the committee stage, in dominating such proceedings.

After that exposition, clearing himself of the charge of tyranny, his third reading speech in any terms confirms his high mana.

Mr Seddon (Premier):[54]

Having succeeded in getting this most important measure through committee, and as it still has to go through the third reading stage, I myself do not wish to say anything that might tend to irritate. But, Sir, I feel that the remarks made by the member for Wairarapa were very uncalled for, for it cannot be said in respect of this Bill that I have been in the slightest sense tyrannical; but I do say this much: It would have been better for both parties if there had been more give and take. We have had during these last few weeks a stubbornness and a determination, and instead of being guided by reason, to simply appeal to physical force.

Now after the time we have been sitting in committee I think members

---

54 *New Zealand Parliamentary Debates (Hansard), Volume 104, page 555.*

on that side of the House will come to the conclusion that ... I am able to stand the physical test with the best of them. But I will say, now that the Bill has got through its committee stage, that the leader of the Opposition has during the course of the Bill ... behaved very well indeed ... he has had to contend against on that side of the House what I have had to contend against on this side — namely a very large number of members who considered the conduct of other members on that side unreasonable ... particularly the honourable member for Wairarapa was acting in the most tyrannical and unfair manner towards them, and my difficulty has been to restrain my supporters from taking extreme steps ...

I hope the debate on the third reading will be a debate which will do credit to our Parliament and to honourable members.

Third reading of the Bill. Mr Seddon:[55]

... there has not been a measure which I have had the honour of introducing in this House that has given me the same anxiety as the one which the House is now being asked to read a third time. During the last few weeks, and whilst the Bill has been in the committee, the ordeal has been trying in the extreme. The Bill was (in) committee something like 11 days, and it has taken 90 long hours in its passage through that stage; and I believe there have been some 1,400 speeches delivered in committee upon it ... when there are so many speeches made and so much information sought, it is the duty of whoever is in charge of the Bill to give that information, and to meet the arguments that are adduced as against any particular clause. But, Sir, tenacity of purpose, a good cause and strength of will to do what is right — supported as I have been on the second reading and in committee by honourable members on both sides of the House — have prevailed.

And I say to the supporters of the Bill that, for the trying position in which they have been placed during the last few weeks in respect to this measure, they will be more than compensated, because they must feel they have done their duty to the deserving aged of the colony. The cause for which they fought so valiantly is the cause of humanity, and there are thousands of

55 *New Zealand Parliamentary Debates (Hansard), Volume 104, page 569.*

Richard Seddon (1845–1906)

people — not only those of today, but those who will come after us — who I feel sure will look back on what we have done for them with gratitude, and will receive what we have provided for them with pleasure.

Sir, it cannot now be urged that this measure has not received the fullest consideration. We were told that it was a bill that was crude and ill–considered, and that it necessitated the fullest and fairest discussion. It has had the fullest discussion; but I may say ... that it is questionable whether or not the discussion had always been fair.

Sir, I am satisfied with the Bill at this present stage ... As to those who have opposed it ... I can only express my regret that their efforts were not in a better cause. Those who have supported it on this side of the House did so under the most trying circumstances. The greatest constraint had to be exercised to be kept, as they have been, hour after hour and day after day; and yet knowing that there were no real arguments to reply to, they were taunted because of their silence ...

And then, Sir, what are the terms that have been applied to this measure? As I have said — first, 'crude and ill–considered', then it has been called 'degraded charitable aid', it has been termed 'skinflint' charity, and ... 'an abortion'. Those too who are to benefit there under have had very harsh terms indeed applied to them. The harshest of all ... that we were legislating for paupers and loafers ... I was sorry for it, because I feel that to those who may hereafter and will receive their pensions those harsh terms will be applied.

It is true we had a difficulty in discriminating in respect to the deserved aged — and in legislating you must provide against abuses that might arise— but whilst we were doing that, we have no right to apply to the deserving aged of our colony, who form the great bulk of those who will receive assistance under this measure, the harsh terms used in respect to pensioners, as it may lead the outside world to believe that those who founded New Zealand— those who have been chiefly instrumental in making the colony what it is —are not a deserving class of colonist ... I have no hesitation in saying that the great majority of those who founded this great and glorious country had no right to have been insulted ... And, Sir, may I say this in answer to the term 'drunkards' that has been applied ... we are the most sober people, I believe, in the British Empire ...

We say, of course we are making provision for the deserving aged of our colony, and we say they are entitled to it, because they have helped make our colony what it is; and this measure, if it is passed, cannot for a moment be correctly termed a measure that is going to provide assistance for the degraded. There are thousands in our colony at the present time who have never touched charitable aid under our existing laws.

There are those who, I admit, under the existing charitable laws, think nothing of spending all their earnings. They are thriftless ... but this measure will not touch them at all. The class I allude to are not 65 years of age, and they are not amongst those who have been some twenty five years in the colony. They are all of more recent origin ...

Sir, there are many in our colony who have felt the pinch of hunger and want at times, and of whom it could not be said for a moment that they are thriftless. There are those who have embraced every opportunity that has been put in their way. They have brought up their families respectably; and they have denied themselves so as to help to place their families in a better position in life than they themselves occupy; but with the intermittent employment, and with the small earnings which they have received, while they are paying their way as honest and good people, they have not been able to make provision for their old age.

I am not saying anything against their energy, or their intelligence, but I say that circumstances have been against them; and when I see those who have been more fortunate, and who have provided for their old age, and who look upon themselves as superior beings, let me tell them that there are hundreds now in our colony who have been unable to provide for their old age.

Through the banking crisis which occurred in the other colonies, and which also slightly touched this colony ... they are left today absolutely penniless, and many of them will come under the provisions of this Bill. I therefore say that we must admit that he who has done all that human hands can do to provide for his future, and who may be forced in his old age to apply for a pension under this Bill, should not have taken from the right of receiving it at our hands. And why should he have applied to him the terms and epithets that have been applied?

Sir, I hope that those who have been fortunate will think kindly of those who in their old age are badly off, and who have not been so fortunate, but are looking forward to severance from the world with pleasure. Sir, we should stretch out to them the right hand of brotherhood, and make this provision for them. What does it come to? Will it all be felt by the taxpayers of this country — the amount we require under this Bill?

I undertake to say that when this scheme is complete and the money is being paid, we shall go on, as we have gone on for other works — as we have gone on with other progressive legislation, in regard to which the colony has received great benefit, while the evils and the dangers prognosticated have never arisen. And I think that after this passes it will be held in years to come that there was no necessity for the anxiety and the bitter hostility that has been shown in the passing of this measure.

Now, Sir ... we have been told (this Bill) is simply an enlargement of our present charitable aid system. Sir, I will be no party to the enlargement of that system ... that system and our present charitable aid legislation has done more to degrade the people of this country than any legislation that had ever been passed by this House. And I say that it has done more than that: it has altogether stopped true benevolence ...

The people say 'You rate us for charitable purposes; we have been rated for charitable aid; and if you take the money from us by laws. We do not feel called upon to contribute voluntarily'. That has been the result of the working of the charitable–aid laws now in force, and therefore I will not be a party to extending them ...

Then, Sir ... A scheme of deferred annuities ... is next to an impossibility ... What I want to say is that we must legislate in a direction we have not so far legislated in, because no contributory scheme can meet the existing circumstances. For those who are now 50 years of age, and for those who are 45 years of age, there is no opportunity. The days of their youth, and the days of their past earnings are gone; consequently it is impossible for them to take any advantage of any contributory scheme ...

Now there is another thing we must take into consideration — namely that it is beyond the power of the class we desire to assist to make these payments to the funds that are necessary before they can secure an annuity. They have not the means. The better class of artisans — the higher paid, and those who are in permanent employment — may take advantage of that; but what you have to do in this country, and in any country, is that you must deal with those who have no opportunities, and whose earning wills not permit them to do it ...

During this period of youth, with its expectations and buoyancy, they never think that they will be in want; they scarcely think they will live to the age of 65, or that at that age they will require a pension ... in any contributory scheme you may have here there will be a large section of the population who will not take advantage of it, and for whom in their old age you must make some provision.

Now I say that a deferred annuity system must and will of necessity be, so far as the deserved age in our colony at the present time are concerned, a mockery ... in any contributory scheme you may have there will be a large section of the people who will not take advantage of it, and for whom in old age you must make some provision.

I take it that this Bill we are now passing is simply the foundation stone; it is the commencement and upon this structure we may have a more complete and perfect scheme which will reflect credit on the intelligence of members of the House and be for the good of the colony ... by and bye we shall extend ... in two directions: Firstly in reducing the time the pensioners are in the colony; and secondly we may bring it down from 65 to 60 years of age.

As regards another amendment ... making the Bill subject to triennial review by Parliament ... is consistent with our experimental legislation ... As against that ... an amendment that the moneys be appropriated annually ... I do not want to have 88 hours again in committee; I do not want to see the time of the country spent again in bickering, or to hear those who are receiving the pensions insulted in the way they have been by those honourable members who, not thinking what they are saying, are doing these poor people a great injustice. I say if the amount were to be voted annually it would do away with the pension. It would not then be a pension scheme at all ...

The passing of this Bill into law will be memorable... We shall be the first Parliament under the British flag[56] that has passed a law of beneficence so widespread, in conferring lasting benefits on the deserved aged of our colony, and they are really entitled to our consideration.

---

56 Chancellor Otto von Bismarck had been the first to introduce pensions as part of his social insurance policies in Imperial Germany in the 1880s to offset the appeal of the Socialists.

'Military Glory'

James Carroll

1899

In September 1899, the arch imperialist Seddon as the Premier 'of an integral part of a great empire' charged off to the war in South Africa. His tub thumping speech to the House in September 1899 focussed on two major points.

'We stand with Britain who defends us. As a free and enlightened people we stand for freedom and civil rights for our oppressed kindred, deprived of the rights of British subjects, in the Transvaal.'

In face of such rhetoric, few noted MPs, like T. E. Taylor, of Christchurch, and Robert McNab, of Mataura, were arguing that the Boers were right, and Britain wrong.

Certainly not the Hon. James Carroll[57], MP for Waiapu, and just taking over as Native Affairs Minister from Seddon. His intent was to put the case — as with the recent Jubilee celebrations — for the New Zealand contingent, going to help a Mother Country 'on the verge of war', to include Maori.

In the 1900s, the passionate, eloquent Carroll emerged as a power in the Liberal cabinet. He put a brake on land spoliation and importantly tied

---

57 *Alan Ward. 'Carroll, James — Biography', from the Dictionary of New Zealand Biography. Te Ara — the Encyclopedia of New Zealand.*

159

James Carroll (1857–1926)

Maoridom back into the mainstream of the New Zealand polity, affirming the place of Maoridom in the New Zealand polity.

Few leaders have done so much, in their own right, nor provided such an example for future leaders nurtured under his shadow, Apirana Ngata, Peter Buck and Maui Pomare.

Addressing the House, Carroll said:[58]

Sir ... I do not think, on this occasion we should inquire into details. It is not for us to ask the reason why this war, and what justifies it. All that we understand is this: that the Mother country is in trouble — is on the verge of war; and as a component part of the Empire it behoves us to consider what steps we should take towards contributing our share in maintaining her prestige.

With previous speakers I also would suggest to the Premier, and to this House that, in selecting this contingent which we may decide to send to the Transvaal, the Maori race of this colony should not be overlooked.

I know there is a yearning in their hearts, induced by loyalty, to add whatever they can towards holding up the military glory of the Empire; and from their point of view I do not think you will be doing amiss if you make selections from their ranks.

About two years ago this House agreed to send a New Zealand contingent among whom were Maoris, to the Mother country to represent this colony at the time of the Jubilee.

They acquitted themselves exceedingly well, and they deserve a great deal of credit for the way in which they rose to the occasion. Now, as the Empire is about to engage in war, we should be prepared to give a practical pledge of what we assumed then, we should be able to do on her behalf.

The time has arrived, and we should not tarry at the question of expense. Let us select the best men available for this particular service, let us give them the best of equipment ... and I am sure our action will rebound to the credit of the colony. As part of the Empire, we will feel the direct advantage of the step we are about to take at the present moment.

---

58 *New Zealand Parliamentary Debates (Hansard), Volume 110, page 90.*

I do not for one moment blame those who differ from us on the subject. I say everyone is entitled to his own opinion, and I recognise to their credit that it will require no little courage to face the stronger force of opinion on a subject like this — that is, to differ from the consensus of public opinion.

This is not however the time for us to inquire into the particular grounds on which members base their opinions. I believe this resolution will be carried by a large majority of this House, and that it will meet with the approval of the people of this country. For the sake of those who volunteer, I say it will be an admirable thing for us to afford them this opportunity. They will have their chances in a new country ... to add additional lustre to our national mana.

Sir, it may happen that there are many in the Transvaal who can claim relationship with us. I have no doubt there are many Maorilanders in that part of the world, and, if they are seriously menaced in the possible outbreak of hostilities between the Boer and British Governments, we at least should not withhold any succour which we may be able to afford them, apart from our Imperial sentiments.

I wish again to impress on the House ... the desirability of making the best selection, so that our contingent may reflect credit on us, giving the preference to our volunteers, and joining with them some of our Maoris, who are eminently fitted for such service. I am sure we can get an efficient corps ... and I am sure our name, our national spirit, and our loyalty will be added to.

Despite Carroll's urgings, and Seddon's proposal to the Imperial Office that at least 100 Maori soldiers be included in the First Contingent, the British government declined, believing native troops should not be deployed in a 'white man's war'.[59]

As for Carroll, he became acting Prime Minister twice in the Liberal Government and in 1911 became the first Maori to be knighted. In 1918, he visited Maori troops serving on the Western Front.[60]

59 Maori and the war — NZ in the South African War', URL: *http://www.nzhistory.net.nz/war/ new-zealand-in-the-south-african-boer-war/maori, (Ministry for Culture and Heritage),*
60 *Alan Ward. 'Carroll, James — Biography', from the Dictionary of New Zealand Biography. Te Ara — the Encyclopedia of New Zealand,*

'Fishing With a New Net'

Maui Pomare

1906

Under James Carroll's tutelage the 'Young Maoris' burst on the scene in the 20th century. Among them, Maui Pomare of the Atiawa proved to be an outstanding orator as well as politician.

As a Minister he struggled for years to secure compensation for the dispossessed Taranaki tribes. It was a tribute to his standing that a sympathetic Prime Minister, Gordon Coates, set up the 1926 Royal Commission to look at the wrongful confiscation of Taranaki lands.

The Sim Commission confirmed that the people were not in rebellion, the Government was wrong in declaring war, and the Taranaki Maori ought not to have been punished by the confiscation of their lands.

It was a significant victory for Maui Pomare, but he did not live to see any effective result. Nor despite some miserly payments did the generation of the Great Depression and World War Two.

The best that might be said of the Sim Commission was that it ate at the conscience of the State, foreshadowing the Crown's acceptance of proper compensation for tribal claimants in the much delayed era of Treaty settlements of the 1990s.

Pomare, witty and good humoured, was in demand as an after dinner speaker.[61] But he could stir emotions too, as he did when he made an address to the Australasian Medical Congress in Melbourne in 1906, in his capacity as Health Officer to the Maori.[62]

Away back in the twilight of fable we find my race parting from our common Aryan mother. Ethnologists tell us we journeyed south and eastward through the ancient Empire of Irania, coming into contact with the Egyptian and Semitic branches of the human race, and then on to Sumatra, coming into contact with the Indonesians.

You Pakehas went towards the setting sun. You had the fortune to strike the metal-key which has opened to you the vast stores of knowledge. You had the fortune to come into contact with superior races to your own, from whom you acquired the arts and sciences which today have made you leader in the arena of civilised nations.

My ancestors, bold, venturous vikings, journeyed across the chartless seas of the east, peopling its many islands and exploring the unknown realms beyond; while yours were journeying overland through Europe, being afraid to traverse the trackless deep for fear of falling off the edge of a flat world.

We were unfortunate not to come across superior races to our own. We were of the stone age, and fate kept us with the stone till today destiny has brought us together once again.

The stone axe has been loosened from its handle: the spirals and works of art cut by our stone and obsidian are no longer to be seen in our Maori village and kainga, but only in the Pakeha's house of antiquity, the museum.

Long before the dawn of Pakeha civilisation one of our ancestors dreamt this prophetic dream: 'Shadowed behind the tattooed face a stranger stands. He owns the earth. He is white.'

Two hundred years before Pakeha feet trod on these shores another dying kaumatua called his children about him, and thus spoke: 'Weep not for me, but rather weep for yourselves and your land, for the time is coming, and now is, when alien white feet shall desecrate my grave.'

---

61 *Graham Butterworth. 'Pomare, Maui Wiremu Piti Naera — Biography', from the Dictionary of New Zealand Biography. Te Ara — the Encyclopedia of New Zealand,*
62 *Legends of the Maori (Volume 2), edited by James Cowan. From the New Zealand Electronic Text Collection.*

Maui Pomare (1875 or 1876–1930)

That time has come.

The tattooed face is now an article of commodity, sold to the highest bidder in civilised England. 'The white stranger owns the earth' — that time has come. The white feet of vandals have desecrated the seer's grave; his children are weeping for their vanishing glory and land. Enough! For are not these sayings old and true? 'Kua kotia te taitapu ki Hawaiki.'

(There is no returning to Hawaiki). 'Ka pu te ruha, ka hao te rangatahi.' (When the old net is full of holes it is cast aside, and the new net goes a–fishing).

The useful net of Maori days, now full of holes, has to be cast aside. We know the old net caught many big fish in its time, but that time has passed. We recognise that the fishing of today must be with the new net our Pakeha brother has brought us.

In the year 1900, our benevolent parent, the Government of the Dominion, after much travail brought forth a son whom we christened 'Te Pire Kiore' (The Rat Bill). This was not a premature child, but its birthmark was a peculiar one, for it was a rodent rampant.

This is not to be wondered at, for at that time our parent was much agitated owing to multitudinous rumours and scares concerning rats and plagues. Indeed these rats were so bold they crossed the Sea of Kiwa, laid siege to some of our cities, and two of our inhabitants died of 'buboes'.

Now, I was chosen from among my fellows to herald the birth of 'Pire Kiore' and to explain his mission. I was much troubled because I knew my people were a sceptical race, slow to change and fixed in their ways. However, with a kind sympathetic chief — a Ministerial Captain of Health — I launched forth in my new duties full of hope, fear, and trembling.

Fear and trembling did I say? Yea! for I knew the deeply–rooted superstition of ages, the strongholds of tohunga–ism, the binding laws of tapu, the habits and practices of centuries, the mistrust of the Pakeha, for these were the Goliaths in the way of sanitary progress amongst my people.

For what did sanitary reform mean? It meant the dissolution of some time–honoured customs, the tearing down of ancestral habits and teachings, the alteration of Maori thought and ideas of living; in fact, a complete revolution in their socialistic, communistic and private life.

It meant more — it meant the gentle persuasion, the authority not of force, but of clear convictions of the evils of the present system of half European and half Maori ways of living, and the benefits of a better, more sanitary and higher and nobler mode of life.

Who cares to have a stranger poking around his back door, condemning the hundred and one things which sanitarians know are detrimental to public health? Who cares to have his habits disturbed, his wrong–doings pointed out, the tapu'd house of his ancestors destroyed?

Was it likely that tribes which were at one time at war with mine would take kindly to the words that I would utter? And yet it was because of the utter hopelessness of the Maoris' sanitary condition — the thought that, unless the flagrant infractions of Hygeia's laws were quickly stopped my people would surely disappear with the moa — that gave me courage and hope to fight the cobwebbed customs of the past and to introduce the new.

Listen, and you will hear in the words of many chiefs as to how I fared: 'Welcome, thrice welcome! Our hearts are made light at last. Our forbears adopted Christianity; but their lands went from under their gaze; it was death. We signed the Treaty of Waitangi, but went to war; it was death.

We send members to Parliament, but death remains with us. We have been disappearing with our lands.

At last, at last there is life!' And thus spoke another: 'Come! Welcome! Come to show your nation the ways of health — the good ways of the Pakeha and other nations of the world you have seen. Come! Our hearts are made glad, our hearts are made light, our wailings shall cease. The light of life dawneth; we bid you thrice welcome.

'Come upon the wings of knowledge. Come and teach us. Give us the ways of health; warn us from the ways of death. Give us to drink of the same cup as the Pakeha. Hide nothing from us that we may live and bless thee.'

'Come! The descendant of Maui! Come and fish for us the great fish of life (health), like your illustrious ancestor who fished up this land from the depths of the sea. Come and behold the place of the people who are no more. Come and see the remnants who are so few of days. Teach us that our tears may cease to flow.'

My reception was surprising as it was cheering. The audiences were most appreciative. Wherever I went I was received with open arms. The new gospel was preached everywhere with practical results.

Yea! have I not seen the smoke of the whare circling heavenward as an offering to the God of Health as the landmark for the parting of the ways of the old and the new?

Now, when our ancestors landed in New Zealand some five hundred years ago they found another race living there, and amongst them a fair-haired people. These races they conquered and absorbed. On the eve of their departure from Hawaiki the people on shore, in bidding farewell to our ancestors, said, 'Depart in peace. Leave war and strife behind you.'

But our people did not give heed to this parting injunction, for as soon as they reached the new land they quarrelled, and so the different crews of the various canoes separated, and thus they spread over the country. They waged continual warfare with one another as in the old baronial days of the Pakeha. Now, this was productive of several things.

First, it made the race active, and thus physically fit. The weaklings and the deformed were often strangled at birth. It made them build their pas or strongholds on inaccessible heights for protection and a good outlook. This resulted in much good, because the air was pure and the pa easily kept clean. In fact, in olden times each pa was almost as well regulated in regard to public health as in some of our more modern villages.

This was so striking that Captain Cook marvelled at their advancement, and bears testimony to it in his journal to the detriment of European cities of that period.

Rubbish of all kinds was swept out at regular intervals. Latrines were properly constructed and placed on the edge of some cliff or hole, the woodwork often being elaborately carved. The water supply was nearly always obtained from some fresh mountain spring, either in the pa or just outside of it. The people had but two meals a day — one at sunrise and the other at sunset.

The sick were attended by duly qualified men who had received their instruction at the whare wananga, the college of learning. The dying were set apart in separate houses which were burnt after death. All clothing belonging to deceased persons were either burnt or buried with them. Corpses were sometimes buried, or more often secreted in some cave. Bearers of the dead were tapu'd for a certain number of days, and had to wash in running water.

Mothers were set apart, and considered sacred till eight days after their accouchements. Lepers were isolated in caves. Tonsils were removed. Poisonous bites by the katipo spider were cauterised. The Caesarean section was sometimes performed. In tutu poisoning the patient was made to vomit, beaten with branches of trees and douched with cold water. In karaka poisoning the patient was buried standing so as to keep the arms and legs from being distorted.

Wounds were washed with astringent juices from several trees, bandaged with leaves and plastered with clay. Splints and clay plasters were used in fractures. Massage was used for stiff joints. Steaming with the hangi (native oven) was employed in cases of amenorrhoea and rheumatism. The hot springs were resorted to in all skin ailments and other affections. Herbs were extensively used as tonics, anti–arthritics, astringents, purges.

Child engagements were entered into, and girls so engaged were called puhi, or virgins. If they, by chance, violated the laws of chastity they were immediately killed. In this way the Maoris lived and multiplied till the dawn of civilisation, when the race became decadent.

At this time a new instrument of warfare came into use which proved most destructive to the Maori population. Hongi, a northern chief, went to England — was presented before King George IV, and given many useful presents. He kept the steel tomahawks and axes, together with a coat of armour. He sold the rest of the presents when in Sydney, buying guns with the proceeds.

With these he devastated hundreds of pas, and killed thousands of his enemies. He, with Te Rauparaha, must have wiped out at least a quarter of the population. The whalers and traders commenced coming in about this time, and they were not all over–scrupulous men, for the gun was their chief article of commerce.

The earliest white men as aforesaid were not the most moral, consequently syphilis was introduced, the results of which are too horrible to mention. It left a terrible mark on the vitality of the race. Riotous living, trading in smoked Maori heads, drunkenness and debauchery were the order of the day till eventually Christianity stopped the marauding expeditions and a good many of the introduced vices. Slavery was abolished, and peace more or less reigned in the country.

This brings us to about the year 1840, when the united tribes declared their independence under the sovereignty of Great Britain.

By this time the race was fairly weakened, and thus the ground was well prepared for the introduction of measles, scarlet fever, enteric, and consumption, the two former being the most disastrous. Typhoid and consumption became more prevalent after peace had been declared, because the natives then commenced to descend into the valleys. They left their healthy homes on the hilltops, and began to build their pas near the plantations and the swamps where eels and birds were plentiful. This produced a state of inactivity, and together with bad drainage their numbers were depleted to a great degree.

When we deal with the statistics of the Maori population we find them to be most unsatisfactory, as in a great many instances the statistical returns are nothing but surmises. Nevertheless, no one for a moment can doubt the steady decrease that has set in within the last fifty years.

The returns were made by conscientious men, but frequently a good deal of the returns were mere guesswork. This was due to two reasons: First, because of the troublous times then existing, and secondly, the unreliable sources of information. So in calculating we have to deal with generalisations rather than the correct figures. The question naturally arises as to whether the Maoris are increasing or decreasing.

And bright as are the hopes held out to us by the last census of their increase, yet the Maoris have been gradually but surely decreasing. Who has not noticed the gradual decay, the deserted villages? What Maori living will not tell you of the numerous inhabitants that were?

The census has only been correctly taken since 1878, and even then several of the tribes were not included, and that is why you will find that the returns decrease and increase in an astonishingly contradictory way. The matter of census taking has now been adjusted with correct returns by the aid of Maori councils.

Since the year 1858 the death-roll has been 12,906, or an average decrease of over 280 per year. Since the year 1874 the numbers have been fairly uniform until 1896, when we find a sudden drop, showing the decrease between the years 1858 and 1896 to be 16,195, at which average it would not have taken very long for the native race to become extinct.

As most of these early numbers were only estimates, as already pointed out, I have grave doubts in regard to the number of actual deaths which are supposed to have occurred at that time. Wars and disease have been accounted as the chief causes, but mainly disease. With the introduction of civilisation came destructive diseases which have proved fatal, and will prove fatal till the natives have acquired immunity like the Pakeha. The last census gives the assuring increase of 4,588, which I hope will now be maintained, and will be the commencement of better days.

While upon these statistics, I will not pass over an important factor in the causation of the ultimate end of the Maori, and that is the half-caste. Whenever two communities live together throughout the world, the weaker must tend to become absorbed in the greater and more powerful; this then will be the destiny of the Maori — not extinction, but absorption. This process will take many years, but it is inevitable. The decrease of the future will be in the purity of the Maori blood. I would like to prove this to you by actual figures, but unfortunately, the Government returns being mere approximations in the earlier censuses, makes it unsatisfactory; however, even allowing for these fallacies, since 1886 there has been a continual increase of half-castes, till today we have 6,516 half-castes in our midst, to say nothing of those hundreds who have already become absolute Pakehas, and thus are not included in this enumeration.

A further interesting fact is that there are 211 Maori women who are the wives of Europeans, besides a few men who are married to European wives. Generally speaking, these women are prolific when mated with Europeans; in fact, much more so than when mated with one of their own. I know families of such unions to range from two to seventeen. Then again, as we progress, the half-caste girls will give more consorts to the Pakeha, who is better able to give them the luxuries of life. The half-castes who marry Maoris are lightening the blood in their progeny, and so the process goes on, till in time we shall have a new race.

That when the old is past and gone,
We still may find its trace
In nobler types of human kind,
With traits wherein there blend

The white man's more prosaic mind,
The poet Maori trend.

Aside from the diseases which are prevalent, there are a few customs which have played a great part in the causation of our decrease. In ancient times clothing was scarce — a man only wore the korowai, or toga; thus a good part of the body was more or less exposed, making the wearer a stranger to colds. It is not the English clothing that does the mischief, so much as the ignorance of the laws concerning Pakeha clothing. Some days 'Madam' can be seen stylishly dressed, even to the waist–squeezer, the corset, and the tight–pinching shoes; the next day you will find her with nothing but a thin print dress on, without the warm under–garments. This half–and–half mode of living has been productive of much harm.

The Maori's food supply in olden times was fairly wholesome, but since the introduction of Pakeha food he has learnt to emulate the Englishman's gamey cheese and pheasant by steeping his corn and potato to such a concert–pitch that their humming could be distinguished a mile off. This eating of putrefactive food has also been productive of much harm.

Smoking among women and children has also been common.

Alcoholism has had its day, though it is still bad in some districts.

The tangi, or wake, is another pernicious custom, as the relatives from near and far congregate to weep for the dead, to eat the family out of house and home, and to spread diseases of all descriptions.

Tohunga–ism, or witchcraft, was one of the worst evils we had to deal with. The strong arm of the law was the only potent medicine that could cure this cancerous malady. A few doses of the lock–up have had the desired effect. It is wonderful how superstitious even the most enlightened are.

Who has not seen a delicate silk–attired lady of fashion sigh her wishes over her left shoulder at the inconstant moon? Who does not dream of bad luck when thirteen sit at a table? And who has not seen an old shoe cast at the happy wedded pair?

And if these things can happen in the far advanced, we can surely excuse some of the peculiarities of the Maori, who has barely emerged from the neolithic night of superstition into this blazing sun of civilisation. However, I do not by any means excuse the acts of the tohungas. The immersion of the sick in cold rivers has been stopped by the councils; not that a bath, even a cold one, is altogether detrimental, but the attending risks in exposure are so numerous, and the result so disastrous, that it has been deemed wise to stop all such treatment.

It is quite a common thing to hear the expression 're mate o ana tupuna' ('the disease of his ancestors'), and there is no hope. The disease has been handed down through generations by a powerful curse. Though the theory has often been advanced that consumption was unknown to the ancient Maoris, and that it was introduced by the Pakehas, yet this was not so.

The Maoris had several names for the disease, the common one being mate kohi (the wasting malady). This term was also applied to the waning of the moon. 'Ka kohi te marama' (the moon is wasting away). And, as in the case of the moon, she was restored to life and health by bathing in the living waters of Taane, in the heaven of lakes, so the individual, by potent incantations to Motiti, the guardian god of the chest, could be restored to health again.

What has been done and what we are doing. At the passing of the Public Health Act of 1900, the Maori Village Councils Bill was also passed. This was practically an Act giving the natives a certain amount of local governing authority. It gave them the power to appoint councils and sanitary committees, and inspectors, further, to make by-laws in regard to sanitary and health matters.

The Health Department, under its native branch, has been in touch with the Maori village councils, for these councils stand in the same position as the ordinary local authorities. There are 46 medical practitioners subsidised by the Government to attend indigent natives, there are nine sanitary inspectors, and two health officers. Within the last three years we have destroyed 1,057 houses, 1,183 new houses have been built. Every village, and practically every Maori house within the Dominion has been inspected. The houses destroyed for sanitary reasons have not cost the Government of New Zealand a single penny for compensation.

Seven-tenths of the entire Maori population have been vaccinated. Lectures on sanitation and hygiene have been delivered throughout the

Dominion and outlying islands. Maori girls are now being trained in our hospitals in order that they may go back to their people to teach and uplift humanity.

The gospel of work has been preached. Already the Maori is responding by milking cows and farming sheep. Communism is being broken up by the individualisation of the land. The new day has dawned. The individualistic idea, the push and energy, the turning of time and sod into gold has shaken the foundation of the old Maori world. Henceforth Maoriland will be the cradle of a new race whose predecessors knew the steel, and, yet, the stone also.

In 1907, Pomare drew upon his Melbourne address when speaking over the body of Te Whiti as a chief of the Atiawa.

What New Zealander cannot be moved by his heart rendingly beautiful oration as he spoke of our 'man of peace and goodwill'?

Depart to the illustrious chiefs who have gone before, the brave comrades of old to the Giver of war and peace. Go to that land from which no man ever returned.

Your words have come true; the lips of children speak to you as 'the man of peace and goodwill to all people on the West Coast.' In your own words you said that war and peace as life and death were foreordained. The sun was overshadowed at times with many troubled clouds, but your sun has sunk gloriously in the West leaving your people desolate ...

A new condition of affairs has arisen. It is not new: it is old. Your predecessors saw years before the feet of white men had trodden on the land that should be.

The Pakeha is not a stranger; he is one in blood with us. Ever bold and venturesome, the Maori conquered the unknown waters, while his Pakeha brother clung to the land, journeying westward through Europe, fearing to cross the unknown waters lest they should tumble over the end of a square world.

One of your ancestors long before the foot of the white man touched this soil said: 'Weep not for me, but weep for yourselves for the time has come and now is when alien feet will desecrate my grave.'

Tiriwiri, another of your ancestors, two hundred years before the white man came said, 'Shadowed behind the tattooed face the stranger lurks. He is white. He owns the earth.'

Now the Pakeha has come, the iron has taken the place of the stone. The lightning flash of the Pakeha's wisdom speaks far and near. The old order has changed; your ancestors said it would change.

When the net is old and worn it is cast aside and the new net goes fishing. I do not want to blame the old net, it was good in its day and many fish were caught in it.

But the old net is worn with time and we must go fishing with the new net our brothers have brought us. We must advance our work, for therein lies our salvation.

'The Status of Our Country'

Sir Joseph Ward

July 12, 1907

How much did origins affect the Liberals Greyhounds who made modern New Zealand? There was Seddon, the Lancashireman who thrust himself into power over the Shetlander Stout, who expected to inherit, and Reeves, the eclectic eloquent orator from the city of the gentry, the most radical of them all, pushing through the administration's social legislation.

After death took King Dick, homing in on God's Own Country, Joey Ward,[63] the Irish Catholic Squireen of Southland, claimed the inheritance. Ward did not have the same oratory skills as Seddon, with the *Evening Post* describing his speech style as 'stiff as his moustache' and his words delivered with mechanical precision.[64]

But like Larnach, another business and political leader in the prosperous South, Ward was a hyperactive minister with a footprint on a vast opus of legislation and public works.

More a practical man of business than a Liberal, he might have felt the conclusion of the main trunk line — with its hilarious opening journey

---

63 Michael Bassett. 'Ward, Joseph George — Biography', from the Dictionary of New Zealand Biography. Te Ara — the Encyclopedia of New Zealand.
64 Evening Post, December 30, 1911.

Sir Joseph Ward (1856–1930)

carrying the whole of Parliament — was his major legacy.

Despite Massey's denigration — 'It will no doubt sound more important to hear himself called the Prime Minister of the Dominion of New Zealand than the Premier of the Colony of New Zealand' — it was his placing New Zealand alongside Canada and the Commonwealth of Australia, as a grown daughter Dominion, distinct from the riff raff of the caste–ridden British Empire, that provides one of our significant speeches.

That Ward in 1907 secured this milestone on the road to independent nationhood is perhaps not as important as the distinction itself.

As Prime Minister Keith Holyoake observed in the House at its Jubilee in 1957[65] ' … this was a remarkable constitutional step, New Zealand was then sparsely populated, and her economic potentialities were far from being developed, and the idea of New Zealand as a nation was not really current in the world of that day.'

By moving so surely in 1907 to claim 'constitutional recognition of maturing nationhood' well before the Great War, this man of manoeuvres secured for New Zealand a seat at the Imperial War Cabinet alongside Canada, Australia and South Africa.

That led then to our signing the Treaty of Versailles, marking New Zealand for the first time as a new nation.

The Rt Hon. Sir J.G. Ward (Prime Minister) moved:[66]

That this House respectfully requests that His Majesty the King may be graciously pleased to take such steps as he may consider necessary in order that the designation of New Zealand be changed from the 'Colony of New Zealand' to the 'Dominion of New Zealand'.

… Now, Sir, … what prompted me to submit a proposal of the character that … will alter the designation of the colony to 'dominion' … (an) alteration … that is not going in the slightest degree to take away from those who have passed away or from any of our old colonists the sentimental association that is attached to that term … the alteration in name would lift us out of what I would term a groove of being included amongst a great number of colonies concerning which no distinction is made …

On looking up the records … I find that Sir James Ferguson foresaw, as also did the late Sir Julius Vogel, the possibility of this country becoming

---

65 *New Zealand Parliamentary Debates (Hansard), September 26, 1957, page 2635.*
66 *New Zealand Parliamentary Debates (Hansard), July 12, 1907, Volume 139, pages 371–382.*

the centre of government for the islands of the Pacific ... and ... 'the head of a new dominion' ...

I want to ask the questions:

First, will the change of designation raise New Zealand in the eyes of the world? Secondly, are we worthy of the title, and does it involve any false pretences?

In the first place I wish to say the Old World ignorance concerning these countries is remarkable ... There exists as to our position geographically in connection with the Australian colonies a very great ignorance ...

The belief that New Zealand is a part of Australia exists in the mind of many people ... and that the two were, practically speaking, one ... that the Commonwealth also absorbed New Zealand.

The idea of New Zealand with its independent Government, and with its independent destiny, being mixed up with the Australian Commonwealth is one of which the minds of people should be disabused.

In the Old World, in the minds of many people a belief exists that we are part of Australia ...

The British Empire consists of 43 colonies and dependencies ... The making New Zealand a Dominion does not alter in any the position or status of either the Governor, or the members of the Cabinet, or members of Parliament ... the object is with the lifting us from the position of being included without any distinction as one of the 43 colonies and dependencies ... when this country is certainly the natural centre for the government of the South Pacific ...

Canada took the title Dominion in 1867, and at the time it contained a little over three millions of people ... Dominion being better than colony to express the State, and so ... add to the influence and position of that country ... Now anyone who knows anything of the march of progress of Canada will recognise the term 'dominion' has done immense good to that country ...

With us too, it will have a similar effect in future — when the federated States of South Africa are brought into existence, as they must be at an early period, and when their representatives and those of the Dominion of Canada and the Commonwealth of Australia meet in the

Old Country, as they certainly will, it will have in the eyes of the world of causing New Zealand to occupy a higher plane than if it were simply known as a colony.

I do not know any reason why the status of this country, even on sentimental grounds, should be allowed to hold an inferior position to the countries the representatives of which we should meet, and do meet, upon even terms ... (Canada selected) a designation that would give a superior standing in the eyes of the world and the people at large. They selected the word 'dominion' ... there is no suggestion or proposition to change the form of government at all ... It is the only term that I could find, if I may say here, that I could find that appeared to be appropriate, if we desire to make the change ... 'realm', 'kingdom', and another is 'polity' ... none is applicable as a designation or would convey the meaning that the term 'dominion' does.

The argument ... that because the Canadians have adopted the terms 'Dominion' already ... does not. I think, amount to much. In the future these great self governing countries will be known as the overseas dominions of Great Britain ... the Press of our country have generally regarded favorably this proposal to change our name ... the Auckland Herald ... gave very strong reasons what we should make the change from 'colony' to 'dominion' ... to improve the status of our country in the eyes of the people of the outside world ...

I know of no solid reason that can be advanced why the change should not be given effect to, and I am certainly of the opinion that good will result from it ... The change will not in the slightest detrimentally affect the Native race ...

We have a right to aim at improving the status of our country ... I think that members generally will admit that since the Commonwealth of Australia has had that term applied to it, it stands out more prominently in the eyes of the world than it did before.

We have this fact to remember: some of the countries in the Old World send out prisoners from time to time, such as in the case of New Caledonia, which is a penal settlement ... You hear it talked of as a colony on the same plane as New Zealand.

Sir ... it would be a good thing for us as a country, and certainly in the interests of our children and those who follow after them, if the proposed change were given effect to.

We have no desire, I am sure, to make a change of this kind with the idea of making ourselves greater than we are ... I am prompted solely by a desire to lift the colony out of the ... list of colonies ... and in order to have the status of our country improved.

It will, I believe, conduce to the well–being of the country that its designation should be changed in the way I suggest, and I know of no serious objection that can be urged against it.

On September 26, 1907, on the steps of the General Assembly Library in Wellington, the Governor, Lord Plunket, invited the Prime Minister to read the proclamation of New Zealand's dominion status.

Having done that, Ward called on the crowd to give 'three cheers for the King'.

Ward issued a public statement in which he spoke of preserving 'the purity of your race' and urged 'equal opportunity to all'.[67] He stated:

Trust the future of our Dominion not to increasing wealth, but rather to an ever higher manhood and womanhood, to a wider enlightenment and humanity disciplined by the needs of industry, by temperate living, and by those healthy and beneficent tasks that beget advancement and which should be the price of promotion in a free country.

---

67 *'Joseph Ward proclaims Dominion status', URL: http://www.nzhistory.net.nz/lord–plunket–reads–the–royal–proclamation–granting–new–zealand–dominion–status, (Ministry for Culture and Heritage),*

Fight for King and Country

William Massey

August 14, 1914

In August 1914, the first troops were ready to leave New Zealand for the war in Europe. Members of the advance expeditionary force were called together at short notice and told they would be leaving from Wellington by sea.

To farewell them, the troops were taken to the Basin Reserve on August 14 where several thousand Wellingtonians gathered to show support. The dignitaries were headed by the Governor, Lord Liverpool and the Prime Minister, William Massey.

Massey made a brief but rousing speech to the troops:[68]

> *Officers, non–commissioned officers and men. When the Empire calls it is for the citizens of this Dominion to respond, and when the Empire calls it is for the soldiers of the Dominion to obey.*
>
> *When you leave the shores of New Zealand, in probably a very few hours from now, you carry with you a very great responsibility, but I am sure you all realise the trust that is reposed in you.*
>
> *You go forth to uphold the honour of New Zealand and to fight for King and country in the greatest crisis the Empire has ever seen.*

68 *Auckland Star, August 15, 1914.*

Prime Minister Massey, Opposition Leader Sir Joseph Ward and other politicians outside Parliament after the declaration of war.

As for our glorious Empire, when this war is ended. I am confident that it will become a greater, brighter, and nobler Empire than it is today.

Officers and men, our hearts are with you. We are proud of you, and we who stay behind to do the business of the country have the satisfaction of knowing that New Zealand has been the first to respond to the call for assistance to the Empire in her hour of need.

We know you will keep the flag flying, that you, will keep your faces to the foe, and, on behalf of the people of New Zealand, I wish you all not goodbye, but au revoir and good luck. God be with you till we meet again.

Massey's speech drew continuous applause and cheers. After cheering for the Governor, the troops sang *God Save The King*.

'The Sun of Liberty'

Robert Semple

December 1916

Unionist Robert Semple[69] became a national figure at the start of the 20th century, organising industrial action by West Coast miners and then becoming a leading advocate for the combining of unions representing miners, transport and waterfront workers into what became the Federation of Labour.

As World War One began, the Australian–born Semple became a high profile opponent of national conscription, addressing meetings of unionists in a flamboyant style that earned him the nickname 'Bob the Ranter'.

In 1916, he was arrested in Christchurch and charged with sedition for comments he made in an Auckland speech. He was denied a jury trial under the newly introduced War Regulations and was held in prison for 12 months.

The following is a reported transcript of his anti–conscription speech that led to his arrest:[70]

---

69 Len Richardson. 'Semple, Robert — Biography', from the Dictionary of New Zealand Biography. Te Ara — the Encyclopedia of New Zealand.
70 New Zealand Truth, December 16, 1916.

I have a message of fraternal greetings from the Australian people. It is the Australian people's message that the people of this country shall not under any circumstances permit this country to be lassoed by that Prussian octopus, conscription.

Despite all the strongest opposition, slander, and vilification and journalistic perjury and hypocritical tongue of that polished wowscristic gang the democracy stood on their feet and wiped from the sun–kissed hills of Australia every vestige of Prussianism.

In years to come generations of the future will look back with glowing hearts and benevolent souls upon the men and women who broke the chains of despotism that were about to be put around their bodies. It is only a repetition of the past, anyhow.

In every war it was the opportune time for the reactionist and commercial vulture to do his dirty work in the name of patriotism. They are doing that now.

What other guarantee could the politicians of the world give to the Shylocks who are lending money to conduct this dreadful tragedy? No other guarantee, only a servile, slavish people.

Conscription and liberty cannot live in the one country. Conscription is the negation of human liberty. It is the beginning of the servile State. It is the one forged chain that can be applied to the legs and minds of men and women.

Conscription was not intended in this country to fight the Kaiser, but to fight trades unionism and the working classes. They are more afraid of the trades unionists, the capitalists are, than the Kaiser. Why? The Kaiser belonged to the same school that they belonged to.

The Kaiser stands for despotism, robbery, plunder, oligarchy. The workers stand for liberty. They fear the rising of the working class population a sight more than the Kaiser because the Kaiser belongs to the same school as the rest of the robbers in the rest of the world.

The psychological effect of my experience in Australia has kindled a name of rebellion in my soul and, regardless of the consequences, I intend to fight, by God, that infamous, rotten law (to wit, The Military Service Act 1916) that has been passed upon the heads of the people in New Zealand. The men who fought the campaign in Australia feared nothing.

Robert Semple (1873–1955)

We have, too, the same kind of soul. I believe similar blood flows in the veins of men and women such as flowed in the veins of martyrs in days gone by. It has got to do things and say things and the time has arrived In New Zealand to do it now. We're not going to allow Australians to say we haven't got a kick. They have said to me, 'Semple, whatever you do, we will be with you morally, financially, in spirit and in every other way.' We are going to make it damned hot for this Government.

How long are the working class of New Zealand going to be the apathetic tools of the employing classes that they are today? Something has to be done in this country to resurrect the fighting energy of the working classes. Miners in this country are ready to pay their share of battle, no matter what it might be. I have a wire in my pocket which I got last night to the effect that every coalminer if he is drawn in the ballot (to wit, the ballot for service under the Military Service Act 1916) has received instructions not to present himself. He is exempted by instructions of the Government. The miners don't want that exemption. They will say, 'Take your bribe back again.' They will say, 'You are not going to bribe us and conscript our labour. You are not going to play us against the other fellow. To hell with your bribery.'

We are going to see before many weeks how much there is in them. We are going to try them. Make no mistake about that I know that everyone talking against this infamous law is knocking at the jail door.

But we have to take these risks. I refuse to have my tongue bound in my cheeks. I have the freedom of my children and the dignity of my wife to fight for, and I am going to do it regardless of what I may personally suffer in the process.

The gong has got to be sounded. The force of manhood have got to be mobilised and things have got to be done in order that the sun of liberty may shine upon the people of this country. This political system has its roots in hell. The wowser churches are infamous dens administering chloroform and dope.

Upon his release, Semple toured the country, speaking of the injustice of his denial of a court hearing.

By the end of the war, he was elected to Parliament as a Labour Party MP representing Wellington South. He failed to hold his seat at the 1919 General Election but in 1926 he became president of the New Zealand Labour Party, returning to Parliament in 1928 and remaining in the house until his retirement in 1954.

As for his campaigning against conscription, Semple was a cabinet minister when New Zealand committed itself to World War Two. He was given the portfolio for national service and drew the marble for the first round of conscription.

He supported the introduction of compulsory military training in 1949 — seen by the political left as an act of betrayal.

The Pledge of Sacrifice

Francis Bell

July 12, 1917

After two years of war, New Zealand was counting the tragic cost of its involvement in World War One. News of fatalities continued to reach home, and a growing number of voices started to question how long it should continue.

Deputy leader Sir Joseph Ward faced a deputation complaining that railway services had been unduly curtailed to free up more men to go to the Western Front.

Ward told the deputation: 'The only thing that passes through my mind, is that we shall have to consider how much further this country can go in sending men at all. The time will come — I cannot say when — when it may not be possible to let any more men go.'

As the war extended into 1917, and the third anniversary of New Zealand's involvement approached in August, the Reform–Liberal joint administration faced increasingly difficult questions about its level of commitment.

It fell to prominent lawyer Francis Henry Dillon Bell[71], known to friends and colleagues as Harry, and appointed leader of the Legislative

71 W. J. Gardner. 'Bell, Francis Henry Dillon — Biography', from the Dictionary of New Zealand Biography. Te Ara — the Encyclopedia of New Zealand.

189

Council in 1912, to defend the case for New Zealand's continued support of the war effort.

One of the oldest members of the Legislative Council, 86–year–old John Ormond,[72] attacked the government war policy, manpower was being depleted and the country's exports were being harmed. Only single men should be called upon and the country should focus on producing food that England could not produce itself, he urged. Another member, Sir William Hall–Jones, questioned whether married men should be going to war.

Ormond: 'At the present time, we have been asked to make greater sacrifices than any other Colony of the Empire. My honourable friend (Bell) cannot deny that.'

Bell: 'I deny that we have been asked to.'

Ormond: 'We have done it.'

Bell: 'That is a different thing.'

Ormond argued that since America had joined the war, it could find all the men needed.

Bell's biographer, William Downie Stewart, said that in reply to arguments such as that set out by Ormond, Bell 'delivered one of the greatest speeches of his career' on July 12, 1917.

Bell immediately sought to identify the issues, arguing that a manpower shortage in the agricultural industry was separate to the issue of whether the country should relax its war efforts because it was on the verge of exhausting the single men available.

Stewart wrote … 'some extracts will serve to convey to the reader the vigour of his thought and language and the deep emotion with which he spoke.' The following extracts were recorded by Stewart:[73]

It is as if we should say that a single man is bound to fight for his country, but if a man marries he is thereby free from the obligation imposed upon us all. It is as if to say that the suffering which is borne by

---

72 *Mary Boyd. 'Ormond, John Davies — Biography', from the Dictionary of New Zealand Biography. Te Ara — the Encyclopedia of New Zealand.*

73 *The Right Honourable Sir Francis H. D. Bell, PC, GCMG, KC: His Life and Times (Butterworth & Co), by William Downie Stewart, 1937. Part of New Zealand Electronic Texts Collection.*

a wife who parts from her husband is greater than the suffering borne by a mother who has sent her son to the front.

It is not right or just thus to cloud the issue of our present convenience, with the question relating to the calling up of married men. If all the men in the country were single men, the first issue would be as present and as pressing as it is today, if it were present at all.

Bell then quoted the pledges made by Parliament on the outbreak of war, expressing the nation's resolve to make any sacrifice to maintain the people's heritage and birthright. The pledges had been repeated on each anniversary of the declaration of war and had expressed an 'inflexible determination' to continue to a victorious end.

Yes, Sir, 'any sacrifice' and 'inflexible determination'; but when the point has arrived that something of our convenience and comfort is to be sacrificed the determination of the Hon. Mr Ormond and of the Hon. Sir William Hall-Jones becomes flexible at once. These, I say, are the obligations to which you and I and every member of this Council are parties — with the Government it is true; but it is not the Government of this country alone — it is the people of the country, the Parliament of the Country, and this Council that have given the promises and the pledges I have read. 'Any sacrifice' of someone else; no sacrifice of convenience or comfort for ourselves.

Why, Sir, the Saturnalia being held near Wellington today, and the clamour of complaint against want of convenience in railway conveyance to the races, and crowds of motor cars going to enjoy pleasure show how many of us yet can sacrifice nothing. Byron, in the last century, in his glorious ode, after appeal to the Greeks to remember their history and to rouse their nation to defence against the oppressor, found them such as the men I have just spoken of:

'In vain, in vain; strike other chords,
Fill high the bowl with Samian wine;
Leave battle to the Turkish hordes,
And shed the blood of Scio's vine.'
The poet in these lines expressed what the minority for whom the

Francis Bell (1851–1936)

honourable gentleman has spoken today in Council really mean. Do not touch the music halls, the picture shows, the races, or the public houses. The time has come when we are beginning to disturb them; the limit of sacrifice is then overstepped.

Well, Sir, at all events, I who speak here am solemnly bound by those engagements that I have read; and if they are to be thrown to the winds, then let some others — let some others be the men to break the faith of New Zealand, but not a man born in New Zealand, proud of New

Zealand, happy in what has been done, feeling that his country has done its duty so far in performance of its obligations to the Mother country.

If our promise is no longer to be the measure of our obligation, then let some other men dishonour our word and the promise that we have made.

But I do not believe, Sir, we have become craven. I will not believe it till the country has so declared. This country, Sir, was the first to enter upon German soil. It is true that we occupied Samoa without resistance, but that was a mere accident of the absence of the great fleet Germany was prepared to defend it with. We were the first country — the first dominion of the Empire — to enter upon German soil. We have that to our credit.

Shall we be the first to quit, and have that to our lasting dishonour and disgrace? And, Sir, the third anniversary is approaching. Are those who have spoken prepared to send a message of shame, or will the honourable gentleman on the third anniversary move an amendment to the twice-repeated resolution?

Shall we not again say that our determination is inflexible or shall we admit that it is flexible, and that our time for abandonment has come, and that we have had enough?'

How can the entry of America into this quarrel make any difference to the obligation of New Zealand? If any part of the Empire was in danger more than another, New Zealand was that part.

It is our New Zealand soil we are defending, and the enemy is at the gates of one New Zealand avenue which stretches to the other side of the seas.

How can the entry of America into the battle make any difference to our duty?

Is it to be said of Englishmen at last as someone said in days of old, 'We will fight with Hessians, but not with our men and our own sons?' Are we to sit behind a rampart of Americans or of any nation? Americans are our brothers, of the same speech and of the same blood, but they are of another nation. They have different aims, different objects, different hopes, and other aspirations.

What test can it be of the question whether we are doing all that we can, and making as much sacrifice as possible, that there are others who are prepared to join England and her Allies in the fight? It will make the end speedier; but shall the end come without us because the Americans are there? The honourable gentleman's claim that we should at this stage make a pause and halt, and cease to reinforce our division, is nothing but a base and ignoble surrender.

I believe that there is no difference of opinion upon that in the minds of the vast majority of the people of New Zealand — that even if we have done more than other countries because we have fulfilled our promise, that which we have done in fulfillment of our promise we shall continue to the end, come Americans, come Russians, come any other nation in the world, and until the breaking point whatever be the sacrifices.

But I declare that it shall never be the case with me, and I declare my firm belief that it will never be the case with the people of New Zealand — that it shall be said at such a time as that, and in such circumstances as I have referred to, that there are no men to spare.

I would ask further; what can such a speech as the honourable gentleman made, moderate as it was, restrained as it was, carefully free from offence to those to whom he addressed himself — what can such a speech mean to the enemy? Has it any other meaning than that we are at the end of our resources, so far as our support to the Empire is concerned?

We are the descendants of men who in the last century bore privation and suffering, almost starvation rather than give way to a military despotism. I do not believe I shall live — I hope I shall not live — to see the day when it shall be truly said that the dogged determination that made England the pilot that weathered the storm in the beginning of the nineteenth century has disappeared from the traditions of our race, and that our heritage and birthright, of which we spoke so proudly when the war broke out, is a heritage and a birthright whose value is to be calculated in money, and to be defended not to the utmost limit of physical endurance, but only until our pockets begin to be affected.

I do not believe there is the smallest cause for the contention that this country will be brought to ruin by the further depletion of its manhood. It may be that it will be brought to privation. It certainly may, and I think should, be brought to privation of many of the comforts, conveniences, and luxuries that we have today.

Sir, the upright man was defined by a poet two thousand years ago:

'The upright man remains ever determined to carry out in full that to which he is pledged, and is not swayed from his determination by the clamour of the crowd demanding base and mean conclusions, nor by the frown of any tyrant, however near.'

That, Sir, I hope will be the maxim of every man and of every woman in New Zealand who at the beginning of this war joined with the rest of the Empire in the fervent determination to support the cause of justice. A pause in it would mean that we had abandoned the cause which we declared we would maintain to the end.

The end has not yet come, Sir, and I trust that no words from the honourable gentleman, long as his experience has been and great as is the respect in which he is held, will prevail to make the determination of the people less, or to make us hesitate in our duty to the cause and to the Empire until the victory is won.

While Bell's words staved off many critics, his commitment to the pledge of sacrifice took a personal toll on his family.

Two weeks after making his speech, Bell's 33–year–old son William was killed in action in Belgium while serving as a Captain with the 1st King Edward's Horse regiment.[74] William had resigned as a Member of Parliament to join the forces.

In 1923, Bell was knighted and in May 1925, he became Prime Minister after the death of Massey but served for only 16 days, turning down the his party's invitation to remain in the role.

---

74 *Archive, Auckland War Memorial Museum.*

Peace and Freedom

William Massey

November 1918

While Joseph Ward was a practical liberal, his Prime Ministerial successor, William Massey[75], proved a liberal in disguise. Like Seddon, he stumped the country. Despite a fraught Parliament — without the elective second chamber he sought — the first full–time Reform politician used the power of the State, like Seddon and Ward, across the spectrum to bring reform.

He strove to provide freehold for the farmers; establish a non–political civil service, break strikes and maintain the arbitration system; recruit and maintain a citizen army overseas; seize a Pacific mandate, and project the future of an economy, including an iron and steel industry, and a national shipping line.

With a non–political civil service, the Massey administration established the pillars of the 20th century economy — Departments of Agriculture, Forestry and Science, Meat and Dairy Boards, and the Road and Hydro electric infrastructure — that underpinned the rapid development of what had become, and would remain until 1970, Britain's offshore farm.

---

75 Barry Gustafson. 'Massey, William Ferguson — Biography', from the Dictionary of New Zealand Biography. Te Ara — the Encyclopedia of New Zealand.

With a somewhat 'harsh delivery', Massey was a broad–based if not spectacular debater.

Quick in repartee and on interjection, the essence of Parliamentary debate, the Presbyterian pragmatist liked Biblical quotes and historical references. His force of character, allied with a quick humanity, helped him command Parliament.

Not for nothing, despite powerful lieutenants like Francis Bell and James Allen, or a forced coalition with Ward, whom he disliked, was he known as the Chief. Not for nothing, when meeting the wounded veterans of 1 NZEF, perhaps the Dominion's finest construct, until 2 NZEF, did he weep.

In marvelling at Massey's long career, we find few Prime Ministers who suffered such vicissitudes — vicious strikes, a numbingly long Great War, deadly epidemics, severe Depression and, on top of all those cataclysms, hung parliaments.

As time separates the generations, we too easily ignore the pressures on a leader in an unprecedented war. With his own son at risk, in 1914 Massey sweated out the news that German naval vessels were a threat to the Samoan convoy. Sitting in the Imperial War Cabinct he led a country that with 42% of its males under 45 on active service, suffered the highest casualties, at 58%, of any Dominion.

Taken together, three of his speeches in early November 1918, on the surrender of Turkey, and then Austria, and on the Imperial Conference, were a Parliamentary tour de force.

What stands out is the nation's pride in the 1 NZEF — at the end halting the last major German offensive of 1918, and earning Foch's Citation of the Army— the strength of the feeling for a stiff peace, the pride in the 'heritage' of the Empire, the concept of Memorial Days fulfilled in Anzac Day, backed by a survey of the development from land to ironsands and pulp mills to carry the 'enormous liabilities' of the war and lift the onward march of the nation.

The following are extracts from Massey's speech, delivered on November 1, 1918, on the surrender of Turkey:[76]

---

76 *New Zealand Parliamentary Debates (Hansard), Volume 183, page 109.*

The Turkish plenipotentiary arrived in Madros early this week and an armistice was signed by Admiral Calthorpe ... and comes into operation at noon of the 31ˢᵗ October.

The events of the past few days constitute, to my mind, some of the most important events in the annals of British history; and ... among the great events in the world's history. It means that civilisation that was being attacked, and was intended to be smashed by those who are opposed to us in the war, has been saved — and saved I hope, for all time ...

Sir, I feel certain that members will agree that if it is at all possible (if Anzacs were sent to garrison the Dardanelles) it would be a compliment which the Anzacs have undoubtedly earned in the Gallipoli campaign, a campaign which will never be forgotten: it will remain for all time throughout the world as a standard of heroism, gallantry, discipline and endurance.

The people of New Zealand and Australia, and of the Empire generally, will never forget that campaign — ill–fated though it was — where the Anzacs established a reputation equal to the best of the fighting men of British stock of which history gives us any record ...

And, Sir, I think I am justified in telling Parliament that ... when the terms of peace came to be arranged ... an earnest attempt should be made by the British government to secure control of the Gallipoli peninsula ... To my mind it would be nothing less than sacrilege if the foot of the Turk was allowed to press to the dust where lie the remains of our gallant men.

We want Gallipoli ... to make it the Mecca of the British citizens from the South Pacific, a place where they may visit, where they can see the monuments to their relatives, and think of the heroic deeds which they performed for the people who are alive today and for all future generations.

Sir, we must not forget ... our gallant Allies ... we should think first of our kinsmen across the Pacific — the people of the United States — and the brave soldiers they sent to assist the armies of Britain and France and of the other Allied countries ... I have no doubt they have done a great deal towards turning the balance in favour of the Allies. Nor can we forget the gallant sons of France ... Then there are the chivalrous people of Italy ... the news ... indicates the very early breaking up of the Austrian empire and ... an early peace ...

And, Sir, we must never forget the splendid part played by the Native races within the British Empire. Our own Maoris — two thousand of them — are engaged at the front, a body of men descended from a long line of warrior ancestors ... there were no better fighting men in the New Zealand Division than the Maoris. And if there were no better fighting men in the New Zealand Division then I can follow that up by saying there are no better fighting men in the British Army ... the native of the islands of the South Pacific ... Rarotonga ... Tonga ... Niue ... have done their share in the war ...

All these natives as British citizens did their share ... we should remember the assistance we have received from the coloured races within the British Empire coming into the struggle ... they have earned from the Anglo–Saxon peoples of the British Empire, their right to a better standing for all time.

... We have got to admit that Japan right through 'played the game' and played it nobly ... What would have happened if Japan had thrown in her lot with Germany? It would have been quite impossible for us to send a single soldier from these overseas dominions ... to keep open our commercial relations with Britain ... and we owe Japan a deep debt of gratitude for her good faith ... for sending a battle cruiser to escort our Main Body when they sailed from New Zealand ...

As I have said, the end is coming. I do not think there is any man in the world who now envies the Kaiser ... It is said that history repeats itself. Thousands of years ago there was a Babylonian king named Belshazzar ... to whom it was said 'God hath numbered thy kingdom, and finished it. Thou art weighed in the balance and found wanting.' It is not finished yet ... but I have no hesitation in saying that it is very near.

And I think it is right on an occasion like this that we as British citizens should remember the Higher Power who has guided and protected us and all the people of our Empire during the four years of this awful war.

It is quite true that much of our enthusiasm has passed ... but that enthusiasm has been succeed by a stern determination ... to carry the war to a satisfactory and successful end ...

And when peace does come, it will be our duty to see that it will be a peace worthy of the sacrifices that have been made — a peace worthy of the men who have died for the Empire. Fifteen thousand New Zealanders — the pick of our population — have laid down their lives for their fellow citizens ...

I hope that when peace comes it will be a peace worthy of the sacrifices made by our soldiers in all the theatres of war. We want to make quite certain that peace will provide for reparation on the part of the enemy ... and just punishment for the crimes that have been committed ... (and) that Germany will not be in a position to disturb the peace of the world for many a long year to come ...

The following are extracts from Massey's speech, delivered on November 5, 1918, on the surrender of Austria:[77]

... Sir, this is an exceedingly important occasion, because Austria is the last of Germany's Allies to surrender in this war.

First there was Bulgaria, then Turkey, and now Austria ... Germany now stands alone against the Forces of the Allies; and I think it must be apparent to every one of us that Germany cannot stand long in that position.

The sands of Germany are running down very fast; it may be a week or it may be a month but within a very short period Germany must follow the example of those associated with her ...

In any case it is quite clear now that peace is not far distant. We have been looking for and long for peace, and we have the satisfaction that we have not very much longer to wait.

We know perfectly well that while the news coming to us has been hailed with delight by the citizens of the empire, it has also been hailed with delight in the different theatres of war ...

We heard no complaints from our soldiers with regard to the dangers, discomforts and hardships which they had to put up, but they did express

---

77 *New Zealand Parliamentary Debates (Hansard), Volume 183, page 185.*

201

the wish that the time would come when they could be sent back to their own country.

... Sir, we are looking forward to peace and I am certain we will not look in vain. There are many people who think that when the war comes to an end we shall have a new heaven and a new earth, but I am not of that opinion, though I believe we are going to have a better state of things so far as the British Empire is concerned, and that a better state of things will prevail so far as humanity is concerned; and speaking of our fellow citizens, I am certain that when the war comes to an end we shall have a better feeling of comradeship amongst ourselves, and ... a better appreciation of what British citizenship means.

As a matter of fact we have forgotten what the freedom and liberty we enjoy has cost, and do not appreciate it as I think we ought to.

I think that we have failed to appreciate the great deeds of the Empire and the men who were responsible for them. In many cases we know nothing about them ...

I am thinking particularly at the moment of the United States.

We had an opportunity of seeing how the United States Independence Day was celebrated in France ... (attending) a meeting of the Supreme War Council at Versailles, and we saw on that occasion the march of fifteen thousand American troops into Paris ... It was one of the grandest sights I ever saw. We also witnessed how the Americans troops ... celebrated what they call Memorial Day. We hear very little about such days in this country.

Memorial Day is the day set apart for patriotic people to do everything that is necessary or fitting in the way of keeping in good condition the graves of the soldiers who fought and died for the United States in the days gone by. The 2,500 troops on board ... understood it, and knew what it meant ... another day they celebrate is the anniversary of the dedication of the soldiers cemetery at Gettysburg ... the occasion on which President Lincoln uttered one of the greatest speeches ... that the citizens should dedicate themselves to the purpose for which those soldiers had died, so that Government of the people, by the people and for the people shall not perish from the earth ...

Millions of young people read and repeat the speech every anniversary

William Massey (1856–1925)

of the dedication ceremony ... patriotism is encouraged in every possible way ... I admire the system, and I take this opportunity of saying 'Go ye and do likewise.' Our rising generation have a great deal to learn;

they want to be taught pride of race — it does not matter what race they belong to in the British Empire — pride of Empire and love of country; they want to be taught what is meant by the Union Jack ... the time has come when there should be another Cross added — a cross indicative of the official partnership between Britain and her overseas dominions ...

We need to teach our young people something of the great men of the past, something of the race from which we have sprung ... the ancient Britons ... who fought for liberty ... the Danes, Saxons, the Jutes, the Angles, the Normans — that wonderful combination that forms the basic structure upon which the British Empire has been built up. Going back to the Saxon times ... Queen Boadicea ... King Alfred ... Richard Coeur de Lion, Henry the Fifth, the great Queen Elizabeth, and her captains and statesmen ... to Nelson and Wellington ... the heroes of the Crimea, and now to the great struggle in which we have been engaged for the last four or five years ...

Sir, the names of those who have played the leading part in this last struggle of all will be handed down to history in the same way as the names of those who fought in the great eras I have mentioned. We must not forget Marshall Foch ... Lord Kitchener ... Field Marshall Haig ... Admiral Beatty ... These are the men whose memory we ought to honour; and I hope they will never be forgotten, and that we shall follow the example of other countries, and do a little more in the way of celebrating the great deeds that have given us the proud position we occupy today.

We ought to revere the memories of the men who were and are responsible for that position. They had their struggles in the past, but they faced the odds and came out successfully.

We have our struggle today but I believe it is nearing the end and that we shall be just as successful in finishing this was as our ancestors were in the years that are past, when they were called upon to defend their liberty and freedom, and to fight for the Empire which has grown up.

Sir, the record of our country, of our Empire is one of which each and every one of us have the greatest reason to be proud. It is a record of a struggle during hundreds of years —a struggle for the liberty and the freedom which we enjoy today —always fighting up towards the light, and always on the side of honesty and truth.

The first thing to consider in a crisis like this, when we hope the great war is coming to an end, is: Are we going to continue building up as our fathers built, or are we going to act as the citizens of the great empires of the past have acted — empires that rose, flourished for hundreds of years, and then decayed?

Are we going to give way to laziness and luxury? I sincerely hope that that will not be the case; I trust that we shall choose the better part, and that we shall go on building up this great heritage, which has come down to us, in such a way that will leave a brighter and better Empire than anything that has every been dreamt of up to the present date.

Massey's third speech, about the Imperial Conference, was made to the House on November 7, 1918. Here are extracts:[78]

I wish, Sir, to make a Ministerial statement ... with regard to the business dealt with by the Imperial War Conference and the Imperial War Cabinet ... Good work was done by the War Cabinet not only in the interests of the Dominions, but of the Empire as a whole ...

Let me say, that as far as New Zealand is concerned the system has on the whole worked well ... We have laid a foundation upon which I believe a great Imperial structure will be built up as time goes on.

We have been taken into partnership ... by the Government and the people of Great Britain ... There is no interference with the autonomy ... of any one of the Dominions ... But the people of Britain say this: 'We extend to you ... the right hand of fellowship and of British citizenship ... And I say it ought to (be) heartily and cordially accepted ...'

This proposal is a tremendous improvement on anything that was possible in connection with the system of Imperial Conferences that were held prior to 1916 or 1917 ... Of course ... there is a section of the people ... who say we should go for a system of federation. With an Imperial Parliament ... I believe I am just about as ardent an Imperialist as most people. But because I am an ardent Imperialist ... I say it would be a mistake at present to attempt anything in the way of an Imperial Parliament ...

78 *New Zealand Parliamentary Debates (Hansard), Volume 183, page 277.*

My reading of history has shown me that Constitutions are not built up in a day — or in many years for that matter. The Constitution under which the British Empire and the British dominions are working has come down to us from the old Saxon Witanagemot ... from the Magna Charta at Runnymnede ... the Bill of Rights ... the Reform Act ... the extension of the franchise in the United Kingdom ... there is no Dominion ... that would submit to be taxed by a Parliament sitting outside its borders ...

... That brings me to another point in connection with the work done at the Imperial War Cabinet ... the question of the Pacific Islands ... the future of the German colonies in the Pacific ... Samoa and New Guinea ... we wanted them simply as a protection for the peoples of the South Pacific ... if they (the Germans) are allowed to re-establish themselves there it will mean the building up of a cruel, unscrupulous, and ambitious nation in the South Pacific which will be a menace to the British peoples now living in the Southern Hemisphere ... the men at the head of affairs in Britain understand (that) position better today than they did ten or twenty years ago ...

There is no country in the world so prosperous as New Zealand today; and so far as the war is concerned, what country has done its part and performed its share better than this Dominion? The soldiers of no part of the Empire have excelled those of New Zealand ...

... One point ... I am sorry that in New Zealand we have not been in a position to commence ship building, and particularly the building of iron ships, and thus promoting the utilisation of the iron ores of the South Island and the iron sands of the North Island ...

I say that we should do all that we can to see that the overseas carrying business remains in the hands of our own people ... I know that in the past, so far as shipping is concerned, that is a matter which has been left almost entirely to private enterprise. There is no question, but that private enterprise did well, and I hope it will do well in the future; but when there is an undertaking of a national character, there should be something in the nature of national control. The sea is the national highway of the British Empire, and we ought to make the most of it ...

I am not finding fault with State ownership ... The business of shipping requires to be managed by experts. At the Imperial Conference I moved 'That in order to maintain satisfactorily the connections, and at the same time encourage commercial and industrial relations between the different countries of the British Empire, this Conference is of opinion that shipping ... should be brought under review by an Inter–Imperial Board' ... It is an attempt to place our shipping under the control of a Board similar to the inter State Boards which exist in America and Canada ...

If we are a wise and an intelligent people ... then we shall profit by the lessons of the war, and in that case it will not be an unmixed evil. We know perfectly well, so far as the whole Empire is concerned, that we have not done justice to it ...

We must do our duty ... to the Empire so that it may become stronger and more powerful than it has been ... (and) see that the emigration that take places from Britain and from any country in the Empire should be kept within the imperial boundaries. We should see to it that British citizens are encouraged to come to this country ...

... With regard to land settlement. Land is the raw material upon which our prospects depend ... I am thinking particularly of wool ... in extending that branch of industry ... I am very glad to find that a start had been made with regard to making iron from the iron sands of Taranaki ... another industry ... is the making of paper ... the sooner we get some paper mills or pulp mills established the better because what an immense amount of paper is imported into New Zealand ...

We may be able to do something ... to deal with the supply of motor spirits ... there is no reason why we should not encourage industry whenever we have an opportunity ... use our own raw material, encourage our own industries, employ our own people, encourage immigration of the British race, and ... establish a satisfactory scheme of preference after the war — the Empire as a whole will enter upon a better era, a brighter era, a more prosperous era ... and we shall have no difficulty in carrying the enormous liabilities which ... we have been called upon to build up in the war period.

Interjection from the floor: 'What about the hydro electrical scheme?'

Massey continued:

That is urgently required. Already the Public Works Department are making the arrangements necessary ...

... There is one other subject ... I believe that the coming of America into the war was providential ... I believe, Sir, it was destiny that brought America into the war. If we ever reach that the time — and I think we shall, not in the present generation or for a long time to come — which is predicted in Scripture, when men shall 'beat their swords into ploughshares and their spears into pruning hook; nations shall not lift up sword against nation, neither shall they learn war any more', it will be by a combination such as already been commenced — a combination such as is in existence today, a combination of the English speaking races — Britain, the British Dominions, America, and along with them France, Italy, Japan, and the other nations ... with regard to Japan, I acknowledge the great part that Japan has played in the war ... our main body ... did not sail until the Japanese battle cruiser Ibuki steamed into Wellington Harbour ...

Sir, I believe that Britain and America have a mission—

I am convinced of it — and it is to punish Germany and the Germans for the crimes of which they have been guilty ...

I do not want anything more than justice, but we ought to get justice for both victims and criminals, and we are entitled to it. I hope too that justice will be done to Germany; and if justice is done to the Germans — and honourable members will understand the justice I wish to mete out to them — I shall be satisfied ...

The war ended on November 11 and a month later, Massey travelled to Europe to represent New Zealand at the Paris Peace Conference. On June 28, 1919, Massey signed the Treaty of Versailles, a defining first step on the road to nationhood, and arguably the most significant event of his chieftainship.

He returned to an exhausted New Zealand and an influenza epidemic that would kill more than 8,500 of its citizens.

Sharks v Minnows

John A. Lee

July 10, 1924

Five years after the Great War, *Hansard* records the emergence of one of our first native–born orators and finest political minds. Combining precise knowledge on issues, and witty takes on his leading opponents, John A. Lee's 'sharks v minnows' speech cut the Reform and Liberal leaders down to size.

No one with any feel for Parliamentary government thereafter could doubt Labour's claim to be a government in waiting.

In a brilliantly constructed speech, the one–armed returned soldier excised the criticism of Labour as an unpatriotic party. It was a party based not just on the book learning of its leader, Harry Holland, but on experience of life's hard knocks. Countering the distinguished Apirana Ngata, Lee[79] then established a principled position for Labour on defence. Critically he turned on the 'Billfoolery' of Prime Minister Bill Massey, and the 'Tomfoolery' of the Liberal's Sir Thomas Wilford.

Quoting the overseas press (as Ngata would do in 1939) he satirised the image of the old leader (for whom he had some respect) as a Humpty Dumpty of imperial statesman, and for breaking promises

---

79 Erik Olssen. 'Lee, John Alfred Alexander — Biography', from the Dictionary of New Zealand Biography. Te Ara — the Encyclopedia of New Zealand.

209

(that Lee himself had heard him give in England) to the influential Returned Soldiers lobby.

He then demolished the Liberal leader. Wilford was a weathervane leader of 'a jellyfish party with no fixed principles, who was not taken seriously, and (who) ... did not seem to take himself seriously.'

Wilford never recovered from the beating.

Here's the speech that used wit in the way a veterinarian would wield a scalpel to dissect a frog:[80]

> *I want to congratulate the member ... for putting on record the fact 'that the financiers are getting away with the swag' ... as speaker followed speaker, even from the Reform side of the House, we had evidence following evidence that indeed, the reformers were getting away with the swag, and a very substantial swag indeed.*
>
> *I want first of all to refer to a circular that was placed in my box this morning. It is a circular from a New Zealand League which claims to comprise many influential men who have in the past supported the Reform Party and this circular appeals to each member of the House to give earnest consideration ... to the desire for a compromise cabinet ...*
>
> *It seems to me that the proposal consists of an attempt to get rid of a cabinet of sharks for a cabinet of minnows or whitebait.*
>
> *The most interesting thing is that only two members of the present cabinet (are) considered to have satisfactory qualifications. Five members of the Liberal Party are budding members of the Cabinet ... and four reformers not present members of the Cabinet are to be included ...*
>
> *It is altogether a most amusing proposal, and a piece of most amusing egotism.*
>
> *The only thing I do not notice about the suggestion is that thought the Prime Minister is asked to go into cold storage, the leader of the Liberal Party is not asked to accompany him.*

Mr Howard: 'He will go ... to some place hotter.'

> *If ... the Prime Minister goes into cold storage and the leader of the*

---

80 *New Zealand Parliamentary Debates (Hansard), Volume 203, pages 360–369.*

Liberal Party into hot storage then we will avoid what the member for Waimarino described last night as 'Billfoolery' and 'Tomfoolery' ... (the Prime Minister) went away with an outstanding reputation ... the sole survivor of the war cabinets; the sole remaining war potentate, a fixed star; and of course when he got to England, and started to tell the people there how they should manage their affairs ... the result reminds me of the little nursery rhyme:

'Humpty Dumpty sat on a wall
Humpty Dumpty had a great fall
Not all the horses and all the King's men
Could put the Prime Minister together again'

As a result of his interference in British politics ... the Prime Minister came back with a reputation sadly addled. Indeed the Cape Times said this: 'Mr Massey is still Mr Massey and still Prime Minister of New Zealand, which means that New Zealand's share in the Conference will be very much what it was last time — amiable, profoundly well-intentioned, and not conspicuously intelligent.'

And that very naughty Bolshevistic paper the Daily Herald (noted of him): 'the only allied wartime Prime Minister remaining is the extremely reactionary but rather unimportant Mr. Massey' ... You can understand why the present leader of the Reform Party objects to people reading the Daily Herald.

... I was most amused and interested in the progress of the Prime Minister. It amused me to read he had gone to Ulster and been welcomed by a special guard of constables ... that he had had a gramophone record made of a speech of his, and that he had proudly boasted of the fact that the record had produced a distinct Ulster accent. It was a most amusing piece of news. But I do not know of any positive good that accrued to New Zealand or the Empire as a result of that Conference ...

The Prime Minister, whenever he was tackled with interfering in British politics, had something to say about the patriotism of his opponents. If an individual dares to disagree ... with the Prime Minister, he has a habit of referring to that individual as lacking in patriotism; and it is the habit of a considerable number ... of the Liberal Party and the Reform Party to constantly charge against our party, that we are not patriotic.

I read something of Horace Walpole's the other day ... at the same time ... as Johnson said that 'patriotism was the last refuge of a scoundrel.' Gentlemen have talked a great deal about patriotism ... that of late patriotism has been so much hackneyed about it is in danger of falling into disgrace. The very idea of patriotism has been lost, and the term prostituted to the worst purposes.

A patriot, Sir. Why patriots spring up like mushrooms. I could raise fifty of them in four and twenty hours. I have raised that many in one night ...

If patriotism is to be made the football of political parties, if individuals are going to charge every one who disagrees with them with a lack of patriotism ... the time will come here in New Zealand ... when honest men seeking the suffrages of the people will be compelled to stand on the platform ... 'I am not a patriot' ... I am sorry to see that the Liberals as well as the Reformers are not above ... (making) patriotism the football of politics ... They are constantly trying to impute a lack of patriotism to the Labour Party.

Last night we heard ... (the MP for Eastern Maori) that we were not unpatriotic but lukewarm (about) the abandonment of the Singapore base ... (about which the British) Labour and Liberal Party had made a closer study than ever the Member for Eastern Maori ... we are brave and intellectual and heroic when we are marching to the shambles, but if we try to initiate a policy which will try to prevent the Pacific turning into a future shambles, we are supposed to be ignorant ...

The honourable member charged us with being too well read ... I plead guilty. I have read the Russian novelists such as Gorky, Gogol, Tolstoy, Turgenev, Dostoevski ... the Labour party has found an economic foundation for its programme, but it has a literary foundation which is British to the core ...

Mr Speaker ... The Government blundered over the settlement scheme (for returned soldiers) ... when I was in camp during the war at the limbless school, Oatlands Park, the Prime Minister came down ... (he) will remember the promises he made ... and will make an effort to redeem them ... we bled them in the trenches for their country; and now they are back here they are bled by their country ... the returned soldier was asked

John A. Lee (1891–1982)

to pay interest ... altogether too high ...

The leader of the Liberal Party says ... the country is turning towards the Liberal Party ... He says there is a wave of Liberalism. It is a very small wave — a brain wave ...

The Liberal Party falls down between the desire to placate Reform and the desire ... to offer something to the people who are being ... politically educated by the Labour Party. One day the Liberal Party cries aloud 'Singapore for Ever'; the next day it is discretely silent about Singapore. The following day we have 'My country right or wrong' ... at Victoria College ... I heard one student declare that the Liberal Party was a party with no fixed principles. Another called the Liberal party a jellyfish ... (which) forgot the two great Liberal principles ... even handed justice and taxation according to means ...

Here in this House the Liberals get up and say we should not squabble with them, and there should be unity between the Liberal and Labour parties to dislodge the Reform party. Now which of the two represents the attitude of the Liberal Party ... I do not know where they are, but to use their own phrase they are in the middle of the road ...

... The leader of the Liberal Party declared in favour of a reduction in customs tax but when it comes to voting he will vote in favour of a reduction in income tax. He declares against strikes, and his party assists to reduce wages and impose conditions, which make strikes inevitable. The leader ... declares in favour of humanitarian legislation.

Last session he placed on record that it was more important that income tax should be reduced than humanitarian proposals should be brought into operation. That he clearly placed upon record in Hansard, just as he foolishly placed on record ... a clear cut statement that he was not in favour of a land policy based on occupation and use ... a statement of that kind must not be passed over ...

The meeting took a jocular note; the honourable gentleman was not taken seriously, and I go so far as to say that he did not seem to take himself seriously ...

I do not know why the Liberal Party should not go through the penitent fold because I believe they would be welcomed — received with open arms. We welcome on the basis of that suggestion of the New Zealand League a Cabinet with five Liberal members; but what would become of the present members of the Reform Cabinet I do not know ...

Mr Speaker during the dinner adjournment I have not been able to discover the parents of the mysterious document that was placed in my locker earlier today. I have not been able to discover its parents at all. Evidently the child is disowned. It has been laid at our doorstep, and undoubtedly it is a foundling. Still–born maybe. I am reminded of the words of a poet ...

> *'Has it a sister*
> *Has it a brother*
> *Has it a mother*
> *Take it up tenderly*
> *Lift it with care*
> *Fashioned so slenderly*
> *Young and so fair'* [81]

And unfortunately dead. We will send along the wreath ...

I think only one thing can save the Liberal Party, and that is that 'piebald moke' ... called the Reform Gerrymandering Electoral Bill ... a system of electoral reform by means of which the two important parties will cut their throats for the sake of the least important party.

The Reform Party has been guilty of all the crimes in the electoral calendar. The Liberal Party has been equally guilty — in the Coalition cabinet and by its support in the House since ...

It seems to me the Liberal Party is turning King's Evidence. The Liberal Party is telling on the Reform Party so that the Liberal Party may escape the verdict.

I think the two parties had better get together ... stand side by side in the dock so that the electors may try both parties and return a verdict of guilty and send to this House a majority of Labour members who will not indulge in what my friend the Hon. Member from Waimarino called 'Billfoolery' and 'Tomfoolery', but will legislate in the interests of all the people.

---

81 *Poem adapated from Thomas Hood's The Bridge of Sighs.*

215

'Warfare is Not Noble'

Frank Milner

June 28, 1933

The records suggest a contender for the status as New Zealand's finest orator may have been a charismatic, revered, long–serving Rector of Waitaki. Between 1910 and 1946, Frank Milner presided over and produced seven cohorts of 'virile citizens' at what became one of the best known schools of the British Empire on which Massey was so focussed.

The Rector's son, Ian Milner, was a Rhodes Scholar. His biography[82] of his father talks of the mana of 'The Man'.

'The Man had mana, a favourite word. What gave it life was his power of speech. The words flowed from his lips as from a permanently welling spring, in perfectly shaped sentences with resonant sentences. He scorned to use scripts or notes …

'There was never hesitation or pause to find a word … The music of his voice, deep toned, capable of a wide variety of timbre, cast an additional spell …

'The words and their music were charged with a dynamic force that came from the inner man … Instinctively, infallibly, he created the

---

82 Milner of Waitaki: Portrait of The Man (John McIndoe and Waitaki High School Old Boys' Association), by Ian Milner, 1983.

Frank Milner (1875– 1944)

intimate rapport with his audience that marked the born (and trained) orator.'

When roused by a serious theme, his eloquence had the commanding ring of the old prophets. A Southland Waitakian, Douglas Brass, who became a distinguished editor in Australia put him alongside the best ones: 'I have heard a lot of famous men on the platform; the only ones who came near Frank Milner, for playing surely and sensitively and eloquently on an audience, were Churchill and Soekarno.'

Milner's son, Ian, continues: 'His greatest oratorical performance was at the 24th annual Rotary International Convention in Boston, June 1933. He spoke to an audience of 9,000 on the need for a new world order. Pleading for international understanding, he warned another war would mean disaster.'

The speech, though musty in the records, gives an insight into the impact of World War One, not only on our nation but, with their eloquent rolls of honour, our schools.

One can stand and weep at the endless names on the memorials of the major public schools of England from Eton to Sherbourne and of its universities from Oxford to Cambridge. The same is true for our schools and universities.

Extracts from Milner's address to the Rotarians at Boston:

Now, many of you are fathers. You have your children who carry on for you, even in this life, some form of immortality. Their mothers went down to the portals of death to give them life. You encompassed them with love and tender nurture. You have fondly imagined lives of honour and usefulness for them. But again breaks in this ruthless cycle of armaments, of fears, and national hatreds, and shatters your dream, and what do you see? Behold I show you the 'nobility' of warfare, for warfare is not noble, though it gives rise at times to noble virtues ...

Here is a noble youth in the express image of his Maker, and in one moment blown into quivering bloody rags; one moment a bright youth, with a wonderful career of usefulness before him, dehumanised to a gibbering idiot, the light of reason gone for ever ...

The answer was for America to look to a fuller association with Europe, and eschewing the extremes of jingoistic nationalism and pacifism, work for a new world order that would render war an anachronism.

So he moved to a peroration based on the inscription on a famous statue on the Chilean–Argentian border pleading for peace:

'Sooner shall the domed peak of the Andes crumble into dust than that the people of Chile and Argentina shall break the peace which here, at the feet of Christ the Redeemer, they have sworn to maintain.'

As he finished his address, the audience rose as one to give him a standing ovation. News of Milner's success rapidly reached New Zealand. A cablegram from Mr T.C. List, Rotary's New Zealand Governor, sent back to fellow members read: 'Frank Milner scored a complete triumph. Address received with unparalleled enthusiasm.'[83]

After Boston, Milner was persuaded to repeat his speech at a series of lectures in North America. He received three offers to remain to work in America, and was given an audience with President Roosevelt.

When he returned to New Zealand, he took his New World Order lecture on tour, starting at the Auckland Town Hall. He went to the provinces and hundreds filled the street in New Plymouth, listening to him through amplified speakers outside a full theatre.[84]

At Waitaki, Milner, in teaching the virtues of liberty and co-operation in human affairs, made as part of his message the building of a remarkable Memorial Chapel.

Then at the opening of Memorial Gates, in 1944, surrounded by his friends and admirers, as he moved into his oration, he fell dead.

Those who were there never forgot The Man. Those who have heard both Churchill and Soekarno can accept Brass' affirmation of his stature as an outstanding orator.

---

83 *Evening Post, June 30, 1933.*
84 *Evening Post, October 5, 1933.*

Woman About the House

Elizabeth McCombs

September 28, 1933

Kate Sheppard was our first successful woman politician but never an MP. It was forty years before another Christchurch woman overcame the prejudice against women Members of Parliament. At the age of 60, Elizabeth McCombs,[85] became New Zealand's first woman MP.

Brought up in the age of progressive liberalism and socialism that nurtured Sheppard, she cut her teeth in the Children's Aid and Temperance movements. With her husband, James McCombs, she helped found the Social Democratic Party in 1911, before he entered Parliament in 1913.

When James McCombs became first president of the second New Zealand Labour Party in 1916, she was elected to the executive. In 1921 she was the second woman elected to the Christchurch City Council. There, she worked successfully for improved civic services for women and support for the unemployed and distressed. In 1928 and 1931, she stood for Parliament with the slogan: 'Vote for the first woman to the New Zealand Parliament.'

When James McCombs died, and despite the prejudice against women,

85 Jean Garner. 'McCombs, Elizabeth Reid — Biography', from the Dictionary of New Zealand Biography. Te Ara — the Encyclopedia of New Zealand.

Elizabeth McCombs was elected with a huge majority to Parliament in September 1933..

Her maiden speech that month proved her 'a skilled and effective orator.'[86] The *Auckland Star* parliamentary reporter notes her 'speaking in clear measured tones'. She made 'a reasoned address, characterised by fluency and neat marshalling of facts, and relieved by subtle thrusts and irony.'

She strode straight into battle, making it clear she had come to Wellington to make a difference. Here's an abridged transcript of her speech:[87]

Mr Speaker, in the first place I wish to express my sincere thanks to the honourable members of this House for the very kind reception which they have accorded me. It seems to me that a very good working basis has been established, and I trust that nothing will happen during my term of office that will disturb the harmony of the relations so created.

I would like to warn honourable members, however, that women are never satisfied unless they have their own way. It happens in this case that the woman's way is the right way.

I should be failing in my duty if I did not take the first opportunity that is presented by the Standing Orders of this House to bring to the Right Hon. the Prime Minister and the members of the Government the message that I believe was given to me in the Lyttelton by-election to be conveyed to this House. The great majority of the electors in my district have expressed the greatest dissatisfaction with the administration of the Government, as it affects various matters that touch the country as a whole ...

... Take, for instance, the question of unemployment. So far as that question is concerned the Government of this country seems to have withdrawn into a kind of mental euthanasia. It sits there sublimely satisfied that all is well. The electors of the Lyttelton constituency have sent me here to say all is not well so far as the unemployment question is concerned.

The official figures — the latest I have, at any rate — for unemployment

---

86 *Auckland Star, September 29, 1933.*
87 *New Zealand Parliamentary Debates (Hansard), September 28, 1933, Volume 236 page 157.*

register 80,000 unemployed. These figures do not include women. If we include women and youths we find that the number is practically double. If we take those and all their dependants, we will find that they constitute a very large proportion of the people of this country; but add to those the number of people who are in employment but who are working only half–time or part–time, and earning no more than relief rates of pay, and we will find that the total practically as many as the total registered unemployed. If we take those and add them to the number of unemployed with all their dependants, we will find that we have a quarter of the population of this country in such a position that they are unable to provide themselves and their dependants with a sufficiency of even the bare necessities of life.

Honourable members have referred to the fact that there has been a great deal of charity. I think I heard the Minister of Employment state that there had been a great deal of charity subscribed, and I was afraid the Government was depending very largely upon the charity of its citizens for the support of the unemployed.

I am reminded of the tramp who was asked if he had never been offered work and who said, 'Only once; apart from that I have had nothing but kindness.'

It is perfectly true that the unemployed have had charity; they have had kindness, and plenty of it; but what they want now is a little real work, with real wages, to vary the monotony. I feel that I am competent to discuss the question of unemployment as I have had a very large experience in connection with the administration of the Unemployment Act. For instance, I am a member of the Benevolent Committee of the North Canterbury Hospital Board ...

... I know just what unemployment means in the homes of the people of this community.

I know how it affects them in sickness and in health. I know very well to what extent their children are fed or starved, and I feel that I can speak with experience upon the subject of the relief of the unemployed.

In addition to that, I am a member of three local bodies which are employers of unemployed labour ... I know the difficulties that have to be encountered in order that work may be found. I know just why the men were originally put to work that very often was unproductive, such as chipping grass from the sides of the streets — humiliating work.

It was not that the local bodies desired to give these men humiliating work, but that they had neither the funds nor the means to provide the funds with which to put remunerative work in hand ...

... I am particularly interested in the question of unemployment and the Government's administration of the Act so far as they concern women and youths under 20 years of age. With regard to the women, the Government is collecting approximately — probably it is more at the present time — £750,000 annually from the women of this community in unemployment taxation. The Government imposes unemployment taxation upon every little girl who is earning 10 shillings a week; and if she is receiving as part of her remuneration board or meals, the Government assesses the value of those meals or that board — at a fantastic figure, in many cases — and taxes the child on that.

Take, for instance, the matter of waitresses. At one of my meetings in the Lyttelton by-election this question came up, and while it was being discussed a restaurant keeper stood up in the audience and made a statement regarding the matter. He said that the customers in his restaurant were charged 9d[88] for meals, that the waitresses partook of the meal after the customers were served, and that the meal they received was not of the same value as that which was given to the customers. But the Government came in and insisted upon assessing the price of those girls' meals at one shilling per meal, and taxed the girls accordingly. That is how the Government regards some of the girls so far as taxation is concerned.

Take the nurses in our hospitals. I suppose that most of them are working for six days a week, and some of them, I know, are working for seven days a week, the day's work amounting to at least eight or nine hours. The Government taxes the wages and the board of these girls, their board being assessed at, I think, £1 a week. The probationer nurses in the North Canterbury Hospital Board's hospital are now receiving 7s. 3d. a week, the day's work being from eight to nine hours, and the Government is taxing those girls on their wages and on their board.

---

88 Nine pence, or three-quarters of a shilling.

When the Unemployment Act was first brought into operation the Government made absolutely no attempt whatever to make provision for unemployed girls. Everyone knew that there were numbers of unemployed girls up and down the country. But the Government made no move whatever to alleviate their position, in spite of the fact that it was collecting taxation to the extent of £750,000 annually from the women and girls of the Dominion.

Elizabeth McCombs then described the efforts of volunteer groups to help young women in need before turning her focus to the problems of young men.

Now, with regard to the question of unemployed boys, so far as this Government is concerned a boy ceases to exist on the day he reaches the age of sixteen years. Up to that point, if his father is on relief work, the father is given work in respect of that boy; but the day the boy reaches the age of sixteen years that work is withdrawn, but no work is found for the boy, who is therefore thrown on his own resources in a country where, at the present time, it is practically impossible to find work for boys, or is thrown on the charity of the Hospital Boards, or upon his own family, and thus becomes an additional burden on his parents.

I wonder if the honourable gentlemen occupying the Government benches realise what a critical stage that is in the lives of these boys. Can anyone imagine a more unhappy state for a growing boy to be in? He is deprived of education and deprived of work. Now, what does this sort of thing lead to? Is that also something that has escaped the minds of the honourable gentlemen opposite?

Recently I heard the head of a very large school state that the most dangerous criminal age in New Zealand was coming to be that between sixteen years and twenty years. So I looked up the figures relating to the matter, and I found that out of a total of 6,742 charges proved in our Police Courts, 3,302 were against boys under the age of 20 years.

The thinking people of this country are disturbed by such a state of affairs. I do not want anyone to misunderstand me regarding this matter. I am not suggesting that the whole of the unemployed boys of this country are criminals, but I do say that the Government's inaction with regard to those boys is driving a large number of them to a form of desperation that will react upon the whole community. In failing to make provision for boys at that age, the Government is displaying an indifference to the welfare of the country both now and in the future. We have to remember that someday these boys will grow up and be a force of some kind in this country. Whether for good or bad rests with the Government of the country today.

I sometimes wonder whether the honourable gentlemen occupying the Government benches have forgotten whether they were young themselves. Indeed, Mr Speaker, I have not really made up my mind whether it is that they never were young, or whether they have really never grown up.

She then addressed changes in education that she believed were particularly harming poor families.

The Government ... has raised the age of admission to school to six years. This, of course, again will react upon the children of the poorer classes. In England the school admission age is three years, and the compulsory school admission age is five years. Many of the honourable gentlemen on the Government benches, I think, are accustomed to a rural life and to the delightful freedom of sunny paddocks. I do not think they altogether understand the conditions of life in the cities today. Many of our people in the cities are now compelled to live in rooms. I know of several cases where a whole family lives in one room.

Not so very long ago the members of a committee of which I am a member assisted a family of eight — the father, mother, and six children — all living in one room. The children of such families as that have no green paddocks in which to play. They cannot be taken out on to the sea, beach or into the sunshine. They play in the streets if they play at all outside their own homes, and in many of the poorer quarters of our cities the only playground is the street. I would like to point out to honourable members that the habits acquired in early youth are very hard to eradicate.

Elizabeth McCombs (1873–1935)

The Government, of course, at the same time has withdrawn its grants to the free kindergartens, so that that source of education also is denied to these children ...

... But while I am discussing education I do not want to pass from it without referring to the effect of the Government's policy upon schoolteachers. We have 1,600 schoolteachers out of work in this country.

Those teachers entered the profession at the invitation of the Department. The Department spent large sums of money on their education, and now that they are prepared to give their services to the community, the Government has no work for them. It is perfectly true that there is a certain amount of rationed work being found, and the allotment of it would be funny if it were not so hopelessly uneconomic ...

... Another reform that is urgently needed in this community is the appointment of women police, a step that the women's societies have been urging for many years. Perhaps honourable members on the Government benches do not realise the importance of this reform. The idea is to have women police appointed particularly in our large cities for the protection of women and children and youths of both sexes ...

... Both in Scotland and in England, of course, women police have been employed for many years ... The Chief Constable of the City of Glasgow says: 'Experience has proved that women can be employed with advantage to the community in the performance of certain duties — police duties — which, until a few years ago, were exclusively performed by men. I would like to emphasise particularly the value of preventative work which police women are better fitted to perform than men.'

The women's societies have been asking that this reform shall receive urgent consideration in view of the large numbers of young people in the community at present without employment or occupation. There is an old saying, 'For Satan finds some mischief still for idle hands to do.'

I hope honourable members on the Government benches will lay that to their hearts.

In the less than two years before her death in June 1935, Elizabeth McCombs continued her special focus on women's rights while pressing for industrialisation to reduce unemployment. The pity was that she could not have entered Parliament sooner, or lived to be part of the first Labour Government elected that November.

Elizabeth McCombs, on the strength of her maiden speech, could have become our first female Minister of the Crown with a role preferably including Women's Affairs.

The Need for Confidence

Gordon Coates

October 24, 1933

Few Prime Ministers have more easily donned and doffed the mantle, and in whatever position, acted with such authority as J.G. Coates[89], New Zealand's first Maori–speaking Prime Minister. Going late to the Great War, he served spectacularly well, rising to the rank of Major in 1 NZEF.

Back in Parliament, Massey used him as a key minister, and dying, bequeathed him the Prime Ministerial seat. This he held for but one term of office 1925–28, our 'jazz age Prime Minister', as John A. Lee called him. In the 1931–35 Coalition Government 1931–35, and at the end, in the 1940–43 War Cabinet, Coates proved, in Peter Fraser's terms, 'a statesman of the first rank.'

In any office of state, Coates showed himself the practical man, with as Carl Berendsen was later to note, 'a certain flair — shared only in my experience by Peter Fraser — of leaping to the heart of any issue by intuition' and the will to act, if not to woo the voter. He was an indifferent speaker, but in the seats of power, a being wonderful to

---

89 Michael Bassett. 'Coates, Joseph Gordon — Biography', from the Dictionary of New Zealand Biography. Te Ara — the Encyclopedia of New Zealand.

229

behold, a decision maker, a 'man of action'[90].

In the 1920s, as Minister of Public Works, and then Prime Minister, he led the completion of the railways system, the development of the Main Highways systems, the centralisation of the vital hydro electricity industry — the sector that lifted New Zealand to its prime place in the developed world by 1950 — and, on the advice of Britain's key scientist and Ernest Rutherford, founded the vastly important Massey Agricultural College. The seven years (1921–28) proved him, with his close links with Apirana Ngata, an effective and influential Minister of Native Affairs.

Did Coates lose power as Prime Minister in 1928 through lack of care of the electorate Seddon had taught was desirable? Being sporting gentry, moving from Liberal to Reform, and surviving the Western Front, perhaps made him an indifferent party man? The proof might lie rather in the Reform Party's chief executive, A.E. Davy, shifting his flag to the Liberal Party barque. Thereafter, however, when the going got specially tough in the Great Depression, and in World War Two, Coates resumed his chiefly mantle.

Nowhere was this more evident than in setting aside party, and personality, in leading the country out of the depths of the Great Depression. Coates did not push a passive Prime Minister Forbes out of the saddle, but in 1932 instinctively understanding the need for action, overrode the able Minister of Finance, William Downie Stewart, out of the Dunedin intelligentsia, and took charge of the Ottawa Conference delegation on Imperial Preference.

On return he then drove through, again against the wishes of the Minister of Finance, with his famous brains trust rather than the Treasury, the devaluation essential to restore momentum to our derelict agricultural export economy.

On Downie Stewart's landmark resignation, he became Minister of Finance and, defying the powerful banks, after lengthy toing and froing within the establishment, passed the Reserve Bank Act Downie Stewart had in contemplation.

---

90 Bruce Farland's 'Gordon Coates', New Zealand Profiles, briefly complements Dr Michael Bassett's fine biography Coates of Kaipara AUP 1995.

Putting 'the deliberate management of the monetary system into the hands of a national institution' sets Coates among our leading Ministers of Finance, and establishes his claim to statesmanship. Astonishingly then, after the Labour victory of 1935, the newly–formed National Party twice passed Coates over as leader.

Was he the victim of being the 'jazz age Prime Minister'? Or simply of being Minister of Finance in bad times? Perhaps there is a gentleman's disdain of ambition? Or did any leader in the Great Depression stand any chance of survival?

And, statesman though Fraser would name him at his death, Hansard suggests the practical, efficient Coates, though an effective enough speaker, was, if this speech is any guide, no orator. Inhibited he may have been by the opposition of the banks and the Social Creditors but there was little to catch hearts and minds in a speech of such significance.[91] Perhaps the capacity to speak with passion and conviction is an imperative underwrite of the Prime Ministership of our intimate democracy.

Here's how Coates set out his plan for a Reserve Bank:[92]

Mr Speaker, in moving the second reading of the Bill I wish to make a few remarks upon the necessity for its introduction, and upon some main points which have I think a close relation to the requirements of the country today ...

I am not discussing the (monetary) theories that have been put forward, but I do say that I cannot see, that some of these proposals have any practical bearing upon the case ...

This measure, in my opinion, in no way conflicts with ideas I have heard expressed in regard to the currency problem.

Therefore the House is called upon to consider on the merits of the

---

91 *Between Governments and Banks, by Professor G. R. Hawke, 1973, gives a vivid account of the lengthy gestation of the Reserve Bank, and the array of ministers and officials, institutions, and interests, involved. This was a democracy addicted to gradualism — at least until the Strewelpeter years of the 1980s.*

92 *New Zealand Parliamentary Debates (Hansard), Reserve Bank of New Zealand Bill, Volume 136, page 623.*

case for the establishment of a reserve bank, and the necessity for that establishment, rather than to concern itself as to what other scheme of currency might be preferable to that now existing ...

The first point to be considered is this: Does this proposed reserve bank interfere with the freedom of government action? I take it what Parliament is concerned about is whether it is consciously passing over to some outside authority a very important matter — the control of currency.

Some time ago I cabled ... to ascertain ... the relationship between the Federal Reserve Bank and the Government ...

The reply stated 'The abandonment of a monetary standard is a Government function, not that of a central bank' ...

I cabled also to the Prime Minister of South Africa ... His reply was as follows: 'The Central Bank has performed successfully its primary function of maintaining the country's currency as by law established. The Central Bank affords machinery for giving effect to Government's currency policy.'

That is another piece of evidence on the matter. I establish this first point because I know it is correct that the Reserve Bank of New Zealand Bill before the House today will if passed into law set up an organisation or machine to give effect to Government policy.

What is the value of an organisation of that kind? It is for the purpose of:

1) Controlling our own currency policy.

2) Strengthening and coordinating the existing banking system or organisation.

3) Providing cheaper credit for the community; and

4) It will show a saving to the State or to the taxpayer ...

Those are four definite objects and I think it can be shown that they give an advantage to the community as a whole — an advantage which at present does not exist ...

The purpose of the measure is to afford unified and disinterested control of currency and credit in New Zealand by New Zealand directors for the benefit of New Zealand. I lay that down as being the purpose of the Bill.

Gordon Coates (1878–1943)

I suppose I shall be asked this question at once; how can that be when it is proposed to have shareholder capital? I have met with that question on a number of occasions, especially from those honourable members who think that the bank, to be a truly national concern, should be entirely controlled by the Government of the country. By that I do not mean the politics of the country, but that the Government should be responsible for the appointment of the directorate and also for the appointment of the governor and deputy governor.

I want to emphasise that in order that the bank may function properly the management must be free of the suspicion of being influenced other than by the general economic and financial condition of our country. Even suspicion must be removed.

Then we come back to the question of shareholder capital. It is proposed in the Bill that £500,000 shall be subscribed by the public of New Zealand and that State assets worth £1m shall be placed, as arranged for, behind this bank as a security ...

Now I come to the question of providing that the bank shall have the confidence and trust of the country. It is definitely essential that the bank shall have the complete confidence of the trading or commercial banks because they can help materially in keeping credit control flexible.

Indeed the proposed reserve bank will be a banker's bank and will, therefore, be called upon to carry out many transactions at present carried out by the trading banks. It goes without saying that the reserve bank should have the confidence of the trading banks. I have no doubt that honourable members will agree that the bank should be free from political control.

The shareholder capital of £500,000 is to be spread throughout the country and it would be desirable to have as many shareholders as possible ...

Mr Lee[93]: 'Why not all the people?'

All the people will have £1,000,000 invested in the bank ... I think the case is almost unanswerable for having shareholder capital with

---

93 *John A. Lee, Labour Member for Grey Lynn.*

shares well spread, for then the institution will be firmly planted in the country. It is not a question of who the shareholders can be ... I believe we shall have the shares well spread. That in itself will be a strong influence in planting this institution firmly with its roots in our country ... It gives confidence, both inside and outside of the country, and that is an important point. It gives confidence to our financial institutions the country. It gives confidence to all sections of political thought in the Dominion. After all the psychological effect of any important move is very definite and very real ...

It is all sections that must have confidence in this institution. It is not merely what different sections think. It is the confidence of the whole people that is important in connection with this institution. As I have said, we must have the trust and co-operation of the commercial banks ... of shareholders ... (of) the general public ...

In addition to these safeguards we have Parliament before which must come the annual report of the reserve bank. Here again we have another representative cross section of the community which will review the activities of the reserve bank.

The annual report will come before Parliament in the ordinary course, and full opportunity will be given for discussing the value and policy of the institution, and whether that policy is in accordance with the wishes of Parliament, for it is this machine that will carry out the monetary policy of the State.

Mr Sullivan:[94] 'If Parliament has an opinion contrary to that held by the reserve bank, how can that influence the position?'

Parliament has the situation in its own hands, for each year Parliament can alter or amend the legislation as it desires ... Parliament has full control of the situation. I wish to reiterate that I cannot follow the argument that this Bill removes jurisdiction from Parliament altogether. Parliament is paramount, and can alter or amend legislation as it thinks fit.

Now at this stage, I want to say — and I am now speaking with

---

94 *Dan Sullivan, Labour Member for Avon and Mayor of Christchurch.*

some little experience as Minister of Finance — that I am definitely of the opinion that any other honourable gentleman in this House, if he occupied my position, would take the very course that I am now adopting. He would have nothing to gain from it, nothing whatever, but his sense of public duty would lead him to foster and endeavour to assist in passing legislation of this kind ...

Now what part can a reserve bank play in the economic life of the country? In the first place ... without an organisation of the kind, it is not possible for the banks as constituted to play the full and important part that they should in the life of the country ...

It is laid down and recognised that in a period of low prices, a proper banking organisation working in conjunction with the Government, should be able to provide ample and cheap credit. Ample and cheap credit is essential in a time of low and stagnant prices. Are we in New Zealand in the position of having a proper organisation today?

Have we the organisation or the institution to make perfectly certain that the country is getting the cheapest credit possible? I think that is a question that must be carefully weighed before we attempt to criticise adversely a measure of this kind ... We have not the organisation laid down time and time again as necessary by experts and politicians — namely an organisation that includes a reserve bank to provide full and ample credit.

The next point is that, if this reserve bank is established, it will be definitely a powerful factor in the negotiating of credit for the New Zealand government when necessary. It is a necessary adjunct to the Government for that purpose and for the others I have mentioned.

We have bad times and then we have good times, better known as boom times. Can this institution play a part in controlling speculation in boom times? Definitely it is a part of its duty, if boom times threaten to endeavour to shorten credit to the extent that it is not easy for people to carry on speculation ...

In times of stress the reserve bank gives all the help possible, and in good times when we are threatened with booms and violent speculation, it calls in all reserves ...

I have pointed out clearly that this institution is a national institution

... The reserve bank will give effect to the monetary policy (of) the Government for the time being — that is one of its functions ...

For that purpose it is necessary that certain arrangements be made with the other banks (for assets to) be deposited with the reserve bank ... Eventually I anticipate the reserve bank will gradually take over all foreign transactions for and on behalf of the commercial banks ...

If we make the institution wholly a State bank. I have no hesitation in saying that might cost New Zealand hundreds of thousands of pounds, by reason of the fact that if the very institutions that we must depend upon for co-operation will not co-operate, there will be nervousness ... only one of these banks operating in New Zealand has its headquarters here ...

Does it not seem reasonable that we should have at least some organisation that can keep in touch with these, and take an entirely independent and disinterested view in relation to the commercial banks doing business in New Zealand with their headquarters in other parts of the world?

I would say definitely that the effect of an organisation of this kind would be to give New Zealand a much more independent status in this regard ... to promote and to maintain the economic welfare of New Zealand ...

Now, Sir, ... I have endeavoured to condense as far as possible the reasons why I think it imperative that New Zealand should have a reserve bank. Like many others I hesitated ... but today I have not the slightest hesitation in saying that, in my opinion, a reserve bank for this Dominion is a necessity ...

Let me summarise the advantages ...

1) Deliberate and disinterested control of currency and credit by a New Zealand board of directors for the benefit of the people as a whole.

2) The strengthening of the banking system by consolidation and co-ordination under a central authority.

3) The provision of effective machinery for carrying into effect any monetary policy decided upon.

4) The pooling of banking reserves which not only gives strength in the face of an emergency but provides a safe basis for an expansion of credit if that is in the interests of the Dominion.

5) Substantial savings to the State and the commercial community through lower discount bills, both Treasury and trading.

6) It enables New Zealand to take effective part in any scheme for co-ordinated action on the part of the banks of the Empire for raising prices or stablising currency.

7) Provides commercial conveniences by a single uniform note issue; and

8) Makes available to the Government, local bodies and other financial authorities, disinterested expert advice on monetary matters generally.

It took Coates more than four hours to state his case for a central bank. Parliament took up the debate the next day and considered and rejected any amendment. After a week, the second reading of the bill was carried.

A Sense of Nationhood

Lord Bledisloe

February 5, 1934

On February 5, 1934, a far–sighted Governor General, Lord Bledisloe, gifted the Waitangi Estate to the Nation. The suspicion is that this highly political head of state took advice not only from historians like Buick and Ramsden, but also from elite critics such as Apirana Ngata, in making one of the more significant speeches in our history.

The gloomy years of the Great Depression saw this pro consular Governor affirm the Treaty of Waitangi as the Magna Carta of the Nation, and establish the Treaty House as our National Marae.

Bledisloe[95] was a skilful, practical, statesmanlike politician, trained in the law, and deeply diversified in agriculture. He fitted warmly and easily into the New Zealand scene, talking up in particular the imperative of advanced farming practices. His ministers thought him too clever and too talkative by far. Bad–mouthing him as 'Chattering Charlie' told more about their limitations than their Governor General. If only they had left their country memorials as practical as the lessons on agricultural science and oil exploration, or as fitting as the Treaty House, and the Bledisloe

95 Russell Marshall. 'Bledisloe, Charles Bathurst — Biography', from the Dictionary of New Zealand Biography. Te Ara — the Encyclopedia of New Zealand.

Cup, of our most significant 20th century Governor General.

At Waitangi in 1934. 'Chattering Charlie' saw off his detractors with his landmark speech.

The speech itself reeks of Apirana Ngata. But it was the Governor General himself who moved beyond warning and advising. Like George Grey, to whom he refers, he put on a pro consular mantle, bought the Waitangi Estate, defined it as our National Marae, and there proclaimed the Treaty of Waitangi as our nation's Magna Charta. It took pro consular arrogation of royal authority to let Bledisloe establish the twin underwrites of the Treaty.

Signing the Treaty saved you Maori from a murderous, internecine extinction. Recognise what the British did for you.

You Pakeha under God, have a continuing responsibility for observing the terms of the Treaty. That means helping your Maori brethren. The trust of 1840, you must note, is much more demanding than any international mandate you may have accepted. Learn Maori language, history and philosophy.

Bledisloe's speech was superbly crafted (even if understandably he ends on the traditional New Zealand view of Marsden) beautifully delivered, and firmly noted. A copy should perhaps stand beside the Bledisloe Cup to confirm, what caballing with Apirana Ngata, Lord Bledisloe did for New Zealand.[96]

E te Iwi, tena ra koutou.

I am deeply impressed and much touched by the enthusiastically loyal and cordial welcome ... on the banks of the Waitangi River, whose waters 94 years ago, witnessed the welding of the two races into one nation under the British Crown. That the Maori race should have signalised our modest gift to the people of New Zealand of the adjoining estate — the cradle of the nation — by these commemorative celebrations is characteristic of their unswerving loyalty to the British Crown, and is

---

96 *New Zealand Governors General in the Inter–War Years in W.P. Morrell: A tribute, by Professor Angus Ross, provides a brief, elegant comparative study on which to base judgement.*

gratifying testimony on their part to the sincerity of British honour and integrity.

This gathering is convincing evidence that the doubts and fears which were prevalent in another bi-racial convention, which took place in 1840 a few hundred yards from here, have been effectively dispelled, and that today the Maori is walking confidently in step beside the Pakeha, and that the Pakeha is walking in friendship and comradeship beside the Maori.

Moreover in bringing together Maoris of different tribes ... from Te Reinga to Murihiku ... this meeting is a proof that the Treaty of Waitangi has served to unify the Maori people. It has quenched inter tribal feuds, softened ancient grudges, and above all, it has for ever abolished internecine wars and thus averted race suicide. On the part of ... the British people this gathering affords an opportunity of renewing our obligations to the Maori people — obligations which have become all the greater since ... our race has become the dominant partner in the possession and enjoyment of this country, the sovereignty of which we hold as a sacred and inviolable trust.

Let Waitangi be to us all a Tatao Pounamu — a happy and precious closing of the door for ever upon all war and strife between race and tribes in this country ...

It is well to remember ... that one hundred years ago British statesmen were confronted by problems originating on the shores of this very Bay, problems which in their solution called for the pledge of a nation's faith to the Maori people. That pledge was given by Britain's then responsible ministers through the Treaty of Waitangi. Towards the beginning of the last century irregular British settlement was taking place in New Zealand. Its wild injustice called for reform and its sporadic character for regulation. The only remedy for this chaotic condition was the intervention of the British Crown.

But the hands of the Crown were more than full with similar responsibilities elsewhere. India, Canada, Australia, South Africa with their several problems and perplexities, were then sources of considerable anxiety. Only the most far-sighted statesmen saw any wisdom in maintaining outposts of Empire at the risk of international jealousies and national impoverishment. Fewer still could appreciate the wisdom of adding New Zealand to these colonial problems. But the dictates of humanity, and the clamant need for ordered government in this country, became so insistent that they could no longer be ignored. Moreover the possibility of some other European nation assuming control, to the detriment of British interests, was naturally not without its influence.

The formidable difficulties facing Queen Victoria's ministers was the fact that New Zealand was a foreign country and outside their jurisdiction. The alternatives open to them were conquest or negotiation. As conquest, with all its horrors, was repugnant to the British mind and conscience, Captain William Hobson of the Royal Navy, New Zealand's first Governor, was invested with consular powers and authorised to negotiate a treaty with the Native chiefs for the cession, upon equitable terms, of their sovereignty to the British Queen.

The honourable intentions of the British Government in this matter are fully and eloquently demonstrated in the instructions furnished to Captain Hobson by the Colonial Secretary, Lord Normanby, before leaving England. Eminently just in spirit, broadly humanitarian in principle, they form a document which any nation might be proud to have enshrined within its archives.

How within sight of this very spot, Captain Hobson carried out his instructions is well known. He was scrupulously careful and transparently honest in all his dealings with the Maori people. His one desire was that they should clearly understand both the pledges given to them by the British government and their own responsibilities in accepting those pledges.

In the three brief clauses of the Treaty the British Government undertook that in return for the surrender of sovereignty it would ensure to the respective tribes their landed possessions, their forests and their fisheries, and that it would ever thereafter cast the protecting mantle of British citizenship over them and their descendants. These terms were accepted, and thus the Treaty of Waitangi became the basis of British settlement in New Zealand.

Inevitably and admittedly the assumption of British authority, with the advent of different ideals and an entirely different code of ethics and law, involved some misunderstandings and some heart burnings, but an impartial survey of the situation as it exists after ninety four years of actual experience discloses the fact that the Maori people still believe that the Treaty has mana of its own and still regard it as the Magna Carta of their political rights, while the European population are resolved to fulfill faithfully their obligations to the Maori people. There is indeed on the part of each, a determination that the Treaty shall continue to be what has been well described as a 'pledge of security to the enterprising colonist, and a protecting garment to the unprotected Maori.'[97]

How different are the sentiments of harmony and mutual trust which animate us all today from those conflicting emotions which stirred the hearts of our predecessors near this very spot on the 5th and 6th February, ninety four years ago!

The Maori people were grievously puzzled and much agitated as to what course they should pursue. Should they yield up the sovereignty of their country and come under the protecting wing of the Great White Queen? Would it, on balance be to their advantage, or would it not? That was the issue they had to decide, and in the face of conflicting opinions and conflicting advice no one could blame them if they approached it with doubt and fear, with mistrust and misgiving.

Fortunately there was among the Maori chiefs who thought with the mind of a sage, who saw with the eye of a seer, and who spoke with the voice of a prophet. That man was Tamati Waka Nene, who after reasoning with his own people that it was now too late to turn the Pakeha away, and pleading with Captain Hobson to remain as 'a Governor and a father' to them, delivered himself of the following eloquent declaration of his confidence in British honour: 'I am walking beside the Pakeha: I'll sign the pukapuka'— a spontaneous expression of trust which carried to the minds of his colleagues the assurance of our good faith and our integrity.

Among the European negotiators two men stand out as champions of British sovereignty — the Reverend Henry Williams, of the Church Missionary Society, and Mr James Busby the former British Resident. What this country owes to the sterling patriotism of these men is scarcely

---

97 Described in The Treaty of Waitangi (S.W. Mackay), by Lindsay Buick, 1914.

yet fully appreciated. Taking their courage in both hands, they faced the opponents of the Treaty, answering argument with argument, and eventually carrying conviction not only by virtue of the strength of their case, but because of their transparent integrity and the confidence which the Natives reposed in their personal veracity. With the aid of such stalwart champions of righteousness, such far sighted pioneers of civilisation and ordered progress, the advantages to both races of British sovereignty was demonstrated, and the Treaty was signed.

Slowly the mists of uncertainty, the clouds of doubt, which confused the issue in 1840 have been dispelled. So that today we look at the Treaty with no doubting or mistrustful eyes. Far from this being the case, our minds are calm and our hearts are happy, because we know that time, the balm that heals so many sores, has softened the asperities of the past, it has clarified our vision, sweetened our memories, and established an abiding feeling of trust and confidence between the two races such as can assuredly never be impaired in the days which lie before us.

The most striking impression which this meeting is calculated to convey is the almost magical effect which the Treaty has had in unifying and pacifying the Maori people. From time immemorial they have been an aggregation of mutually hostile tribes. Each with its own honoured ancestors, its own territory, and its own tradition. There inevitably grew up among them causes of quarrel and strife which brought about an almost incessant state of internecine war.

With the introduction of firearms, and just before systematic British colonisation took place, the Maori race seemed to be advancing towards self extinction. Then came the Treaty of Waitangi, bringing with it British sovereignty, and the majesty of British law, together with the Pakeha system of adjusting disputes, and from that day to this no tribal wars have taken place.

Who can estimate what immense benefit this respite from incessant strife has conferred upon the Maori race or what the resulting sense of security has meant to a people who are essentially cultivators of the soil? Formerly the sower did not know who the reaper would be. Today all can sow their land in the sure and certain knowledge that in due course they will reap what is theirs under the protection of the Treaty and that

Lord Bledisloe (1867– 1958)

no one will dispute the title. So too, has their horizon been widened, for they have moved about with greater freedom, as gradually the barriers between the tribes have been broken down, until today we see mingling together with courtly dignity men and women who a century ago might have been engaged in deadly warfare. Indeed, less than a century ago nothing short of a miracle could have brought together tribesmen from as far asunder as the North Cape and the Bluff, but that miracle has happened today.

To the beneficent teaching of the Christian missionaries we largely owe this softening of ancient animosities, this radiation of trustful friendship, this reign of peace, which are the outcome of the Treaty of Waitangi. It is but meet, therefore, that we should offer up our grateful thanks to Almighty God in that He has afforded the British nation the privilege of being the humble instrument in His hands of bringing about so marvelous a change in the lives of His Maori people.

If there is one conclusion more than another that I draw from this gathering today, it is that nothing has occurred ... since 1840 to relieve the Pakeha population of the responsibilities then solemnly undertaken. On the contrary, these responsibilities have increased, rather than diminished ...

Upon us, therefore devolves, in a larger sense, the obligation of seeing that we observe the terms of a Treaty which not only places the Maori on a footing of political equality with the Pakeha, but enables him to march forward side by side with us in social life, in education, in industry, in sport.

Upon us devolves the responsibility of seeing that our Maori brethren are given the chance of living their lives with some reasonable prospect of success ...

The surest way to make the Maori a good citizen and a real asset to this heaven blessed country which you share in common is to train him how to use his own land to the best economic advantage rather than allow him wholly to divest himself of it.

In this connection my Native Minister, Sir Apirana Ngata, has inaugurated developments of incalculable benefit to his race which will earn him the gratitude of posterity.

Let us then encourage the Maori to cultivate his own land, to grow his own food, to preserve the purity of his language, the poetry of his race, the romantic beauty of his folklore — to cultivate, in fact, not only the soil but also a love of the Polynesian arts of his ancestors ...

Let us moreover, encourage our Maori compatriots, in consonance with the advice of their late eminent rangatira, Sir Maui Pomare, to develop in their own settlements all those wholesome conditions which contribute to good health and long life, and thus we shall have played a worthy part in assisting them to perpetuate their ancient distinctive nationality, which is in no way inconstant with their status as free citizens of our Great British Empire, proudly anxious with us to maintain its greatness.

My distinguished predecessor, Sir George Grey, insistently urged that the most certain way to ensure full justice to our Maori people and their heart-whole co-operation in the forward progress of this country was to develop among their European countrymen a wider knowledge of their language, their traditions, and their outlook upon life and its problems. His sage and far-sighted counsel merits nowadays the earnest consideration of all true patriots.

It is not usual in modern times to commit the weaker peoples of the world to the tutelage of stronger nations under an international mandate, as a means of preserving their nationality and their nationhood. Our obligations, however to the Maori people lie deeper than any which even a mandate from the League of Nations could impose.

We came to the Maoris with our hands extended in friendship, and we ourselves persuaded them to place their future with us. Our duty then is to see that the trust which they placed in our honour in 1840 is never betrayed as long as our Empire endures.

Let me in conclusion, express the fervent hope that a nationalised Waitangi may be instrumental in developing through the whole community of this Dominion a greater sense of solidarity, a deeper spirit of nationhood, based upon pride in its not unworthy beginnings, and a past history of which has no reason to be ashamed.

The initial sources of civilisation, culture and economic development in New Zealand were two fold and at first mutually unsympathetic — namely in these northern latitudes the missionaries, and further south the separate organised groups of British settlers, under the ingenious plan of Edward Gibbon Wakefield, the far-sighted founder of prudent Empire colonisation.

In consequence there has inevitably been in the past a segregation of those separate and benign influences ... (that) have through their separatism checked complete national solidarity and the healthy national sentiment which is so valuable an inspiration to all self governing communities. Waitangi, the birth place of this nation, now belongs to all alike, Pakeha and Maori, North and South Islanders, and the descendants and champions of both sections of its courageous pioneers. All are represented on its Administrative Board. Shall not this fact conduce appreciably to the spirit and consciousness of nationhood.

On a spot clearly visible from the Waitangi Estate, Samuel Marsden, the pioneer of Christianity in New Zealand, preached his famous Christmas sermon 119 years ago to a fascinated Native congregation, bringing the cheerful message of peace and goodwill to a people sunk in heathen darkness.

It is the earnest hope of my wife and myself that peace and goodwill between both races and all classes, based upon national unity and steadfast faith in God, may ever flourish and abound in this Dominion, and that Waitangi may not be without its influence in perpetuating them in days to come.

'Ka nui taku aroha kia koutou.'

Maori people, you have our affectionate regards. Kia ora. Kia ora.

A haka was performed the same day. It was *Te Kiri Ngutu*, written by Tuta Nihoniho in the 1870s and contains the words 'Ponga ra! Ponga ra!', used by Derek Llardelli when he composed the All Black haka *Kapa o Pango* in 2005.

Ponga ra! Ponga ra!
Ka tataki mai Te Whare o nga Ture!
Ka whiria te Maori! Ka whiria!
Ngau nei ona reiti, ngau nei ona take!
A ha ha! Te taea te ueue! I aue!
Hei!
Patua i te whenua!
Hei!

248

Translation:

The shadows fall! The shadows fall!
There is chattering in Parliament
And Maori are being plaited as a rope
Its rates and its taxes are biting!
A ha ha! Its teeth cannot be withdrawn!
Alas!
The land will be destroyed!
Alas!

To Build, Not Destroy

Michael Joseph Savage

December 17, 1935

The first Labour Prime Minister, Michael Joseph Savage[98], was like Britain's Clement Attlee after him, 'a modest man with much to be modest about'. He was not an orator like John A. Lee. When the intellectual Harry Holland died in 1932, Savage, at the head of the line and fortunate that Lee was out of Parliament, pre–empted the leadership.

After seizing the mantle, the quiet, soft spoken and unassuming Savage still found Parliament claustrophobic. So he took to the homely stump. At the risk of his life — in the event — he toured and toured and spoke and spoke in virtually every township in New Zealand.

At best, Savage rated as an effective platform speaker. He had indeed called in Lee in the 1920s to lead Labour's first stump campaigns. Labour intellectuals like Ormond Wilson confessed to embarrassment. Poets made fun of his jumbled rhetoric.

Devoid of demagoguery Savage's trademark was a deliberative 'now then' that gave him time to pick up the next argument.

Out of a woolly Christian socialism and a vague concept of a Christian Commonwealth, his speeches in 1934 and 1935 tuned in to the exact pitch

98 Essential reading on Savage includes From the Cradle to the Grave: A Biography of Michael Joseph Savage (Reed Methuen), by Barry Gustafson, 1986.

251

of a 'war on poverty'.

'Our task is to help the poor and needy, restore pensions, provide work and build a sound economy.'

Savage's humane sincerity (and humanity) in the midst of the Great Depression provided its own eloquence. His peculiar personal appeal to 'commonsense' in the event made him Labour's first Prime Minister and in his lifetime a secular Saint. This is all to be seen in his early speeches.

To celebrate his appointment as Prime Minister, he addressed a rally of supporters at the Auckland Town Hall[99] on December 17, 1935, calling it 'the greatest moment of my life':

A great political transformation has already been accomplished but a great economic and social transformation remains to be accomplished. It is going to be done. I say that with the friendliest feeling in the world. There is no reason on earth why anyone should be hurt in the process. When we start to break things, we won't be helping anyone.

Our job is to build, not to destroy. The day of the destroyer has gone, and the day of the builder is here. Building is not always done in Parliament.

For the most part it is done outside. It is done by you. Our job is to make it possible for you to carry on with the structure. We can do that with your encouragement and goodwill. We cannot do without your assistance.

You are the men and women who have to do the work, and I say again the great transformation that is necessary is in your hands. There is no power on earth that can stand between you and liberty. You have the right to govern in New Zealand. There is no limit —at least, I cannot see any. We have one of the most fertile countries on earth. We have a liberty-loving people.

There is nothing between you and a standard of life if you can combine to produce. Up to now you have been able to produce, but you have not been able to get access to it. It may be that we will get into disfavour with some when we begin to give you access to the means of life, but one cannot help that.

---

99 *Auckland Star, December 18, 1935.*

We are not going to hurt them in the process.

It is going to be a peaceful transformation.

When Labour fails to do your bidding, when we fail to remove the barriers there have been between you and liberty, it will be your privilege to remove us. But it is my privilege tonight in the name of the new Government to again reassure you that you have no cause to worry.

We are going to do our share all right. Some of us have spent the greater part of our lives looking at distress and poverty amid plenty. There is no reason why that should continue one day further.

You have never known what political liberty has meant in the past. The time has come when you should understand what it means and set out with the utmost goodwill towards each other in order to 'accomplish it'.

'The purpose of a nation will decide its destiny' were the words of a great American. What was the purpose of this nation? It was to remove the barriers that stood between them and liberty.

Liberty meant more than to be able to get up in an open place or public hall to address one's fellow citizens.

Liberty meant the right to earn one's living and to be able to get access to it without any force. Those were ideals. They meant a definite programme, they meant something worth living for. They saw in their midst little children and they thought of the nation that was to be, Surely they could not forget their responsibility.

We have a tremendous responsibility and if we can only live a life along the lines I am speaking and go down to the grave with the knowledge that we have left this world better than we found it, we will have no cause to worry.

I thank you from the bottom of my heart, not only for the privilege of meeting you here tonight, but for the privilege that I have enjoyed at your hands over long years.

I have met you on the highways and the byways, and I did not need any protection either. I had the protection of the people, and I believe I will have that same protection today.

When I am unable to meet you on the highways and the byways, I want to get down and make way for somebody else.

This is the greatest moment of my life — to be able to meet my fellow Auckland citizens after the struggles of the last 28 or 30 years, and to be able to see the progress we have made in that comparatively short time.

I stood in this city, without friends, without money. But the schoolmaster has been abroad.

The minds of the people have been moulded as the years have gone by. It has taken some of us a lifetime to develop the thoughts that are in us now. Some of us have had our education in the bowels of the earth, in industry, and in other places, and our minds are moulded perhaps in a different way from others. The world is moving while men and women sleep.

The inventor is producing the machine and the scientific process is thrusting human labour into the stream. The work ahead of us is to see that the machine is the servant of mankind.

After all, I do not know that this is a question, of politics. It is just a matter of plain, common sense. The machine is there doing the job. We can have more production if we need it. It is a problem now of making the product of labour go to the labourers.

The thing seems so plain to me that I sometimes wonder why it takes so many others, so many speakers, to lay the thing barer than it is now.

The machine is there taking the place of mankind, multiplying wealth as the years go by, and as wealth is multiplied, the people are poorer.

What a contradiction! The problem in front of the Government of New Zealand is not only to be able to make it possible for the people to be able to produce the necessities of life but also for them to be able to enjoy those necessities.

I value my word as a man just as much as I value my word as Prime Minister — highly.

I appreciate the great honour that has been bestowed upon me by the people of New Zealand, but I can never afford to treat lightly my word as a man.

I want to be able to meet you in the days to come and to be able to meet you as friends, to be able to meet you as comrades in a common cause. If we can only live to be that, there is no power on earth that can stand between us and liberty.

Michael Joseph Savage on the hustings in 1938.

In Parliament, he continued his theme of building. His first address in reply debate in April 1936, is as good an example of his 'going on' style as we could wish for:[100]

> *I cannot do better than begin where the Leader of the Opposition left off. The right hon. gentleman declared that in its present state the ground is not likely to carry the weight.*
>
> *I admit that the ground is boggy, but nevertheless I have never been more confident than I am tonight. We are not likely to turn back ... I am not going to turn back. I am going on ...*
>
> *At the outset we had a huge army of unemployed on relief works and the payment they received was quite inadequate to ... anything approaching a decent standard of living.*
>
> *Ministers went to any length to balance the Budget, no matter what happened to the people ... A balance sheet that holds tens of thousands of our people — hundreds of thousands in fact — in a state of semi*

100 *New Zealand Parliamentary Debates (Hansard), 1936, Volume 244, pages 62–68.*

255

starvation does not seem to me to be a good dividend payer so far as the people are concerned. After all the problem is a human one. It is not merely a question of pounds shillings and pence — it is a question of dealing with humanity and making the best possible use of a fertile country ...

We promised that the legislation would be ready. It is ready; we are ready to go now ... we are ready for action. We want to get down to work and put our legislation on the statute book so that we can start our public works and industries going. The right honourable gentleman said we are full of hope. Of course we are full of hope ...

The problems ahead of the country today is to make it possible for the people to be buyers as well as producers ... If the machine is doing more work than it used to do, humanity will naturally do less. People should not work such long hours, surely ...

The right honourable gentleman referred to public works ... public works will never cease. I cannot imagine that humanity is going to stand still.

I have been all over this country, and for a start, New Zealand is going to need painting from North Cape to the Bluff ...

The same thing applies in the building trade, and we have people huddled together in what are called homes. The right honourable gentleman seems to be afraid that public works will come to an end.

If we can get the good things of life without hard labour, I cannot imagine we are going to worry about that ... but I cannot imagine a state of society in which work will disappear altogether.

I can easily imagine that science, machinery, and human intelligence are gradually getting rid of the drudgery of work. We want the people — the rank and file — to get the benefit of that.

But that means shorter hours and more wages for the hours we work. But the right honourable gentleman says we are raising the cost of living and what is going to happen to our overseas market?

The overseas market and the internal market have their foundation in New Zealand, and not outside ...

Whether the things are produced here or overseas, so long as they are sold here, we must have the money to buy them. What is the use of arguing about it? There is nothing left to argue about ...

Now let me turn to the question of public works. Why we have all kinds of public works to be done. I wish I could start the men tomorrow to pull down this old building here ...

But the right honourable gentleman will say 'We have not got the money'. We have the men; the timber; a country capable of producing anything in abundance ... we have the men here capable of building a new railways station in Christchurch ... we are going to use the public credit for the purpose of putting men to work building railway stations wherever they are needed ...

There is work everywhere to be done but the old bogey is trotted out: 'Where is the money to come from?' It does not matter how we raise the money, the public credit is pledged. Why cannot we use the public credit straight out, by direct means, for the purpose of building our own country? Will anyone tell me ... it was the way to perdition.

Surely it is not. It seems to me it is the way to prosperity. But the honourable gentleman opposite wants to go back over the old road — the road leading to the bog.

It is not good enough so long as we have men and women ... willing to work ... what is going to stand in our way? I am going to promise ... that nothing will stand in our way ...

... I have a vision of the future. I think that we can have smiling homes in New Zealand; that we can use the public credit for the purpose of building homes worth living in — homes for the native race; homes for their Pakeha brethren.

Why not? We have got the timber here, the mills, and so on. We have the mill at Mamaku which ... his Cabinet closed down. We will re-open it ... and the housing factory ... we are the Government of this country ... we appreciate the difficulties ahead, but we are not going to run away from them.

We are not going to turn back ...

I cannot see public works ceasing. I can see mankind all the time going onwards and upwards, mentally and in every way, and raising the standard of living ... and in all that progress upwards and onwards I cannot see an end to public works ...

Here we have the right to govern ... we can use our powers of government for the purpose of serving each other. Has not the time come for basing our money system on the goods we produce and the services we render ... I do not suggest we can ... over a weekend; but we are going to begin as soon as the Opposition ceases talking ...

... The coalition Government did its best in connection with unemployment. I agree. That is the reason it was defeated at the last election.

The right honourable gentleman says we are hoping, and he is hoping with us. Well the people had been hoping for years and years, and they had despaired of the Government ever doing anything.

The result was that it was turned out ... 50 per cent of the dairy farmers were going bankrupt ... We have not got much to beat. All we have to do is to guarantee to the dairy farmer and everybody else a standard of life based upon the aggregate power of New Zealand to produce that standard of life ...

We have got to organise and protect our own economy in New Zealand. We are living in New Zealand, not overseas ...

I would still want to go to Great Britain, and be able to say to the British people: 'After all we are brothers, we are of the same flesh and blood, and we should stand and fall together.'

But what is the point of saying that to them if we are going to some one else the next? I have listened to a lot of bunkum ... There is only one foundation for preferential trade and that is the investment of our surplus wealth in our own country or the British Commonwealth.

We cannot invest money in Timbuctoo, or in China, or in Argentina ... A country must trade where its money is invested ... The best method of marketing our products in Great Britain will be used ...

We did not come down in the last shower day ... The best machinery to be found in Britain will be used by this Government ...

I have already referred briefly to the control of currency and credit and I think the right honourable gentleman will be able to wait in patience until the Reserve Bank of New Zealand Amendment bill is brought down. We shall then have an opportunity to discuss our financial proposals ...

There are two main things to do in this connection — to stop robbery, and to make it possible for the people to enjoy the things they are capable of producing.

The Leader of the Opposition says that we are retarding business because of the legislation we are proposing. The business people do not tell me that ... things are flying ... business has improved since the 27th November last.

The right honourable gentleman referred to the rate of exchange; but I am going to lay the blame for the present high rate at his door, because after all raising the rate of exchange, did not bring any more money into New Zealand ...

The Government by raising the rate of exchange puts us up a tree, and we have to get down. But it was easier to get up the tree than it is to get down, and it does not matter how we try to get down, someone is going to be injured; but we have to get down, we cannot remain indefinitely up a tree. However there it is, and I want to tell the members opposite there is no need for them to be worried about that ...

... We have a greater amount of goodwill behind us today than the last Government ever had. I think I can say that without egotism. The people know the best and the worst about us ... while my friends opposite had the advantage of the press during the election campaign, we have gained all the representation.

Now, Sir, I think I will have mercy upon my friends opposite. I appreciate their spirit of goodwill — I do sincerely. I appreciate the attitude of the Leader of the Opposition. In the hour of defeat he proved himself the same man as he was in the hour of victory.

'The Chains That Bind'

Wiremu Ratana

April 22, 1936

Sometime the shortest speeches are the most important. Nor need they, if they claim the future, be the fruit of oratory. In 1936, a Maori prophet politician, Wiremu Ratana[101], became a national leader.

Since 1928 he had been working out where the Maori people were, and how to redress the failure of the Treaty of Waitangi. In retrospect many of his prophecies for Maoridom were to come to reality.

Five months after Labour's 1935 first landslide election, Ratana travelled to Parliament to meet the new Prime Minister, Michael Joseph Savage. His focus was on linking the Biblical story of righteous government to a full redress of the Treaty of Waitangi that Lord Bledisloe had placed on the national agenda in the first Waitangi day celebrations in 1934.

In the Maori affairs room, Ratana called on Savage to fulfill promises his predecessor Harry Holland[102] had made to help the Maori people. In prophetic terms, he called on the new Prime Minister to remedy the wrongs and injustices, and remove 'the chains that bind and restrain the Maori people'.

101 Angela Ballara. 'Ratana, Tahupotiki Wiremu — Biography', from the Dictionary of New Zealand Biography. Te Ara — the Encyclopedia of New Zealand.
102 Patrick O'Farrell. 'Holland, Henry Edmund — Biography', from the Dictionary of New Zealand Biography. Te Ara — the Encyclopedia of New Zealand.

Wiremu Ratana (1873–1939)

Prime Minister Savage picked up the challenge. In return, Wiremu Ratana locked his powerful Ratana movement into the Labour Party. His sea change speech was built not on oratory, but on the authority of a prophet. It gifted Labour the Maori seats for the next 70 years.

Ratana brought Savage a set of gifts, and explained their meaning:[103]

The first of my gifts are these three huia feathers and their waka. These feathers are emblematic of the heritage of the Maori in this land.

103 *Ratana the Prophet (Raupo Press, Penguin Group), by Keith Newman pages 186– 187.*

The huia was a native bird. When a person is seen wearing this feather it signifies that person is Maori. As it happens this bird is now extinct, having been destroyed by the weasels and other preying animals, introduced by the Pakeha.

The waka that carries the feathers is a kumara. We have no land in which to plant these foods. This greenstone tiki represents the power, richness and nobility of the Maori people, which I place in your hands. This greenstone represents the power and authority of the Maori people which, in this day and age, has been lost to them through European laws.

Here next is the broken gold watch and chain that belonged to my grandfather, Te Ratana. Te Ratana was loyal to Governor Grey, and to Premier Seddon of New Zealand.

I am now his descendant who professes loyalty to the government of this time, your time. As it happens, this te wati koura has no glass. My ancestor had no money to replace the glass, and as it happens, I have no money either to replace the glass. I give these objects into your hands.

Here too is this emblem of the Ratana movement, he tohu o te mara matanga, that represents the Ratana people, the 40,000 people of my organisation. I hand this over to your safekeeping and care, that you may be their father, in justice, in the physical world.

My boys are here with you attending to their duties. If you should need more of them, let me know, and I will provide you with more of the same. May you never forget your responsibilities to the Maori people, for when you forget this, your government will fall.

These items had such a profound impact on Savage, it is believed he had them buried with him at Bastion Point, in Auckland, when he died four years after his autumn meeting with Wiremu Ratana.[104]

---

104 *'Ratana and Labour seal alliance', URL: http://www.nzhistory.net.nz/page/ratana–and–labour– seal–alliance, (Ministry for Culture and Heritage).*

'War, I Hate It ...'

Walter Nash

November 1936

Walter Nash[105] was an English–born Christian Socialist. As the National Secretary from 1922, and an MP from 1929, he was a key figure in the rise of the New Zealand Labour party to power. In 1935, as the powerful National Secretary, he had drafted the manifesto for Labour's election victory.

Nash himself was an inveterate speech maker. His simplicity and sincerity, and a distinctive gravelly timbre of voice gave confidence and reassurance. His *Dictionary of New Zealand* biographer Barry Gustafson wrote of Nash: 'He did not always discriminate between important and trivial matters, and although a fluent and authoritative speaker, he was also often long–winded and verbose.'[106]

With a keen interest in international affairs, he helped found the Institute of Pacific Relations and the League of Nations Union in the 1920s.

By 1933, he was preaching, typically but startlingly, in money terms, to Wellington Rotarians, the need for the League of Nations:[107]

---

105 Essential reading includes Walter Nash (Auckland University Press) by Keith Sinclair, 1976.
106 Barry Gustafson. 'Nash, Walter — Biography', from the Dictionary of New Zealand Biography. Te Ara — the Encyclopedia of New Zealand.
107 Evening Post, May 30, 1933.

The Great War cost £27,000,000,000. If a road from Auckland to Wellington was paved with sovereigns it could be built 28 yards wide; and if the number of war dead marched six abreast from Auckland to the Bluff a yard apart, the last would not have left before the first reached the Bluff.

In 1935, Nash, 'the Labour Party's most persuasive intellectual force,'[108] took the third place in the Savage Cabinet as the Minister of Finance. He moved quickly to nationalise the Reserve Bank and his major achievement was to introduce guaranteed prices for farm produce. To back up this guaranteed price scheme, he sailed on the *Aorangi* to England in October 1936 to negotiate bulk trading agreements.

His farewell speech in Auckland on October 12 focussed not on finance, but on the importance of democracy, and the concept of the rights of the individual in the world:[109]

The one thing that is apparent in the world today is that there is a great fight between two conflicting ideals. I do not mean the fight between socialism and capitalism, which is inevitable.

What I mean is the fight between dictatorship and domination on the one hand and democracy on the other. The conflict is intense, and solution of it is hard to find.

Dictatorships such as those in Russia, Germany and Italy suppress the soul of every man who comes under their power. It compels him to acquiesce in that which, left free to express his thoughts and feelings, he would not approve.

It is an old and basic principle that British citizens have the right of freedom to choose their freedom and shape the laws under which they live.

The people of a free country need economic freedom, so that each might express himself spiritually and materially. And that is what offers the brightest hope for the future, especially to the young people who will be the citizens in time to come.

---

108 *A Short History of New Zealand by J.C.Beaglehole.*
109 *Auckland Star, October 13, 1936.*

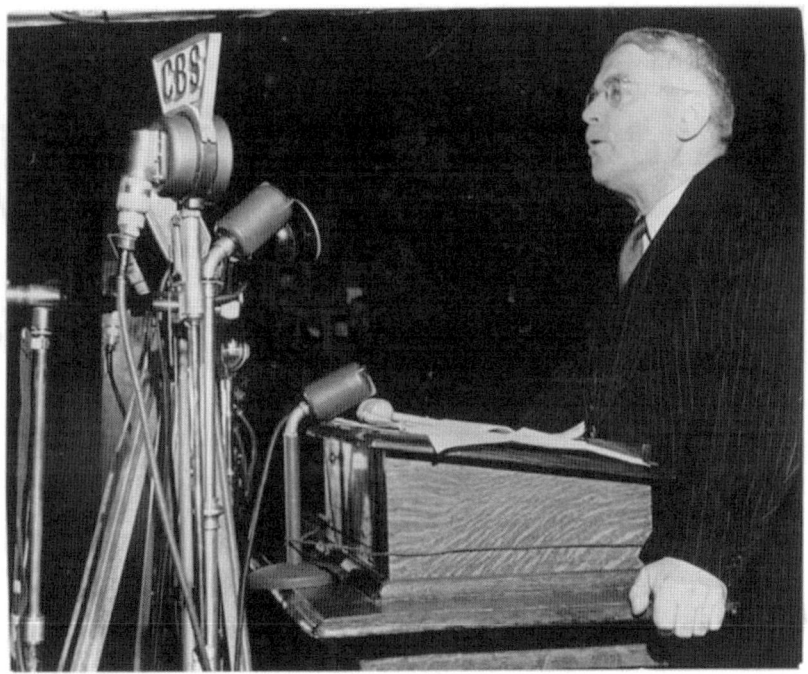

Walter Nash (1882–1968)

The ideal of all who uphold democracy should be government by persuasion, not by force. Their aim should be to grow the plant of liberty, nurture and strengthen it to give all the right to be themselves. That is the goal of life.

When he reached England, he visited his native Kidderminster where he was guest speaker at the annual dinner of the Old Carolinians Association of his Kidderminster Grammar School.

Nash explained the danger in the world lay not between Britain and Germany, or between Hitler and Mussolini, but between the ideals they represented.

The fortune of our race might be determined for good or ill in the clash between democracy and dictatorship. I believe that if the latter triumphed all would be lost.[110]

110 *Auckland Star, November 25, 1936.*

More extracts of his speech were reported by the *Evening Post*'s London correspondent:[111]

War, I hate it — good can never come of it.

Up till 1933, as I see it, it was impossible for a Christian to take sword or gun in hand and destroy another soul. Then in one of the mightiest nations — Germany — much that was good and noble refusing to fight was crushed and nothing left of it.

Then I did not know where I was. But I felt that serious thinking was required to find some way to combat the type which was endeavouring to force itself not only on its own people but on everyone.

If dictatorship wins, as I see it, we are lost. Inherent in all human beings, of whatever class, is the desire to think for themselves and express themselves.

If that desire is suppressed, even if the individual himself or herself acquiesces in the suppression, it is only for a time: The desire for self expression will arise again, and before the century is out their children or their children's children will fight once again for the right to be free.

What we call 'democracy' is the guardian of that freedom of the individual. I am glad to be associated with that section in the world today which is fighting for democracy in the real sense.

It is difficult to see the path along which we must move but I hope that all sections of the free people of the British Empire 'will hold on to the ideal of the right to freedom'.

Nash was preaching while Rome burned. Caught up in his 'fight for life' in London, he clung like Savage too long to his hopes for the League. As a result, the Savage Government sent young New Zealanders away ill–prepared for blitzkrieg (lightning) war.

His major war contribution was as our wartime ambassador in Washington. He was at the height of his powers.

Washington hailed him as its 'Pacific New Dealer'. His work helped prepare the ground for co–operation in the South Pacific and in the international organisations of the post–war world.

---

111 *Evening Post, December 21, 1936.*

With all his political sagacity and abilities, Nash proved in the 1950s a poor Leader of the Opposition and an inconsistent one–term Prime Minister. In retrospect, history suggests Nash managed to translate a good deal of his Christian idealism into our society but that his Christian pacifism saw him fall short in 'fighting' for democracy.

Long ages before, the sages had warned: 'Let him who desires peace, prepare for war.'

Politics in Retrospect

William Downie Stewart

1936

The Great War changed the whole world. One of the few voices describing its impact on New Zealand was a Calvinist Scots New Zealander from Dunedin, William Downie Stewart. After a brilliant maiden speech in 1915, he left Parliament, with Richard Seddon's son, for the Army. He returned in 1917 gripped by an eventually crippling arthritis. William Massey was keen to have him in cabinet.

He might, but for his health, have followed Massey as Prime Minister. Even so, his stellar career saw Gordon Coates — who did become Prime Minister — refer to him, such was his influence, as 'almost a dictator'.[112]

Downie Stewart was a trenchant speaker. This he demonstrates with remarkable modesty and wisdom, in a speech in 1936 to the Otago Historical Society.

Politics in Retrospect[113], in its range and insight, sets Downie Stewart with his record as Minister of Finance, Customs and State Advances, and Attorney General, as among the wisest and most principled of our Ministers of the Crown. Despite him 'seeing with terrible distinctiveness the disadvantages

112 Stephanie Dale. 'Stewart, William Downie — Biography', from the Dictionary of New Zealand Biography. Te Ara — the Encyclopedia of New Zealand,
113 William Downie Stewart, Speech to the Historical Society, Dunedin, titled 'Politics in Retrospect', 1936. MS–0985–009/024. Hocken Collections Uare Taoka o Hakena, University of Otago.

of everything'[114] he is perhaps the nearest approach in our lexicon to Plato's philosopher king.

Here are extracts from his address:

It is natural to make the Great War the pivot point in this retrospect because it not only produced great changes in our external relations but it dominated all our legislation and political outlook both during the War and post–war years, and many of the problems it raised are not yet solved.

Taking first the wide circle of our external contacts, namely, our relations with foreign countries, it is well known to you that the War resulted in a marked change in important fields in our international relations. We have the right of membership of the League of Nations and the right to express our individual views in its deliberations, and we have all become deeply involved in the maintenance of an effective collective system of international relations. The chief point to note is that New Zealand has been more reluctant than any other Dominion to claim the new status that may imply.

Mr Massey always declared that he never had any idea of altering in any way our previous status as an integral part of the Empire. I think it will be found, as a matter of practical politics, that each Dominion magnifies or minimises the importance of its position in the League of Nations according to its degree of dependence on Britain and the British Navy for defence and security.

The Canadians and South Africans and the Irish Free State lay all the emphasis on league membership and seem to subordinate their Imperial connection to their new role. Australia occupies a mid–way position owing to the fact that she is more vulnerable than Canada or South Africa, and hence she is less emphatic on her League status than the previous Dominions.

While New Zealand is represented in the League of Nations yet being the smallest and most isolated Dominion, with a lesser consciousness of nationality, has acquiesced in the theoretical claims of the other

---

114 *J.C. Beaglehole quoted in 'Indirections A Memoir' by Charles Brasch, 1909–1947 p295.*

Dominions that this gives us a new status with a shrug of the shoulders largely for the sake of uniformity, but with her face still largely turned towards Britain as her mainstay and security.

Perhaps the real question of how far we have reached a new international status will be determined broadly by how far and to what extent any such change is recognised by foreign powers.

... My immediate object is merely to remind you that the War did greatly increase our responsibilities in our relations with the outside world. I will not therefore weary you by any debate as to the legal and constitutional problems that arise from our position on the League.

What is clear is that the people of New Zealand are now called on to take a far more active interest in world affairs if they or their representatives are to express well–informed views on the problems that arise.

Let me illustrate this by one example. When I was in London in 1932 the League of Nations was deeply involved in an attempt to solve the China–Japanese conflict. A point was reached where the members of the League were called on to vote on the side of China or Japan.

Our then High Commissioner consulted me as to how he should vote and what I thought New Zealand opinion on the question might be. What was I to say? I had never heard any real discussion on the problem in New Zealand.

It was not possible to suggest that the Empire representatives should confer and speak with one voice as at the Washington Conference; and indeed they had different views and interests according to their geographical locality and all the countries had to vote in alphabetical order. In the net result, the difficulty was not very material and the League could only give an expression of opinion as to what the world thought because Japan took the bit in her teeth and flouted the League.

The greatest danger of war in the future will arise from the failure on the various parts of the Empire to make quick and unanimous decisions and to show a united front.

If each Dominion has to summon parliament and debate the issue at length the decision may come too late. If an immediate decision is to be made by the Government and Parliament disagrees later with the decision arrived at, it could of course dismiss the Government.

So long as Britain bears nearly the whole burden of Empire defence and foreign diplomacy, it is difficult how we can ask more than that we should be consulted, as far as practicable, in all matters of general interest, but the present interminable discussions in the League of Nations, against sanctions and peace negotiations, while a bloody war is raging in Abyssinia, affords a good illustration of what I am pointing out. Apart from the effect of the war in expanding our responsibilities first to the League of Nations and secondly within the Empire by express recognition of equality of status, it also had the effect thirdly of greatly enlarging our responsibilities in the Pacific.

First, in 1920 we accepted the mandate over Western Samoa with a population of over 50,000, and this led to the creation of a new department known by the misleading name of External Affairs Department. One would suppose that an External Affairs Department would deal with all overseas problems but it dealt only with Samoa, until in 1932 the very interesting island of Niue was taken out of the Cook group and put under the Minister of External Affairs. We already had responsibility for the large and scattered group of about fifteen islands in the Cook group with a population of near 12,000 — but as these were acquired in 1901 they do not enter into my story.

Secondly, in 1923 we were also given jurisdiction over the Ross Sea Dependency which has no permanent population but we are supposed to control whaling operations there and get 2/6^d a barrel royalty from licensed whalers who pay an annual fee of £200. Of course, most of the whales are taken outside territorial waters controlled by our regulations and thus avoid the fees, but a few years ago we collected nearly £14,000 in one year.

Thirdly, we also took over from Great Britain in 1926 the Tokelau or Union group and administer from Western Samoa. These islands have a population of over 1,000.

I mention these extensions of our control, although they seem to have little bearing on politics, because I think we have a great responsibility for the welfare of these scattered islands, and they may become of immense importance.

... Let us leave external affairs and consider briefly the effect of the war

on our internal politics and economics.

Naturally the war raised a whole crop of new and urgent problems related to finance, price fixing, profiteering, the commandeer of supplies, conscription and so on. Its direct effect on the political situation was that it caused the creation of the National Government in 1915.

My own view, which I expressed at the opening of the 1915 session[115] was that there was so little difference between the political principles of the Reform and Liberal parties that they ought not only to combine for the War but I hoped it would be the beginning of a permanent fusion.

This hope, however, was not realised and, at the end of the War, the parties split asunder again, and went to the 1919 election in separate camps. It was believed by the Liberals that there would be an immense reaction against the War Government by a war–weary people, and that they could avoid the unpopularity of the War measures by breaking away.

In this they were strangely mistaken, as the electors not only returned Mr Massey with the largest majority he ever had, but the Leader of the Liberals, Sir Joseph Ward, actually lost his own seat. Of the post–war fortunes of these two parties I will say nothing further as although I had a great deal to do with the creation of the National Government in 1931, I could only tell how it came about by making public many things which are better left private in the meantime.

Broadly speaking, both in New Zealand and elsewhere, the effect of the War was to bring about a large extension of State activity and State intervention in our economic life. There is nothing essentially new in planned economy, and discussion really turns on the degree to which State intervention should occur, and this differs with time, place, and circumstances.

But it seems to me that the end result has been to narrow the areas of conflict in politics. There has in fact been a double process going on. The older parties have been driven towards the left by force of circumstances, and have been compelled to use the powers of the State in coping with various economic problems.

---

115 *William Downie Stewart, Maiden Speech; New Zealand Parliamentary Debates (Hansard), 1915, Volume 172, page 63.*

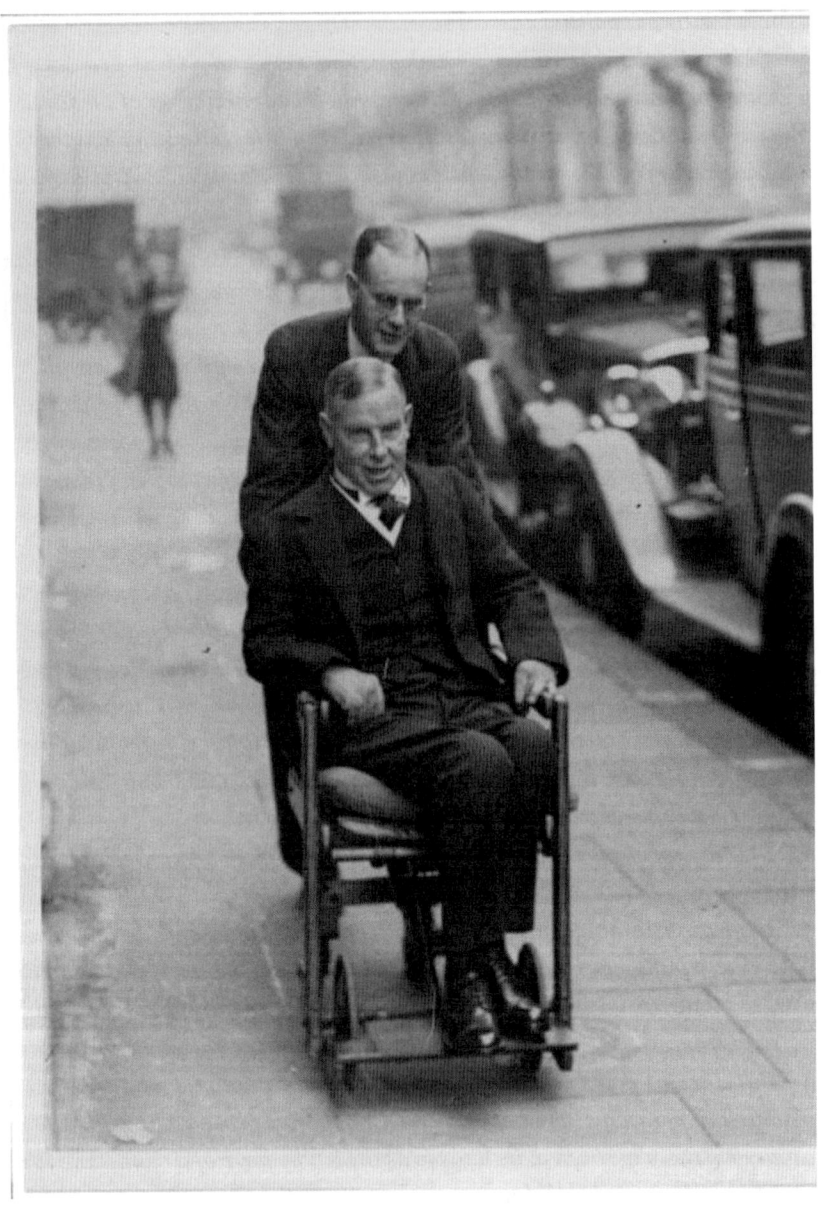

William Downie Stewart (1878–1949)

On the other hand, the Labour Party has been moving to the right, and is more concerned now, with questions of practical policy, than with the old theoretical doctrines of Karl Marx and others, which were so constantly advocated by its late leader, Mr Holland.

... In fact the more the Labour Party has reached responsibility in politics, the more it has tended to shed its theoretical programme and adopted an opportunist policy directed towards redistributing the national income. In other words, except for a small section which has moved towards communism, the general trend of the radical parties has been towards the right. The older parties have been driven towards the left by force of circumstances, and you have only to look at the steps taken to try and save the dairy industry to see how far the parties, which regard themselves as parties of private enterprise, have been forced to use the powers of the state in coping with various economic problems.

... Our parliamentary system, though severely criticised, still functions more satisfactorily than in most countries but apart from the intervention of the State in banking, as for example the Reserve Bank, and marketing, as seen in the Ottawa Agreement and further trade agreements with Australia, Canada, Japan and Belgium, there has been a large movement aided by the State towards marketing boards and similar bodies to organise and rationalise production and sale, for example the Meat, Dairy, Honey and Fruit Boards.

Of course there are marked distinctions between many of these schemes; for example our marketing boards, while they have statutory authority, are organised and controlled largely by the producers to ensure markets or stablised profits, whereas the Italian corporations try to draw in the workers and consumers and are directly responsible to the State. It is often supposed that all these organisations are an intermediate step towards complete State ownership and control; in other words, towards Socialism, but it is not clear yet what their ultimate effect may be.

In fact, in so far as they are self-governing bodies built up and controlled by the producers they may in the end enable these producers if they so desire to offer a stouter resistance to State ownership and Socialism than the individual farmer and producer could do so by his own unorganised efforts. All one can say at present is that they are in a transition stage and, until they transform themselves into some permanent system, it is idle to prophecy what their effect may be.

Downie Stewart then commented briefly on the New Zealand's adoption of conscription and Australia's refusal before venturing some personal impressions of Parliament that contains an invaluable portrait of Mr Massey.

Mr Massey was an Ulster man who commenced life in humble circumstances, but by force of character he succeeded in raising himself to the position of Prime Minster and held that office right up to his death. But before that he had been in opposition for 18 years, fighting against overwhelming odds and leading what appeared to be a forlorn hope ...

Once Mr Massey attained office he rapidly expanded in breadth of outlook and grasps of affairs. During his long tenure in opposition he had learned to dig out his own facts, to study the Blue Books[116], and he knew where to look for material. This is a great advantage to a public man ...

It seemed hard luck that after his long fight to attain office Massey should have had no period of easy sailing, but was almost immediately faced with the great industrial upheaval of 1913, and the following year, with the terrible problems arising from the Great War. After the War, post war problems which went on until his death were almost equally difficult ...

I have said that Massey was a great parliamentarian and knew every mood of the House. One night I was held up by the House on a tariff item and a weary debate went on until after midnight. Massey had been out at some function or working in his office and when he came in he stopped at the table to ask what was wrong. I said I was held up without reasons and was not clear what to do. The old man said 'I will let you know in a minute'. He lay down in his seat and appeared to go to sleep. In a few moments after listening to part of the one speech he came across and said, 'You stand to your guns. They are bluffing you. I know this House. They will give way in a short time.'

---

116 *Reference to Hansard.*

To my astonishment he was right and in a few minutes the debate stopped and the vote went through. Another night the same thing happened. Massey came in and after listening for a few moments said, 'Look out, this is dangerous. There is a nasty current running. You had better compromise on the best terms you can ... The House is a funny animal with strange moods. When you have been here as long as I have you will know that it must be humoured sometimes and driven at other times.'

But he himself had a magnetic power over the House. I have seen him come in with his slow rolling walk to a tired, listless and bad tempered House. Suddenly he would intervene in the debate with a slashing vigorous speech; chaffing the House, bantering some members and trouncing others. Instantly the whole temper of the House was altered; members were alert, laughing and interjecting, and thoroughly enjoying Massey's repartee. For example on one occasion a dispute was raging about some carpenter's award and a member said to Massey, 'You know nothing about this problem. You never were a carpenter.'

'Good gracious!' replied Massey in a flash, 'Why I am the best and only cabinet maker in the House!'

The Nuclear Age

Baron Rutherford

1936

History suggests a Nelson–born scientist was the greatest New Zealander. The grandson of illiterate Scottish weavers, Ernest Rutherford[117] began the age of modern big science. Before his sudden death in 1937, Rutherford 'crested the wave' as a hero of civilisation. But, like a good New Zealander, he was a team player. He liked people. Not once, but three times, Rutherford changed the world. In 1908, he won the Nobel Prize for chemistry, establishing the complexities of radioactive substances and confirming the enormous energy involved in radioactivity. This led to the concept of radioactive dating and Geiger counting. Deducing the nuclear model of the atom, Rutherford then launched his second and biggest revolution, atomic physics. His third seismic move was to split the atom. Atomic physics may be the foundation stone of his fame, but any one of the three was worth a Nobel Prize.

In the 1920s, Rutherford predicted the neutron, which his team at the Cavendish Laboratory would discover in early 1932, at the same time as they split a lithium atom, the first step to a chain reaction and the design of atomic weapons.

117 John Campbell. 'Rutherford, Ernest — Biography', from the Dictionary of New Zealand Biography. Te Ara — the Encyclopedia of New Zealand.

Rutherford was an 'imposing, tall, well–built man', robust, exuberant, excitable, an 'animated speaker' with a booming voice.

His Nobel Prize lecture sounds dry and technical, but his speeches during his 1925 New Zealand visit were punchy, inspirational and visionary. Rutherford came with a leading British scientist to advise on establishing the New Zealand Council and Department of Scientific and Industrial Research. A year later, his star New Zealand student, Dr Ernest Marsden, became the first Director General of our deservedly famous DSIR. In a brief speech[118] at the Wellington Town Hall, Rutherford summed up his vision:

If we are to hold our own in the struggle of tomorrow it will be by applied science. After all, science is merely organised knowledge, and we want to investigate each principle to see if it cannot be improved, and there is nothing in the world that cannot be improved by scientific methods.

Rutherford was not always right. In 1933, he picked up on the work of Cockcroft and Walton, out of his Cambridge team. They had been splitting lithium into alpha particles by bombardment from a particle accelerator. Rutherford noted in a speech at Leicester:[119]

We may in these processes obtain very much more energy than the proton supplied, but on the average we cannot expect to obtain energy in this way. It is a very poor and inefficient (way) of producing energy. Anyone who looks for a source of power in the transformation of atoms is talking moonshine. But the subject is scientifically interesting because it gives insight into the atoms.

Rutherford was wrong. People immediately began to wonder how such tremendous energy might be released to make explosives, and so atomic weapons. His speech is thought to have inspired Leo Szilard in developing the concept of a controlled nuclear chain reaction that would, in the

---

118 *Evening Post, October 27, 1925.*
119 *The Times, September 12, 1933.*

following decade, see the Hungarian physicist develop, and co–patent the nuclear reactor.

Some sense of the excitement and passion of Rutherford's oratory can be taken from an excerpt from a lecture in 1936, in Cambridge, England, titled *The Development of the Theory of Atomic Structure*:[120]

I would like to use this example to show you often stumble upon facts by accident. In the early days, I had observed the scatter of alpha–particles, and Dr Geiger in my laboratory had examined it in detail, He found, in two pieces of heavy metal, that the scattering was unusually small, of the order of one degree.

One day Geiger came to me and said, 'Don't you think that young Marsden, whom I (am)training in radioactive methods, ought to begin some small research?'

Now I had thought that too, so I said, 'Why not let him see if any alpha–particles can be scattered through a large angle?'

I may tell you in confidence that I did not believe that they would be, since we knew that the alpha–particle was a very fast massive particle, with a great deal of energy, and you could show that if the scattering was due to the accumulated effect of a number of small scatterings the chance of an alpha–particle's being scattered backwards was very small.

Then I remember two or three days later Geiger coming to me in great excitement and saying, 'We have been able to get some of the a–particles coming backwards ...'

It was quite the most incredible event that has ever happened to me in my life.

It was almost as incredible as if you fired a 15–inch shell at a piece of tissue paper and it came back and hit you.

On consideration I realised that this scattering backwards must be the result of a single collision, and when I made calculations I saw that it was impossible to get anything of that order of magnitude unless you took a system in which the greater part of the mass of the atom was concentrated in a minute nucleus.

---

120 *In Background to Modern Science: Ten lectures at Cambridge arranged by the history of science committee, 1936 Edited by Joseph Needham and Walter Pagel (Macmillan, 1938).*

Lord Rutherford (1871–1937)

It was then that I had the idea of an atom with a minute massive centre carrying a charge.

Soon after, Lord Rutherford (he was knighted in 1914 and became Baron Rutherford of Nelson in 1931), at the height of his fame, died as a result of delays in operating on his partially strangulated umbilical hernia. His ashes were interred in London's Westminster Abbey.

The English–Canadian physicist Arthur Stewart Eve once observed to his colleague Rutherford that he always appeared to be riding on the 'crest of the wave.' Rutherford replied, 'Well! I made the wave, didn't I?' [121]

Surely Rutherford is the only New Zealander we can unquestionably nominate, since Gutenberg and his printing press, to the top 500 makers of the modern world.

---

121 *Being the Life and Letters of the Rt Hon. Lord Rutherford, O.M. Cambridge (Cambridge University Press), by Arthur Stewart Eve, 1939. Page 436.*

284

Anticipation of War

Carl Berendsen

April 1939

As the Head of the Prime Minister's Department (1926–43), Carl Berendsen[122] established a New Zealand foreign policy. In the 1930s, he warned unheeding governments and the nation of the approach of war. In the countdown to war, it was he who drafted the independent interventions New Zealand made at the League of Nations and at the 1937 Imperial conference.

He then led the preparation of the War Book for a conflict that after the Munich crisis all recognised as inevitable. His ability to speak for New Zealand is powerfully contained in a masterly exegesis at a belated and badly attended South Pacific Defence Conference held in Wellington in April 1939.[123]

It is not my intention to touch on anything strategical or tactical or technical but I propose to confine my remarks to one subject ... and that is the question of knowing the strength of the reinforcements and the time in which they can be expected to be available in the Pacific.

122 *Mr Ambassador: Memoirs of Sir Carl Berendsen (Victoria University Press)*, edited by Hugh Templeton, 2009.
123 *Blue–Water Rationale: The Naval Defence of New Zealand 1914–1942 (Government Printer)*, by Ian MacGibbon, 1981.

In considering the problems ... we must in ordinary prudence assume the worst situation that appears to be possible, and that is war against Germany, Italy and Japan simultaneously; a conflict in which Japan, notwithstanding her preoccupations elsewhere, present and potential, has joined from the very commencement. We must also assume that as the enemy would no doubt himself fix the date of commencement of hostilities, he could and probably would, have his forces in their chosen positions before the inception of hostilities.

I proceed to set out certain very elementary propositions which are probably self evident, but which may serve to clear the ground.

Firstly, all British Dominions and territories are at present safe from attack except by sea.

Secondly, the degree of naval protection is therefore, the very foundation of the defence schemes of all of them.

Thirdly, no valid conclusion from the points raised ... can possibly be reached until an estimate as definite as possible has been made of the extent to which naval protection is available.

Fourthly, Singapore distant and western though it is, is accepted as the basis of naval defence, (of) British trade routes in the Pacific.

Fifthly, it is impracticable to station permanently an adequate fleet at Singapore.

Sixthly, and finally, the vessels of the New Zealand Division of the Royal Navy are intended to defend and (are) not capable of defending New Zealand against a naval attack.

Having stated these as foundation propositions, one draws the conclusion ... that the strength and the time of arrival of naval reinforcements from the old world is of primary importance in our defence system.

The strength of these naval reinforcements is obviously important from the point of view of holding naval forces, and the time is of importance in at least three aspects — firstly, that the possibility that if reinforcements are delayed the fleet may not be able to reach Singapore without fighting its way in; secondly, the possibility that Singapore may be attacked and might be reduced before the fleet's arrival; thirdly ... the period during which the enemy would have a comparatively free hand in the Pacific before the arrival at Singapore of adequate naval reinforcements ...

From the time when the development of Singapore as a naval base was first proposed, and certainly from the time of New Zealand's decision to contribute to its costs, it has always been understood that an adequate naval force would be based (at) Singapore during hostilities in the Pacific.

At the Imperial Conference in 1937... the Prime Minister and Mr Nash, holding the view that the question of naval reinforcement of Singapore was, necessarily, the foundation point of their own domestic defence policy, endeavoured to clarify the position as far as possible, realising, however, as they did and they still do, that a complete indication of what might happen in the varying circumstances of a future war, and probably still is, impossible.

As a result of their inquiries on this matter the New Zealand Government was shown an appreciation of the position based ... upon a war with Germany and Japan but not Italy. The timetable of the fleet's dispatch to Singapore was set out according to the route to be followed, with a maximum of 70 days from the date of departure. Again I wish to stress these words, 'date of departure' for the paper added that in a certain contingency, which appeared to be not improbable, the fleet could not be allowed to depart until after 'a very considerable delay' ... I quote: 'If in these circumstance ... we have to deal with Japan ... in which German ships were abroad in the Atlantic, a very considerable period may elapse before the progress of our operations against Germany and the redistribution of our forces permit of a fleet arriving in the Far East' ...

It is also worth noting that 'a very considerable delay' contemplated as a possibility in a war against Germany and Japan might well become a more considerable delay in a war against Germany, Japan and Italy.

In June, 1937 the Chiefs of Staff ... was asked ...

'Can HMG (His Majesty's Government) in New Zealand obtain a positive statement that a British fleet of sufficient strength will move out to the Far East in the event of Japan taken offensive action against us, even if we are also embroiled in Europe?'

In reply, the COS Sub Committee said:

287

'In the event of Japanese aggression occurring simultaneously with, or subsequent to, an act of aggression against British interests in Europe, it would be our policy to send to the Far East a fleet which at least adequate to contain that of the Japanese. The establishment of a fleet at Singapore as soon as possible after the outbreak of hostilities with Japan is the accepted basis of our Far Eastern strategy and is recognised as a vital necessity ...

(I would like you to note this paragraph because it is the centre of my remarks.)

'Our existing naval strength and present programme will permit us to satisfy this requirement until 1939 ...

a) placing a fleet in the Far East fully adequate to act on the defensive and to serve as a strong deterrent against any threat to our interests in that part of the globe.

b) to maintain in all circumstances in home waters a force, a force able to meet the requirements of war with Germany at the same time ...

The COS Sub Committee was good enough to supply us with the names of the ships which in the case of war with Germany and Japan (but not with Italy) would be dispatched in the period 1937–40 ... At the same time the COS Sub Committee said:

'A Japanese overseas expedition aimed at capturing New Zealand may consequently said to be a highly improbable undertaking so long as our position at Singapore is secure, and the fleets of the British Commonwealth are maintained at the standard outlined.'

It might be noted particularly that the Sub Committee's view as to the improbability even of such a huge undertaking as an attempt to capture New Zealand, was made conditional on the fleet of the British Commonwealth of Nations being maintained at the standard outlined.

May we pause ... to consider the effect of this. In June 1937 the COS Sub Committee said ... that an attempt to capture New Zealand was improbable only if the British fleet was kept up to a specified standard, and in July 1938 the CID stated that this standard had not yet been approved.

The logical deduction ... is the assurance of the COS Sub Committee as to the improbability of an attempt to capture New Zealand becomes

Carl Berendsen (1890–1973)

completely invalidated. This is a startling reflection, especially having regard to the fact that ... Italy must be accepted as an additional potential enemy.

Berendsen then updated the delegates on further communications from the sub committee, with the latest being received on April 5. The latest missive read:

'In the event of war with Germany and Italy, should Japan join in against us, it would still be HMG's full intention to dispatch a fleet to Singapore. If we were fighting against such a combination, never envisaged in our earlier plans, the size of that fleet would necessarily depend on a) the moment Japan entered the war and b) what losses if any our opponents or ourselves had previously sustained. It would however be our intention to achieve three main objects —

1)The prevention of any major operations against Australia, New Zealand or India.

2)To keep open our sea communications.

3)To prevent the fall of Singapore.'

That is the very latest indication, this month. It is still — no doubt quite inevitably — indefinite ... There is (nevertheless) no disposition in any quarter of New Zealand to question the basic fact that in any war in which the British Commonwealth was involved the decision would be reached in the European theatre, and no one in New Zealand would dream of suggesting that a fleet should come to Singapore if such a step might prejudice the situation there.

We entirely realise that the defence of New Zealand depends on the defence of the Commonwealth, so the single reason for this summary is to isolate the facts of naval reinforcements in order to enable a proper estimate to be made of the time in which they will be available, and if the facts, when ascertained, should be found to be unpalatable, then I suggest that is more reason why we should look at these facts with a clear eye and a clear head.

Now, what are the facts? It is suggested that the following deductions are inescapable. Firstly the strength of the naval reinforcements we may expect. No indication is given — perhaps none is possible.

We can be absolutely sure that HMG ... will dispatch a fleet to Singapore as soon as possible, and in as great strength as possible, but we cannot ignore the possibility that in circumstances which may arise HMG may find it impossible to send to Singapore a fleet of sufficient strength, and this is particularly true of the early stages of the conflict.

Secondly, as to the time. For a certain period during the war with Germany, there will not be adequate forces in the Pacific to match, or at least to detain, the Japanese. This period must be at least 70 days, and will probably be considerably more ...

During that period the Japanese forces would have unquestionable naval control in the Pacific, and the only limitation for all practical purposes to Japanese action during that period, 70 days plus X, would be the strength of the Japanese forces, their choice of objectives, the dictates of prudence, and caution that may be important in their minds.

If those are the facts ... what bearing, if any have these facts on the possible scale of attack on British territory during this period, and secondly what special steps, if any, can or should be taken for defence purposes, during this period, are matters for discussion by technical experts, and not by me.

The 'Gospel of Equality'

Sir Apirana Ngata

July 25, 1939

Apirana Ngata of the Ngati Porou may yet stand — like Te Whiti in the 19th century — as the greatest New Zealander of the 20th century. Historian J.C. Beaglehole wrote of him: 'Ngata brought something like genius to the office of Native Minister.' [124]

On July 25, 1939, some forty days before the outbreak of war, Sir Apirana Ngata[125] gave one of the most powerful if sardonically eloquent speeches ever laid out to the House of Representatives.

Echoes still resonate. Sir Apirana was a measured, logical but 'magnetic' speaker, aware that when he stood to speak it was to do battle on behalf of those who he believed to be oppressed.

After the customary references to movers and seconders and new members, Sir Apirana opened, eloquent as a Demosthenes by reference to the existence of a Maori King. As subtly then as Ulysses he picked up on the approaching war to demand a place for Maori — a Maori Battalion.

Maori were prepared to fight for their country so why then did the Labour government fail to include Maoridom in the Centennial celebrations?

124 A Short History of New Zealand, by J.C. Beaglehole, page 141.
125 M. P. K. Sorrenson. 'Ngata, Apirana Turupa — Biography', from the Dictionary of New Zealand Biography. Te Ara — the Encyclopedia of New Zealand,

Are we cannibals? he asked.

Then to underline the strategic failure of the Treaty of Waitangi he focused on a serious and public Maori grievance. Australian newspaper criticism gave him the launching pad for an onslaught on the festering sore of dispossession in the Orakei village nestling in a swanky Auckland suburb. From that emerged the vision — and the lines of redemption — for the future. These indeed after the perhaps inevitable delays of post–war reconstruction and generational passing led to reinterpretation of the Treaty of Waitangi in the 1980s and effective Treaty settlements in the 1990s.

Ngata, if able to contemplate events since his ground–breaking speech, might be the first to endorse that evolutionary aphorism: 'Governments always make the right decisions after they have tried every other alternative.'

Using the immediate issues of peace and war, and calling up the powerful image of the Maori Pioneer Battalion, Ngata weaved every complementary issue into the most compelling case for Maoridom, as valid today as then.

The speech was a work of art and of high forensic oratory. Developed in the hot house atmosphere of imminent and dangerous war, and showing direct understanding of the threat of invasion, Hansard provides few such splendid examples of 'living history'. In laying out the blueprint for the progress of a bi–racial and increasingly multi–racial nation, Ngata's speech made history.

In the light of his own drastic experience at the hands of Pakeha judges and civil servants, we might ask whether its spirit comes as close, as his distinguished biographer claims of Ngata, to that of 'a God Among Men'.[126]

It is worth recalling one of his last commands that the nation now somewhat abstractedly obeys:

I leave you to dream the dream
that my many friends and I have treasured through the years,
that the potent elements of our culture,

---

126 *He Tipua: The Life and Times of Sir Apirana Ngata (Viking Press), by Ranginui Walker, 2001.*

294

those things which belong to this beautiful land,
should be preserved as a heritage to New Zealand.

Sir Apirana Ngata's speech to the House of Representatives:[127]

One of the most remarkable events in later Maori history was the opening of King Korokia's house at Ngaruawahia ... it was a strange feature — a very remarkable one — that the representative of the King of England should be performing the opening ceremony of a private dwelling built by his people for the person called by the Waikato tribe, the Maori King. One could see a long history of misunderstanding, of armed clashes between the two peoples, following by a confiscation of land and a great deal of soreness on the part of many Pakehas. The misunderstanding lasts up till this day — the misunderstanding that in setting up the Maori King, a large section of the Maori people throughout the North Island did in fact, seek to establish a rival to the Sovereign in England.

History is a peculiar thing that solves many problems; and it came about that in the later representatives of the sovereignty of the British Empire in New Zealand we should have English gentlemen like Lord Jellicoe, Lord Bledisloe and our present Governor General (Lord Galway), interpreting in a much broader fashion the institution of the Maori kingship and showing that there was nothing that the Pakeha could cavil at, and no ground for the misconception that an attempt was being made to provide a rival for the King of England (but) deem it to be his rightful duty to be opening the private dwelling of one recognised throughout Maoridom as the representative of their highest and oldest aristocracy. In view of their impending departure, the Maori farewell to their Excellencies should take place, if possible on the occasion of the Maori celebrations in Auckland, very suitable recognition of the broad minded attitude of our present representatives of the Crown towards the relationship between the two races in this country.

We all read with pleasure of the visit of their Majesties to the American continent, and right through the British Commonwealth —

---

127 *New Zealand Parliamentary Debates (Hansard), July 25, 1939, Volume 254, pages 723–733.*

the expression Empire I heard in the debate is not in favour with some — there was a hope there would be a display of that co-operation and friendly feeling, between the two branches of the Anglo Saxon people, which would have a direct and beneficial influence on the complicated and difficult international situation, where the fortunes of the human race are concerned.

I come now to the debate, the overshadowing feature of which has been defence. After listening to my friend the Minister of Agriculture I felt more optimistic that some of the plaints of the Maori people, which I hope to put forward, would not be considered malapropos.

While the world is talking in terms of aeroplanes, artillery, battleships, here we are debating about butter and cheese, accusing one another of offences in the past, taking all the credit for what God Almighty sometimes gives us, in the form of good grass, but when we do not get the grass blaming God Almighty for giving us droughts. I have heard that story in this House for over thirty years. In the end we hope that New Zealand will go on and that she will prosper. Our grass areas should become more extensive, our butterfat should increase. There should be more of all those things being produced today than twenty years ago ...

These things however, seem small compared with what is happening on the other side of the world. Are not we in a humiliating position today as an Empire? One does not know what has happened at Tokyo, but the position is very alarming. We are beginning to retreat from the position the British Commonwealth of Nations has consistently taken up since before I was born.

What is happening today? There was some attempt ... to apportion blame as between the previous and the present government. That is not the question at all. After the war that was waged to end war one could feel a relaxing all over the world, and particularly among the English-speaking peoples.

The whole talk was of disarmament. At the foundation of all the talk of the League of Nations was the assumption that some radical change had taken place in human nature — the world was better, Christian principles were at length dominating the universe.

That was the kind of fool's paradise we built for ourselves after the

Apirana Ngata (1874–1950)

war of 1914–18. But right at the termination of that war the so-called Christian nations laid down the seed of discontent which has since produced Hitler and Mussolini and all that is occurring in China today.

An Hon. Member: 'And the Labour Government.'

No, I will not say the Labour Government. Civilised countries conspired to carve up the territory of the Teutonic peoples and to arrange an impossible kind of Europe. I do not want to justify dictatorship but someday history will be written from another angle and will seek to justify the ambition of a man imbued with a determination to put together again the pieces broken by the Treaty of Versailles.

And the whole world was forgetting the eternal truth that man was put here in a world of strife and he will have to continue in a world of strife until one predominates sometimes the other, but the two are always present.

The whole trouble with the British Empire is that in its self conceit it says that the good in the end had always prevailed over evil. We are the chosen people; we are the people to carry the banner of Christianity — we the British Empire. But conditions have changed. They forget that there are other peoples, and to the extent that our Empire has expanded, it has trodden on the corns of all sorts of nations; it has called up the jealousies of all kinds of peoples; it has established precedents that other people are attempting to follow, and we are trying to tell them they must not follow the bad precedents of the last two or three centuries.

An Empire founded upon blood and rapine! An Empire extended by iron ruthlessness, the treading down of primitive people! That is the Empire which is saying now to its latest rivals, 'You must not do it. You must accept the principles of Christianity.'

What fools. What should this British Empire remember. It was built on the gospel of might, and it will survive only so long as it keeps its armour bright. So when after the Great War it relaxed, made peace with the world and established the League of Nations, it was entering a fool's paradise. We must blame the whole English speaking race for this for the poison went right round the world.

The Minister of Defence tells us the government is acting on the best advice of experts ... Well I will leave that to the experts. But I cannot follow the member for Waitemata when he says we are only going to get raids. If all this bother is about defending the country against raids, that

298

is not a very serious problem. But I hold that it is invasion that we must prepare against; and history says that once we lose our seapower, all sorts of raids and invasions take place. New Zealand may not be raided at all. A hostile power can take New Zealand by taking Singapore. This country would fall into the lap of any Power that was strong enough to take Singapore or neutralise the strength of the British Navy.

When I heard the Minister of Defence speak about the Highland regiments, stating that every city was to have one, I began to have hope of the Maori people to revive the Maori Pioneer Battalion.

Although the Maori people have a good fighting record in this country, that is in our intertribal wars and in the fighting years ago against the Pakeha, the only occasion on which they were given the opportunity of distinguishing themselves abroad in the service of the British Empire was during the last war and among the NZ units that represented this country at the front I do not think any had a more honourable record than the Maori Pioneer Battalion.

It can be accepted on all sides of the House and by all races represented here, that there will be no hesitation in that appeal to the manpower of New Zealand; and having said that I think it would be a waste of words to give any assurance that the Maori will be with the Pakeha, as the Maori is so much part of the New Zealand nation now that that can be taken for granted ... and I do suggest to the Minister of Defence that so far as a substantial section of our people are concerned the best appeal would be this: 'A Maori Pioneer Battalion went overseas? Will you today give the State two, three, four or five Maori Battalions of the same kind?' The Maori of today is one that his ancestors might well be proud of, and I hope this country will be equally proud of him.

That is the offer we make; that is the sentiment of our people now — they have only the one past to look back to so far as service to the British Empire is concerned overseas, and that is the work of the Maori Pioneer Battalion at the Dardanelles and on the battlefields of Flanders and in France.

That brings one to a contemplation of the centennial celebrations. We have got into a difficult position in regard to the forthcoming celebrations, owing to the attitude the government took up, by simply stating to the

Maori that he should take his place in the celebrations like his Pakeha friend. The Maori is asked to co-operate. Our job as Maori members is to sit down and interpret what the statements mean, how I as a Maori am going to take a suitable part in the centennial celebrations.

My friend for Northern Maori told Parliament what is a fact — that the Maori is approaching the centennial year in anything but a jubilant mood. I told my Pakeha friends in the Wairarapa on Sunday that we would forgive them for all that happened in the last hundred years, and that would be the best way of disposing of the whole thing. I said you can break out the history books, and so on. Well, I may break out before I finish. But that is the mood of the Maori people as they approach the centennial. Why? Leaving the past aside, this is our puzzle.

The Native Department was asked by the Centennial Exhibition people what sort of scheme would portray Maori participation in the life of New Zealand in the last hundred years and they deprecated ... 'depicting the background — the starting point'. I agree so far as cannibalism is concerned. We do not want to start there. Let us start a little further this side. Fortunately there was no cannibalism in 1840, therefore we can start with a clean sheet so far as that item of Maori culture is concerned. But so far as those other things which characterise our people are concerned we were told that background was not to be displayed. We were to show how far we have progressed from that ... there were in fact restrictions from doing anything outstanding in regard to the Centennial Exhibition.

I accept what the oneness of the two peoples means. The Maori and the Pakeha can be considered entirely one, but each one can display his characteristics in his own fashion. This is how the Maori interprets the approaching centennial Exhibition we are going to have an easy year during the centennial. All we will be required to do is to sing God Save the King ... For He's a Jolly Good Fellow ... Auld Lang Syne, and that will be the end of it. Somehow we got the idea that for whole tribes to strip the only way our ancestors did, and which their descendants still do, was being deprecated.

It has got to this exasperating length, the only way to show the progress of the Maori race is to display the influence of civilisation on the Maori

— a gentleman dressed in plus fours with a bag of iron sticks behind him, fooling around acres of paddock. We presented that picture to the Exhibition authorities. When the question was raised that we should display carvings and stage hakas we were told that carving can be seen in the museum ... (But) where are the Maoris? And we would have to tell them they were in the museum.

There is still time to put things right. The position today is that they are going to do something although not nearly enough for a Centennial Exhibition which is to be one of the most prominent features in the jubilations of New Zealanders, Maori and Pakeha over the fact that we have reached the hundredth year of our constitution as part of the British Empire.

Let us consider the historical reasons for the hesitations of Maori people to take a pronounced part in the 1940 celebrations. After the Treaty was signed ... an old chief called Panakareao asked a number of questions, as also did others; but the reply to his query as to what was going to happen to his land in terms of the Treaty of Waitangi was that he could retain his land. That which went to the Queen was something invisible, a thing called mana. He made one of the most eloquent speeches made in any part of New Zealand by any Maori at that time. He said: 'All right. After all, the shadow goes to the Queen, but the substance remains with us.' He adjured his people to sign the treaty. In the middle of January this year, at Tokaanu, the people of the Lakes District had been reviewing what civilisation had meant to them in the last hundred years. One old man rose and said: 'We can reverse what was said one hundred years ago and say today that the substance has gone to the Queen and the shadow remains with us.'

Can any one conceive of a generation of Maoris agreeing that that Treaty has been a good one from the Maori standpoint? Will the Maori throw up his hat and sing God Save the King and will he say that His Majesty and the white men are jolly good fellows? Can he say that with any heart in the light of the experience of one hundred years?

What is the position at the present time (with) the work of various governments to put the Maori on the same footing as the Pakeha?

Have we succeeded? I should like to read an extract from the Sydney

Apirana Ngata speaking outside Ngati Raukawa meeting house, Otaki.

Daily Telegraph dealing with Orakei. 'Orakei is a fresh sparkling green hillside which overlooks the panorama of Auckland harbour. It is quiet, peaceful and happy. When the Englishmen came to Auckland four generations ago Orakei was the pa of the proud and brave Ngati Whatua tribe. Today one hundred dirty disease ridden Maori, wretched descendants of that great tribe, live in ugly dank whares at the foot of Orakei hill. They are the doomed survivors of the Auckland Maoris.

'Their squalid ramshackle settlement sprawls over 38 acres of the hillside, below the 700 acres on which aristocratic Auckland first built exclusive homes ten years ago, and on which a Labour Government is building 200 workers homes today ...

'A young and intelligent Maori commented: "Government build houses for Pakeha? Why government no build houses for us too?" Today one looks for an answer to the question put by the young Maori. Where have we got to at the end of one hundred years. All over New Zealand one will find small patches still occupied by the Maoris but dangerously situated with regard to civilisation and the relentlessness of civilisation.'

But getting down to the latest position. The question was whether anything could be done to make the Orakei Maori Pa worthy of the Auckland waterfront and justify the expenditure in that regard by the hope of some revival in the spirit of the Ngati Whatua tribe. I argued all round the matter and in the end arrived at this solution; that if they wanted to rehabilitate Orakei Pa, the Crown could have given an area, readjusting the boundaries, gone for a housing scheme, established a branch of the School of Maori Arts and Crafts. The City of Auckland could have put behind these Maori its economic resources ... By those means I think, the situation would be saved for the Orakei Natives.

The task is nothing if the government wishes to do it, and it could be completed in record time. The question is whether the Pakeha wants the Orakei Natives and, as it is described, the squalid pa there. Or does it want them out of the road. These are questions that could be asked about every little patch occupied by the Maoris all over New Zealand.

The question I now ask is this: Does this Parliament echo the views of the Australian writer? I am not speaking of apportioning blame; I am asking whether that is going to represent the views of the Pakehas on the Maori race, and particularly the views of officials when it comes right up against the problem at Orakei, Waiwhetu, and those other places.

What is the Pakeha going to do about it? Is the only solution that we should get out of the road? We have been getting out of the road for a hundred years.

Is that the only solution? Is the only solution to get Orakei out of the road? Waiwhetu is out of the road. If with the growth of the population the Pakeha finds us in his road, are we continually to get out of his way?

Those are questions that may well be asked at the end of a hundred years. It all arises out of the Treaty of Waitangi and its gospel of equality.

It arises, incidentally, out of what the present government says about equality. Take the matter of pensions, the injustice being done at the present time to the Maori old age pensioners in the differentiation between what they receive and what the Pakeha pensioners receive. Here is another instance of inequality, on the Native land development schemes, on housing, that some of these houses cost too much, that interest is a very substantial item in connection with housing, and should be made comparable in respect of houses built by the same government under other schemes.

Many of these houses are not of a type as suitable as they might be for Maori, who would be more comfortable with an architecture more in accord with their own race. I would like the Cabinet to see what Te Puea is doing. They are only half the cost of those being built under any other scheme. It had been decided to discontinue assisting the marae, the communal buildings of our people, proposals by the Wairarapa natives for the reconstruction of the Maori marae in the Wairarapa. The same thing is taking place at Te Oreore near Masterton, on the West Coast, up the Whanganui River, the Bay of Plenty, in North Auckland and right through. It is one of the signs of returning pride — that is a sign of revival, a sign of revivified interest in the things of which our ancestors were proud in their time. The young folk of today feel they ought to take a pride in those things too.

I cannot let the occasion go without making reference to one more matter, and that is the request made by Maori communities that there should be some authoritative definition of the effect of the Treaty of Waitangi, that the Government signalise in some way the fact that this Treaty has been in existence for a hundred years.

The position may be the correct legal position, that the Treaty of Waitangi is a 'gentleman's agreement'. I do not think the Maori people will be satisfied with that, I can say that they are not. It will not be satisfactory if we have to accept the view that this is a 'gentleman's agreement' — that it has no effect in law; that even where the government passes a law that is contravention of the Treaty, there is no recourse to the Court of Appeal.

The Honourable member for Northern Maori referred also to Maori grievances, and urged that during this centennial year the Government make a signal gesture by the settlement of those outstanding grievances. I support (him) in asking that something be done in settlement of these problems as part of our centennial ...

Now I will tell the Minister of Education (Peter Fraser) why after all we are going to enter wholeheartedly into the centennial celebrations. I go back to where I started, in regard to the question of defence, and what was happening abroad, and was likely to prejudice us in common with the rest of the British Empire.

The one thing the Maori has to be thankful for is that in spite of everything that had happened in the last hundred years — in spite of the loss of land; in spite of jeerings such as appear in the Sydney newspaper, instead of coming under some other flag, New Zealand, the Cook Islands, Niue and Western Samoa came under the British flag.

When we look abroad and compare the position of the Natives' races in these lands, we must be truly thankful that we have lived in this country, under the British flag, with the least unsympathetic of the representatives of Western civilisation.

That fact is sufficient in my opinion to justify our appealing to our people to bury their grievances for a moment, and enter with our Pakeha friends wholeheartedly into these celebrations.

Maori participation in the coming war, mainly through the 28th Maori Battalion, saw more than 16,000 men enlist in what Sir Apirana Ngati described as 'the greatest demonstration of the highest citizenship.'

He wrote: 'In this war, he (Maori) asked to take his share in the front line, and in this he has fully been indulged. Has he proved a claim to be an asset to his country? If so, he asks to be dealt with as such. An asset discovered in the crucible of war should have value in the coming peace.'[128]

---

128 *The Price of Citizenship: Ngarimu, VC (Whitcombe & Tombs), by Sir Apirana Ngata, 1943.*

A Band of Brothers

Michael Joseph Savage

September 3, 1939

Ironically, it was the Pacifist Prime Minister Michael Joseph Savage who announced New Zealand was standing alongside Britain to fight German aggression. Despite the advice of the Head of the Prime Minister's Department, Carl Berendsen, the first Labour Government had done little to prepare for the coming war.

Collective security had failed in Manchuria and Abyssinia, but Savage had held to faith in the League of Nations until the Munich crisis. As late as 1938, barely 3,000 of the 9,000 Territorial Army went into camp to train with antiquated equipment, poor communications and an airforce equipped with Vickers Vildebeste that went backwards in a decent breeze.

In 1939 (Major Haddon Donald reported) there were but three regulars to provide stiffening for the 900 citizen soldiers of the 22nd battalion who marched into Trentham Camp where their fathers had trained for the Great War.

Savage rose from his sick bed — he was suffering from cancer of the colon — to make his famous declaration of war.

Written by Solicitor General H.E. Cornish, a close friend of Berendsen, (who may well have helped in the drafting) it held more than a touch of

Henry V's call to battle at Agincourt. With its famous peroration, this speech certainly ranks as one of the most moving of the 20th century.

A pensive nation heard the Prime Minister's live broadcast on the national radio service. He began with an impromptu reference to his illness:

In this critical hour of our own and the world's history, I feel that I should abuse my privilege of addressing you if I were to speak of matters affecting myself personally. For that reason, and that reason only, I say no more of a certain recent experience that I have had than this, that it has taught me, as nothing else could have done, how quick to kindness the people of this country can be, and how easily political and other differences are extinguished by sympathy and good will.

Tonight I feel that I can say to all of you, with a sense of certainty that I have never quite felt before, 'Thank you, friends, for your kindness that you have so generously shown to me.'

Then began the formal announcement that New Zealand was about to go to war:[129]

The war on which we are entering may be a long one, demanding from us heavy and continuous sacrifice. It is essential that we realise from the beginning that our cause is worth the sacrifice. I believe in all sincerity that it is.

None of us has any hatred for the German people. For the old culture of the Germans, their songs, their poetry and their music, we have nothing but admiration and affection.

We believe that there are many millions of German people who want to live in peace and quietness as we do, threatening no one and seeking to dominate no one. But we know alas! That such a way of life is despised and rejected by the men who have seized and hold power in Germany.

We know that those men have done and are doing incalculable harm to the true interests of their country; and that they are wasting and

---

129 *Documents and Speeches on British Commonwealth Affairs 1931–1952, edited by N. Mansergh, Volume 1, pages 489–91.*

308

Michael Joseph Savage (1872–1940)

destroying the intellectual, artistic, moral and spiritual resources that their people have built up through the centuries.

In doing this, they have, for the time being, cowed the spirit of a large number of their best people. Their work of destruction they have already carried into other countries; and, despite denials, now intend to carry into Poland. If they succeed they will next attempt the overthrow of France and Britain.

Let us make no mistake about that. Of course they repudiate any such intention, but fortunately for the world, we know now, what it has taken us a long time to learn, that their promises are worthless, are made only to gain an advantage for the time being and are broken as soon as the advantage has been secured.

Not a moment too soon have Britain and France taken up arms against so faithless and unscrupulous an adversary.

The fight on which we are now engaged is one whose issue concerns all the nations of the world, whether as yet they realise it or not. We are fighting a doctrine that springs from a contempt of human nature — a doctrine that government is the affair only of a self elected elite who, without consulting the people, may irrevocably determine what the people shall and shall not do.

The masses are used to be as instruments of power in the hands of their masters. They are to be given slogans and directed towards this or that objective approved by those masters. But never are they to be treated as free men, as individual and responsible souls. The individual man is submerged and forgotten — the intrinsic worthiness of his personality contemptuously ignored. Freedom of action and expression is denied to him. Dissent or criticism is brutally suppressed. These are a few of the incidents of the Nazi Philosophy that is seeking to thrust itself everywhere over Europe today and the rest of the world tomorrow.

Nazism is militant and insatiable paganism. In its short but terrible history, it has caused incalculable suffering. If permitted to continue, it will spread misery and desolation throughout the world. It cannot be appeased or conciliated. Either it or civilisation must disappear. To destroy it, but not the great nation which it has so cruelly cheated, is the task of those who have taken up arms against Nazism.

My God, prosper those arms.

I am satisfied that nowhere will the issue be more clearly understood than in New Zealand — where for almost a century, behind the sure shield of Britain, we have enjoyed and cherished freedom and self government. Both with gratitude for the past, and confidence in the future, we range ourselves without fear beside Britain.

Where she goes, we go; where she stands, we stand.

We are only a small and young nation but we are one and all a band of brothers, and we march forward with a union of hearts and souls to a common destiny.

The Habit of Loyalty

Col. Edward Puttick

September 27, 1939

New Zealand went to war ill–prepared in 1939 but with a martial tradition to which to aspire. Colonel Puttick[130] (by 1942 General Sir Edward Puttick, DSO) put that to the officers and NCOs of the forces gathering midweek at Wellington's historic Trentham Camp in September 1939.

They were to form part of 2 NZEF, following in the footsteps of 1 NZEF, one of our young nation's finest constructs. Puttick's knowledge of the French army orders of 1919 suggests that he might have been with the Division in March 1918, or if not, home again in 1919, proud to note the place the French Ministry of War gave to the Division.

Puttick's address holds real irony against the lack of preparedness with which men joined their nation's citizen army. Despite the obvious countdown to war, about which Carl Berendsen had been warning successive governments since 1934, the Territorial camps in 1938 were badly attended.

So troops, as Puttick's address indicates, went into forced training, with inadequate supporting arms, makeshift clothing, and significantly few

---

130 W. David McIntyre. 'Puttick, Edward — Biography', from the Dictionary of New Zealand Biography. Te Ara — the Encyclopedia of New Zealand.

Edward Puttick (1890–1976)

professional officers. Haddon Donald, later Major Haddon Donald, told of there being only two professional officers allocated to the Wellington battalion of 900 citizen soldiers. Their lack of preparedness was to wreak havoc in the early disastrous campaigns, best told in Sir Geoffrey Cox's[131] book *Two Battles — of Crete and Sidi Rezegh.*

Only out of those painful fields did the 2nd NZEF emerge, like its predecessor, with pride. By the end of the Italian campaign, Donald called it the best and most versatile heavy division in the world. In Geoff Cox's term, and he was a part, NZ Div was 'the Xth Legion of the 8th Army'. Its soldiers wore the black flash with pride.

It all began with the rousing call to arms by Colonel Puttick, Officer Commanding the Central Military District, at Trentham on September 27, 1939:[132]

War demands efficiency, especially efficiency in leaders. We need have no doubt about the quality of our men. They will be equal to any in the world. The need is for you leaders, as far as possible, to measure up to the same heights.

So far as I have any part in this Force, I would like to make it quite clear that no considerations whatsoever other than those of efficiency in the officers and NCOs will have any influence on me. If an officer or NCO is not up to the standard required, I shall have no hesitation in taking him away and substituting a better man.

In welcoming you to this historic ground for our military forces, you should remember the big part Trentham played in the last war, when assemblies like this were frequent, and since the war, in the courses of instruction that have influenced the military efficiency of our country.

You yourselves are now to enter on a course of instruction.

It will prove valuable learning for you, and for setting the standard of instruction when training your men. You will find it a very hard course, with long hours, but as time is all too short, you will welcome the opportunity to fit yourselves for the very responsible task which will

---

131 *Geoffrey Cox', URL: http://www.nzhistory.net.nz/people/geoffrey–cox, (Ministry for Culture and Heritage).*
132 *Adapted from the Evening Post report of September 30, 1939.*

confront you in the future. The course provides a means of acquiring knowledge but it requires each of you to make a special personal endeavour to benefit to the utmost from it ... in matters such as word of command, methods of instruction ... and improving your own methods.

On the arrival of the men on October 3, all of you, officers and non commissioned officers, must, in your own sphere, make a special effort to ensure that all the arrangements work smoothly. Avoid fuss and excitement ... use your imagination, think well ahead, know your job, and be prepared for all eventualities.

With regard to uniforms ... you should remember that everything was in train for the provision of better uniforms ... Your duty is to see that the uniforms fit properly and pay particular attention to the fitting of boots. Nothing is more trying than ill-fitting boots. They can cause infinite harm to the feet and interrupt training.

You yourselves as leaders have a duty to maintain the highest possible standards. You must cultivate self-discipline in order to be able to maintain, as is your duty, good discipline throughout the force. You must take special care to see that orders are properly promulgated, so that the men know them.

You yourselves must scrupulously obey all orders you receive, and similarly must insist upon those under you also obeying orders.

So far as training is concerned, unless you make a prior study of the work to be done each day, you will not get the best results. You must cultivate the habit of loyalty to the organisation to which you belong, and loyalty not only to your superiors but also to the men under you.

As an indication of the high standards we must aspire to, our responsibility is to maintain the tradition New Zealanders established during the Great War ... a tradition that is recorded in Army Orders in Paris November 1919:

'The President of the Council of the Ministry of War mentions the name of ... Major General Sir Andrew Russell of the New Zealand Expeditionary Force, who has led a splendid division to countless victories. Its exploits have not been equaled ... its reputation was such that on the arrival of the division on the Somme battlefield during the most critical days of March 1918, the flight of the inhabitants immediately

ceased. The division covered itself with fresh glory during the battles of Ancre, at the Sambre, at Puesceux au Mont, Bapauame, Crevecoeur and Le Quesnoy ...'

Now I ask you to take notice of one fact: that on the arrival on the battlefield of these soldiers the flight of the inhabitants immediately ceased. It was indeed one of the most critical periods of the war. The line had been broken, the enemy was pressing through to anticipated victory, and the unfortunate people of the countryside were fleeing in terror from the horrors of the Boche invasion.

Figure to yourselves what it all meant. The road was crowded with fugitives, old men, despairing and weeping women and children, bearing with them such few household treasures as they could drag along. Then the arrival of troop trains with reinforcements — company after company of khaki men detrain and hurry into the firing line.

'Qui sont ces gens,'[133] the people ask? It was then the flight was stayed. The officer directing the evacuation sent his aide de camp to inquire the reason. 'General, the people say they are not going any further. These soldiers are from New Zealand et tout va bien.[134] They will soon be back in their homes — in fact they are getting ready to return now.'

Such was the reputation of our men for valour and manhood, and conduct, that these war–stricken countrymen knew that they could confide their goods and chattels, and their lives, and the honour of their women in their safekeeping.

I can hold up to you no finer model as soldiers than was shown by the men that a little nation in a far off island in the Pacific sent to the aid of France in her hour of peril.

Puttick's words continued to inspire long after the war.

His son–in–law, Ralph Mullins, a brilliant External Affairs officer (1953–70) kept a copy of the General's Trentham address at his desk to provide inspiration in advising on our complex military involvement in South East Asia after World War Two.

---

133 *Translation from French: 'Who are these people?'*
134 *Translation from French: '...and all is well.'*

National Unity

Peter Fraser

June 7, 1940

Peter Fraser, acting Prime Minister during Michael Joseph Savage's last months, was a messy decision maker but his steerage of the country through World War Two inspired British leader Winston Churchill to observe that New Zealand 'never put a foot wrong'.[135]

Adroit and astute, he underwrote the 'care, skill and courage' of the born leader, with a priceless ability to sense trouble. Heavy handed and domineering he might be,[136] but he put that to good purpose. In 1941, in Alexandria, at lunch on the Warspite, he leaned on an exhausted Royal Navy to rescue a last cruiser–load of Kiwi infantry from Crete.

Fraser's wartime and United Nations speeches confirm the accolade, in limited use in the New Zealand context, of statesman.

Churchill praised him as staunch and clear thinking, vital assets in peace and war, and in the sweat and tears of the political arena.

Fraser's clarity of thought shone through in the first major crisis of the War, the Fall of France in June 1940. Britain had just established

---

135 *Tomorrow Comes the Song: A Life of Peter Fraser (Penguin Books), by Dr Michael Bassett, with Michael King, 2001.*

136 *His colleague, the Attorney General and Minister of Justice in the first Labour Government, Rex Mason, was to call Fraser 'a sadist' for his vicious treatment of opponents within the Labour Party. Page 110, Sacred Cows and Rogue Elephants (GPO Publishing) by J.L. Robson, 1987.*

a government of national unity. With the Opposition calling for a Parliamentary Coalition, the Labour Government argued for a broader based nationwide coalition. Fraser's view prevailed.

After a Secret Session of the House in June 1940,[137] the Leader of the Opposition, Adam Hamilton, called for a Great Council of the Realm, based on the House of Representatives:[138]

This is the time for inspiring leadership through which our work and feelings may be absolutely united. In this crisis the lead must come from the Government and Parliament ...

Our present disunited condition cannot be allowed to drag on ...

The Prime Minister appreciates as I do the extreme gravity of the situation ... We must act swiftly as one great force. Two things are essential — unity and action. This House has to become in my opinion the Great Council of the Realm, uniting the people.

Peter Fraser held to the need, imperative in his view, if somewhat clumsily stated, for a broad–based institution of national unity. What shows is his masterly appreciation of the House and his uncanny nursing of its susceptibilities in insisting on the course of action on which he had determined.

Fraser responded to Hamilton:[139]

In regard to the necessity for national unity, prompt action and efficient administration, there is no difference of opinion. The question is how to bring that about in the most efficient way ...

I cannot imagine that anyone will take the view that national unity begins and ends in this House; and I would ask that the Government's proposals ... be examined ... and that the matter be decided during the course of the next week.

In regard to the necessity for action in regard to the Government's legislation, the House's legislation, the country's legislation — the

---

137 *War time Secret Session PM 22/5/1.*
138 *New Zealand Parliamentary Debates (Hansard), Volume 148, June 7, 1940.*
139 *New Zealand Parliamentary Debates (Hansard), Volume 148, page 149.*

legislation that had become known as the 'all in' legislation — if it is to be left on the statute book without being implemented, that would not do ... because it be just a delusion and a sham.

Consequently the Government proposes, whether in company with the Opposition in the way it has suggested, or in any way which recommends itself to both parties, and to others who are interested and ready to help, or just as the Government is at present, to push forward that legislation as fast as is absolutely necessary ...

What the Government has been anxious to ascertain from honourable members is in what way, if any, the measures of the Government have fallen short, and in what ways if any they can be improved; and I leave it to the House to say whether we have gained a great deal from the secret session.

That session was conducted in a good spirit. There was incisive criticisms — and rightly so — and there was a considerable number of suggestions. The sum total is that the Government feels stronger than ever in its war efforts. That is the sum total of the result of the secret session.

Fraser's argument carried the day.

'Stand for New Zealand!'

Lt. Col. Howard Kippenberger

May 1941

At the outbreak of World War Two, New Zealand reconstituted the famous Silent Division of the previous war. Its finest citizen soldier proved to be Howard Kippenberger.[140] After serving as a young private in World War One, he became a Canterbury lawyer, and continued to study military history.

During the first desperate campaigns in Greece and Crete, 'Kip' (as he was widely known) made perhaps the best short speech since the Maniapoto defied the Redcoats in the Waikato Wars.

As the New Zealand Commander, Lieutenant Colonel Kippenberger — later a Major General, and knighted after the war — stood among his soldiers as they retreated during the running battle of Galatea, with its famous bayonet charge, in May 1941.

Kippenberg stood firm, rallying his men with his steadfast cry:

Stand for New Zealand! Stand every man who is a soldier! Stand for New Zealand!

---

140 *Further reading — Kippenberger: The Gift of Leadership (Random House), by Denis McLean, 2008.*

Lt. Col. Kippenberger (1897–1957) receives the Distinguished Service Order from General Auchinleck, Commander–in–Chief of the Middle East Forces, at Baggush on November 4, 1941.

History tells us his actions, and the rearguard resistance of his men, helped save the Allied situation in Crete, allowing most of the expeditionary force to withdraw across the mountains, to be evacuated by the Royal Navy to Egypt.

'Winning the Peace'

Peter Fraser

August 15, 1945

As World War Two moved to its conclusion, Prime Minister Peter Fraser was already looking to the future — something he excelled at, according to his Labour Party colleague Walter Nash who said of him in his valedictory in Parliament[141] that he had an uncanny sense of vision.

'His intuition was something out of the normal, and greater than that of any other man I have known. Perhaps it had something to do with the land he came from. The Scots seem to have some more highly developed faculty than others, and Peter Fraser had a remarkable intuition as to what was likely to happen under given circumstances. This faculty enabled him to give forecasts of war developments more accurately than any other man I know. He used to talk to me of things that were likely to happen, and I do not think I ever found him wrong.'

Having suffered the death of his wife in March, Fraser shrugged off a succession of minor health ailments to wait for confirmation that the war was over, and to his and New Zealand's role in establishing a new world.

On August 15, news came from London that Japan had formally surrendered and having already announced a two–day public holiday in

141 *New Zealand Parliamentary Debates (Hansard), Vol. 204/30.*

Peter Fraser (1884–1950)

celebration, Fraser broadcast a victory message over the national radio airwaves from Wellington:[142]

---

142 *Evening Post, August 15, 1945.*

Throughout the world as in New Zealand, the people will greet the news of the Japanese capitulation with deep relief and thanksgiving.

Its victorious conclusion will bring joy into many New Zealand homes. It means that our servicemen and servicewomen, after their magnificent record in every sphere of warfare, will now turn towards home and families. The people can be assured that the Government will do everything possible to facilitate the earliest return of our armed forces from overseas.

This morning I am able to announce that that war is won — finally and completely won.

Japan has surrendered unconditionally. She has accepted the terms put forward by the United Nations on behalf of the Allied Powers.

Nearly six years — six long, anxious, worrying, dangerous, tragic years have passed since the announcement of war — since New Zealand stepped unhesitatingly and proudly to the side of our Mother Country to fight for worldwide freedom, democracy, and international justice.

Fraser reminded his radio listeners that because of Michael Savage's illness, it had been he who had made the formal declaration of war in 1939.

That morning, speaking with a heavy heart, with regret and sorrow that the way of war was the only way to freedom, that the alternative to fighting was universal slavery under a heartless, hideous, and murderous tyranny such as the world had never previously known, I said: 'We cannot depart from the principles of freedom and justice in international affairs. If we do not stand by those ideals our civilisation will collapse and crumble into dust. We address ourselves with sad hearts but with firm determination to the immediate task in hand — the task of rallying all the forces and resources of our land so that we can stand side by side with the United Kingdom and the other nations of the British Commonwealth in their struggle for international righteousness. The conflict is between international friendship and international brute force; between reason and ruthlessness, between democracy and despotism. Not in anger but in sorrow, not in lightheartedness but with heavy hearts, not in hatred but with a grave sense of great responsibility to mankind and to the future of humanity, not in malice and revenge, but with a prayer for peace on our lips, the British peoples today dedicate themselves to the work of overthrowing the oppressor and freeing the peoples of the earth from bondage and slavery to a ruthless and cruel tyranny.'

Some months later, Mr Savage expressed his view of the war position when he said: 'Unless Britain and her Allies win all is lost.'

Again in words that will live for ever in the history of New Zealand, he said: 'Both with gratitude for the past, and with confidence in the future, we range ourselves without fear beside Britain. Where she goes, we go, where she stands, we stand. We are only a small and a young nation but we are one and all a band of brothers, and we march forward with a union of hearts and wills to a common destiny.'

Now, we have marched with hearts and wills united to victory. When the Japanese sign the terms six terrible years of war will be over. The surrender of Japan means at long last the achievement of final victory. It is the triumph over the formidable and treacherous enemy which threatened our shores so closely and the last of the members of the terrible triple tyranny of Nazi and Fascist powers which aimed at world domination and dictatorship and which has been crushed in the dust.

It marks the ignoble but thoroughly deserved fate of the nation which began the era of aggression 14 years ago in Manchuria. From that point the forces of evil, emboldened by their first success, grew in arrogance and power. Italy and Germany followed Japan in the path of aggression and barbarism, and to all of them there has come a terrible retribution.

Today we think with gratitude of China. For eight years she fought an heroic fight against great military odds, never yielding an inch from her firm determination to resist the Japanese aggressor.

We think of the gallant and effective part Australia has played in the Pacific war. Her forces inflicted the first defeat at Milne Bay and in the mountains of New Guinea and later in Borneo.

We think of our friends the Americans, treacherously attacked at Pearl Harbour. Then, without even pausing to take breath, rallying her mighty forces, military and industrial, and sweeping westward ever, ever westward and northward until Japan began to crumple and crumble under her overwhelming attacks. Bataan, Corregidor, Tarawa, Saipan, Midway, Leyte, Lingayen, Iwo Jima, Okinawa, are among a list of imperishable deeds.

The Battle of the Coral Sea stemmed and turned back from New Caledonia, Fiji, and New Zealand what seemed to be an innumerable and invincible host, swarming like locusts over the islands of the Pacific. We think of the Netherlands East Indies and the fine, defiant, unflinching stand of its Government, its forces, and its people.

Our neighbours of New Caledonia and Tahiti and of Indo–China kept the flag of Free and Fighting France flying in the Pacific.

Today we can acknowledge with pride the loyalty of the native peoples of the Pacific islands. They showed as much hatred and detestation of Japanese domination as the Australians or Americans or British or New Zealanders.

We are glad that British troops and British ships and British planes have played such a noble part in the war against Japan, particularly in Burma and in the battle of Japan, and that India has been able to contribute to the victory so conspicuously in brave men and essential munitions.

New Zealand took its full part in the Pacific war as it did in the Middle East and in Italy. Our Navy, Army, and Air Force engaged the enemy wherever they met them and won the admiration, praise, and complete confidence of American, British, and Australian commanders. But the war was a world–wide war. Let us glance at some of the names and deeds made immortal by the valour and the blood of the men of the free nations.

From the first to the last, from the battle of the River Plate to the battle of Japan, the New Zealand Navy was in the war, fighting most gallantly and effectively. Our Second Division bore the brunt of the battle in Greece, Crete, the Libyan desert, Sidi Rezegh, Sidi Assiez, Minqua Quam, Mareth Line, Cassino.

Our Air Force has been invaluable in the Pacific, but in every land and over every sea where blows were struck for freedom men of our Air Force or New Zealanders in the British Air Force were flying and fighting as New Zealand airmen can and have done —second to none.

Fraser finished the broadcast with one last plea for New Zealanders to look forward:[143]

Let us rejoice and lift up our hearts in gratitude to God ... Let us prove ourselves by our industry worthy of winning the peace so that fear from want and aggression will be abolished and our great victory will endure.

As the end of the war had approached, Fraser had been positioning New Zealand so it could, in his words, 'win the peace.' He saw opportunities in developing a peacetime co–operation with Australia, born from the Anzac spirit in war, and establishing new styles of relationships with Pacific nations and the United States.

In autumn 1944, the Tasman neighbours signed an Anzac pact and agreed to establish a South Pacific regional organisation, to which the great powers might graciously accede. Fraser's vision enveloped the widest range of ongoing and practical regional co–operation and he laid the seeds for free trade agreements.

In March 1944, Fraser put forward his plan for closer co–operation in the form of the Australia–New Zealand Agreement. Here are extracts of his speech to Parliament:[144]

I want to emphasise that ... there is no sinking or subordinating of one to the other, or discarding the opinions of either country. Collaboration? Yes. Co–operation? Yes. Unity where unity can be achieved, but where unity of opinion cannot be achieved, then there shall be friendly agreement to differ. This is the position. Neither country is subordinated to the other....

In regard to the post hostilities period, the governments of both countries feel that it is only right that we should express vital interest in possible armistice and armistice terms ... While there is nothing of the Uriah Heep about either government or their peoples, we have a sense of responsibility, and there is a realisation that without the co–

---

143 *Auckland Star, August 15, 1945.*
144 *New Zealand Parliamentary Debates (Hansard), Volume 264, page 792.*

operation and help of our larger allies we and our efforts and ideals will be stultified.

Therefore there is nothing in the way of seeking to differ from, or quarrel with the other United Nations. On the contrary, the Agreement makes the widest possible provision for the greatest measure of co-operation. In fact all the nations of the Pacific are invited to express their willingness to co-operate with us; but we do say if an Agreement is signed in Cairo, in Teheran, or in Moscow, then such agreement affects us, and ultimately our countries should have the right to express opinions upon them ...

... We see a defence zone in which Australia and New Zealand must take great responsibility. Nobody can say dogmatically at the present moment as to what the position will be in connection with the necessity for defence after the war ... But we have to make provision for whatever arrangements there are required in the future and, without bowing down to militarism, without becoming slaves of any military conceptions or military caste or militarism in all its repulsive features, we will have to co-operate and arrange with our friends of the United Nations — with all of them — for the security, in the sense of defence, of the South Pacific and the South West Pacific.

The Agreement provides for a South Seas Regional Commission. The idea of an area Commission is not original. In the Caribbean Sea area there is a regional Commission ... It is a Commission of a similar nature which is proposed for the South Seas ...

Australia will also be glad to come into this arrangement ... the French people of New Caledonia ... the Netherlands Government will be prepared to discuss closer collaboration in (health) and in the direction of education.

... We will be very pleased if the ... United States of America ... Portugal, or any of the powers ... in the Pacific, will collaborate and co-operate with us ... it is essential that our friendship (with the United States) should be cemented as closely as it is possible for two nations to celebrate a friendship.

The Chicago Tribune tries to misrepresent the Agreement as being directed against the United States of America. Nothing could be more untrue; nothing more stupid ... we are entitled to be heard in peace as in war ... We had a true appreciation of the position our two countries occupy in the world ...

The Agreement stands for (co-operation and mutual assistance). The Australian Government stands for that. The New Zealand Government stands for that. The New Zealand Government stands for that friendship with all the nations of the Pacific — indeed with all the nations of the world, particularly with the great ally to whom we owe so much.

.... the Agreement has been an important step in democratic progress. It has brought the two British nations in the South Pacific closer together. Provision is made for consultations and conferences with Ministers at periods of six months ... for the interchange of opinions of departmental officials when such consultations are needed.

The right hand of fellowship is held out by the two British democratic nations to our great neighbours in the Pacific, to the United States of America, to Russia, to China, to the Netherlands Government, and to the French Committee of Liberation.

We believe that the document marks a great epoch, by emphasising the right of the two nations to be considered in all matters of international importance which will affect our lives ...

I believe that the Agreement is a great step forward in fulfillment of the Atlantic Charter, because no two governments on earth stand more for freeing the world from fear and want than do those of Australia and New Zealand.

In July 1945, a month before Japan capitulated, Fraser addressed Parliament on the establishment of the United Nations Charter, after he had returned from a conference of world leaders in San Francisco. Again, his focus was on carving an international profile of New Zealand based on the future peace, rather than based on wartime allegiance.

Extracts from Fraser's speech:[145]

Sir, I beg to move that the House of Representatives of New Zealand in Parliament assembled approves and recommends the ratification of

---

145 *New Zealand Parliamentary Debates (Hansard), July 1945.*

the Charter of the United Nations ...

My report (is) ... the decisions of 50 united nations ... I do not know if there has ever been in the history of mankind a more important document than the Charter of the United Nations ... important because ... it marks a great opportunity, and perhaps the last great opportunity, that the nations of the earth will have of forming an organisation to maintain peace, to prevent aggression, and to make impossible in the future the sort of attacks that were indulged in by the Nazi and Fascist powers.

The United Nations Organisation can only succeed if nations decide to implement its principles and provision honestly and determinedly with singleness of mind and purity of heart. If that is not done, success will not accompany the adoption and ratification of the Charter. If the nations do enter into their obligations with a determination to honour them, and do honour them, then it will provide the means of permanent peace.

The genesis of the Charter is really contained in two documents, the first being the 'four freedoms' — freedom of speech and expression, freedom of religion, freedom from fear, and freedom from want enunciated by the great leader of the American people, President Roosevelt, whose loss was felt by the whole free world ...

The second document is the Atlantic Charter, which will live beside the American Declaration of Independence as one of the great documents of the human race ... Following on those declarations came the Dumbarton Oaks Conference ... of the three powers — the United States of America, the United Kingdom and Russia ... Their officials ... laid the foundations of the Charter ... Those decisions were conveyed to San Francisco, where the 50 nations met. Prior (to that) we visited London, and discussed matters ... with the representatives of South Africa, of Australia, of Canada, and of India ... The United Kingdom did not expect that the British dominions would necessarily accept all the United Kingdom representatives had accepted at Dumbarton Oaks and at Yalta ... It is a paradox of the British Commonwealth that the freer we are the more we are bound up together ...

At the Conference there were 46 nations to start with, and there were

50 at the conclusion. The nations admitted were Argentina, White Russia, Ukraine and Denmark ... The Presidents who presided were Mr Stettinius,[146] Mr Eden,[147] Dr. Soong,[148] representing China, and Mr. Molotov,[149] representing Russia ...

Altogether there (were) 12 committees operating, and that sometimes placed a strain on the New Zealand delegation ... we felt we acted in accordance with the democratic and progressive spirit of New Zealand ...

In regard to the purposes and principles (we) presented an amendment. We felt that there was a grave defect in that no provision was made, as had been made in the Covenant of the League of Nations for preventing aggression ... Of course, we know the weakness of the League; but ... there was nothing wrong with (its) principles ... it had many weaknesses. It had not the military power and force that the new organisation I hope, will have, and must have, if it is to exist at all.. But the League ... failed because many members ... did not carry out their obligations ...

I am not going to say that the new organisation is perfect, or will function unless the actions determine that it will function ...

Therefore we moved collectively to resist any active aggression against any member ... the decision was the majority should be two thirds ... the (New Zealand) amendment ... received 26 votes for it and 18 against. It fell just short of a two–thirds majority, and therefore was not carried.

Try as I could, I never understood why it was not agreed to by the sponsoring parties, and I cannot understand it now. It seemed to me so simple and so open that we should make a declaration that, if aggression was contemplated or took place, it should be stopped, and that power should be used to stop it. As a matter of fact that is the whole purpose of the Charter; and there is provision for steps to do that very thing; but that such a declaration was not made was incomprehensible to me, unless it is that we have not yet reached the stage where the great nations of the world fully trust each other.

In spite of that, I have the greatest hopes for the success of the Charter. As

146 Edward Stettinius, Jr.,United States Secretary of State.
147 Anthony Eden, Leader of the British House of Commons, and future Prime Minister.
148 T.V.Soong, Minister of Foreign Affairs, China.
149 Vyacheslav Molotov, Minister of Foreign Affairs, Russia.

the organisation is formed and as the nations work together, confidence and trust will grow. While we sat in conference, however, things were happening ... that showed the need for an international organisation to stop aggression ... we must exhaust every effort to establish an organisation that will promote discipline as well as peace and goodwill among nations ...

Now the powers of the Assembly ... as adopted at San Francisco are much wider than was projected at the Dumbarton Oaks Conference ... we had a conception that the Assembly should have more power ... Senator Vandenberg[150] made the suggestion that the Assembly should be the town meeting of the world ... that any question should be discussed in the General Assembly ... and finally that was agreed to ... For some reason Russia thought that the discussion provisions were too wide. On the other hand we thought that they could not be too wide. We felt that the Assembly, which ought to be the parliament of mankind, should have even greater powers.

We felt that the Security Council should have great powers, and it has, and it agreed to report at every meeting of the Assembly.

Fraser then explained the relationship of the Assembly with the Security Council and the composition of the Security Council with five permanent members and six elected periodically.

... (the Security Council) is of course the executive body, the cutting edge of the Charter, as it were, and it wields very great powers indeed ... with obligations ... in connection with the Armed Forces. The Security Council is to be the body that will operate for the United Nations in connection with disputes, questions of aggression, sanctions, and the use of military forces to prevent aggression and war.

One question that caused a good deal of discussion was the veto. If there had been an entirely free vote ... the rule of unanimity among the five permanent powers (agreed to at Yalta) would have been swept aside by a very large majority ... the New Zealand delegation took up a strong

---

150 *Arthur H. Vandenberg, United States Republican Senator, Michigan, and later appointed chair of Senate Foreign Relations Committee.*

stand against the use of what became known as the veto by one Power. That is exactly what it amounted to — the veto of one of the permanent powers ... it appeared so utterly ridiculous that a large power could stop its own condemnation that it was agreed by the representatives of the large powers that if that actually was done, then there was an end of action under the provisions of the Charter, and any action would have to be taken outside, and the Charter would fail.

In that case we said: 'Why have it there?' The reply to that seemed to be: 'It was agreed to and we are sticking to it.' Then we said: 'We will agree to conforming to the unanimity of four — that there must be four of the five powers of members unanimous.'

That is the reason we tried to amend the Charter ... at what point (indeed) can the veto be exercised? ... it was agreed no power could prevent (discussion) but there could not be a formal investigation ... one power can ... flout the conscience of the world ... We thought that was wrong, that it was untenable, undemocratic, and we did all we could do to prevent it.

But ... finally it was seen that the veto, the rule of unanimity among the five permanent powers was just immovable, that it was a condition of the Charter. The Charter had either to be accepted with that provision, or there would be no Charter at all. So therefore at the final voting, after doing all we possibly could ... 15 of the countries., including our own delegation, stood aside from voting, and the provision was passed. Finally of course every nation voted for the Charter ... (of course) we could ... have prevented the two thirds majority that was necessary, but if that was done the grave responsibility of preventing a Charter of any kind being arrived at would have been on our shoulders ...

'Better some form of international organisation, with whatever defects, than no organisation at all.'

The latter would mean the loss of all hope (in face of) ... the destruction and devastation that will be wrought ... for future wars, if there are future wars. With that terrible knowledge in our possession ... any one of us would vote for any organisation, if only a debating society, where people would come together, where the nations of the earth would come together, and try to understand better; for its seems to me to be either this Charter, this organisation of mankind or the complete destruction of civilisation and mankind together (this before the Atom Bomb) and that justifies us in supporting any form of international organisation that will hold out any hope to the world.

The speech then dealt with provisions for regional arrangements (such as the Pan American Conference) and for the Economic and Social Council, the Trusteeship Council, and the International Court of Justice. Notably the Security Council and the United Nations Organisation were not to interfere in questions of a domestic mature and mandated territories; and colonies had to be looked at as a trusteeship aimed at self expression, self government and independence.

Fraser summed up:

The New Zealand delegation went to the Conference feeling that it would first have to do all that it could to advance the creation among the nations of an international organisation. We did that.

Never at any moment did we deviate from our expression given by myself at the plenary session that there must be an international organisation or there will be no hope for the world. We went with the desire and determination to do what we could to improve the provisions made at Dumbarton Oaks and Yalta. We failed in many of our major efforts, but we succeeded in some. We worked along with other of the smaller and medium sized nations, particularly our neighbour Australia. There was the closest co-operation and unanimity in regard to the vast majority of questions ...

Were we right in feeling that in working for a definite pledge against aggression; in opposing the rule of unanimity called the veto among the great powers; in advocating social and economic advancements; and particularly higher standards of living and full employment, and in endeavoring to make the trusteeship provisions for the people that have not yet attained to the status of self government as humane and comprehensive and generous as possible? In doing all that, I say we asked ourselves if our feeling was correct and that it reflected the Government's policy. We replied as best we could in the affirmative and that we were acting in the spirit of New Zealand, truly representing the Parliament and people of this country in the stand we took.

We (certainly) fought ... to make the Charter as democratic, progressive and effective as possible. When we achieved the maximum that it was possible to achieve ... we had to choose between Charter or no Charter, and we could not hesitate for one moment ...

President Truman ... said that the Conference had framed a document that would have a lasting effect upon the world; if it was administered in the right spirit it would confer lasting benefits; if it was not entered into in the right spirit ... there would be another disappointment, another failure ... that the great nations had great power ... if they used it right it would be a blessing, if they used it wrongly and unjustly in their own interests, then it would be curse to the world ... the UN was not the solution of the problems but it provided the way.

To use words I have used before, the road has been laid towards world peace. The road has been laid towards better standards of living, towards full employment, towards proper, humane and responsible treatment of the subject races of the earth, towards the enlightenment of backward peoples, and above all the road is laid to complete goodwill and understanding and friendship among the nations of the earth, and that road is based on freedom, particularly freedom from fear and freedom from want. The road is there. It is for the nations to say whether they will take it.

I hope we will take the first step along that road by adopting the motion I have moved.

New Zealand was ready to take its seat at the international table.

The Sacrifice of Others

Capt. Charles Upham, VC

October 11, 1945

New Zealand war hero Captain Charles Upham returned from battles in the desert and three years as a prisoner of war to find himself much in demand by newspaper journalists and groups who wanted him to speak of his exploits.

But the double winner of the Victoria Cross — a man who could have won both medals 'several times over', as one officer noted — was reticent to talk about his experiences. His wife, Molly, told the English *Daily Mail*: 'He used to get awfully annoyed when I spoke of his experiences. He didn't even hint that he did anything special in the desert.'[151]

His first VC was awarded after he was wounded in battle in Crete in May 1941. When told of the award, he said: 'It was meant for the men.'[152]

His second VC (the Bar) followed his part in the first Battle for El Alamein[153] in July 1942.

Upham's modesty was proverbial. In September 1945, when handed a telegram advising him of the Bar, Upham told a reporter: 'Naturally I feel

---

151 *Evening Post, September 28, 1945.*
152 *Mark of the Lion: The Story of Charles Upham VC and Bar (Penguin Books), by Kenneth Sandford, 2003.*
153 *A Tale of Two Battles: Personal Memoir of Crete and the Western Desert 1941 (Kimber), by Sir Geoffrey Cox, 1987.*

337

Charles Upham (1908–1994)

some pride in this distinction, but hundreds of others have done more than I did. They could have given it to any one of them.'[154]

The story is that he refused a knighthood. When comrades revived the proposal, Buckingham Palace (whatever the view of the New Zealand Government) refused the request. The Queen's Honours, once declined, are not renewed. Was the Queen for once wrong? Or did New Zealand not press the case?

As much as Upham wanted to dodge the limelight, there were times when he had no choice but to face an adoring New Zealand public.

Such was the case when he attended a State lunch for Victoria Cross winners in October 1945.

The Toast was moved by Acting Prime Minister Walter Nash, and by the Leader of the Opposition, S.G. Holland, a World War One veteran and future Prime Minister. As the most distinguished soldier, Upham was expected to reply to the Toast.

Upham, as always, used the opportunity to promote the welfare of others, rather than himself. Upham replied, not about heroism, but about the morale and leadership of the Division, and the needs of soldiers returning to civilian life.

His words bring to mind Abraham Lincoln's phrase from his Second Inaugural about the stress on returning soldiers:

'To care for him who shall have borne the battle.'

We have taken the liberty of transposing the report of his speech from *The Press* into direct speech.[155]

You do me great honour, but you also embarrass me.

The only circumstance that has brought me to this function is this. I am the representative of a 100,000 others. Their exploits are as fitting of the reward as mine.

My exploits were only made possible through the sacrifice of others. There were many others who did more than I did.

A New Zealander may not appear very formidable in the street. But you can be very proud of the New Zealand soldier and of the Division.

---

154 *Evening Post, September 26, 1945.*
155 *The Press, October 12, 1945.*

We earned so great a reputation overseas that a New Zealand soldier flash[156] would take us anywhere. That success and high morale was due to splendid leadership.

My belief is that the morale and leadership of the Division were higher than that of any other division in any army.

Discipline was good. The fellows were always looking for a stoush. The key was our confidence in our leaders. We had no messing things up as we had in some theatres of war. Our men went into action full of confidence.

There is one thing I want to ask.

When our men come back, people who are in a position to do so, should show their thanks in a practical way. There will be among us men who are maimed, suffering from wounds, ill or mentally ill. They will need homes, furniture, jobs. Please show them your practical help and your greatest patience.

The following year, Charles and Molly Upham bought a farm at Rafa Downs, beneath the Kaikoura Ranges and where they could raise a family in relative anonymity.

Forty years after his wartime valour, he told a television interviewer he would have been happy not to have been awarded a VC at all as it made people expect too much of him.

'I don't want to be treated differently from any other bastard,' he said.[157]

---

156 *A piece of material sewn onto uniform to signify rank.*
157 *The Telegraph (UK), November 24, 1994.*

340

Liberty and Liberalism

Jack Marshall

1947

In 1946 Labour won a tight election with a majority of the four Maori seats. Several returned servicemen stood for and entered Parliament. In the National Opposition three, all liberals, and at times radical liberals, were to prove outstanding figures — Jack Marshall[158] and Ralph Hanan[159] of the 2 NZEF and Tom Shand[160] of the RNZAF.

All became ministers in the Holland Government in the 1950s and returned in the 1960s as the influential core of the Holyoake administration, arguably the most effective since the Seddon era, and of the 20th century.

Marshall, who rose to the formidable rank of Major in the NZEF was a young lawyer of equally formidable intellect and energy. He knew who he was and where he had come from, and had the intellectual capacity to establish where he was going, and the principles by which he would travel. His maiden speech in 1947 was the finest expression of New Zealand's basic liberal highway since it was outlined by George Grey. Marshall's

---

158 Barry Gustafson. 'Marshall, John Ross — Biography', from the Dictionary of New Zealand Biography. Te Ara — the Encyclopedia of New Zealand.
159 G. P. Barton. 'Hanan, Josiah Ralph — Biography', from the Dictionary of New Zealand Biography. Te Ara — the Encyclopedia of New Zealand.
160 Hugh Templeton. 'Shand, Thomas Philip — Biography', from the Dictionary of New Zealand Biography. Te Ara — the Encyclopedia of New Zealand.

exposition established the clear line of evolution the country would follow after World War Two.

Interestingly, in reply to Marshall, Labour put up its able resident intellectual, who had just returned to Parliament, Ormond Wilson, at heart a social democrat, who proclaimed ... 'that socialism has come to stay, and we cannot go back on socialism in the progress of mankind ... that we have accepted the philosophy of socialism, whether we belong to the National party or the Labour party ... And that the only way of dealing with our troubles ... is by planning better and more adequately; by more socialism, and not less.'

It was Marshall, with hands on key levers of power for two vital decades, who caught the flow of the river. In its depths, his career confirmed New Zealanders were in heart and hand, liberals and not socialists.

Marshall's maiden speech[161] was, in the words of historian Barry Gustafson, 'a carefully crafted exposition of the political philosophy of liberalism.'

... I did want to take the opportunity of my maiden speech to state ... the political principles in which I believe and in the light of which my political judgments will be made ...

Edmund Burke[162], a very great parliamentarian, speaking from a wealth of experience, once said that 'the greater part of the measures which arise in the course of public business are related to or dependent on some leading general principles in government.'

I want to say at once, and without any reservations, that the great leading principles to which I adhere are the principles of Liberalism ... But since there are many who lay claim to such principles, and are in fact, far removed in thought and action from Liberalism, I want to define ... just what I mean by the Liberal outlook; and I say the Liberal outlook because it is not a fixed and definite creed, or a rigid social system.

It is rather a state of mind, an attitude towards men and public affairs, which guides one's political judgment without confining them to a set formula. The Liberal tradition goes far back into British history.

---

161 *New Zealand Parliamentary Debates (Hansard), Volume 276 pages 293–7.*
162 *Irish–born statesman and politician in the British House of Commons, in the mid–18th century.*

It transcends political party and it is not necessarily confined to those parties which call themselves Liberal. It begins with a view of man that is both elevated and realistic. It affirms the infinite worth of human personality and each individual man, but at the same time it realises that in the same man there is a want of original righteousness, so that many of us are not as good as we ought to be ...

The Liberal sees man in all his imperfections, and with all his possibilities, and he sets to work to do the best he can with that human material ...

The Liberal is opposed to those who consider people primarily as a class and not as individuals. He regards the idea of rigid and definite class distinctions as incompatible with the full development of personality, and he regards the idea of class war as pernicious ... (as) absolutely unjustifiable in New Zealand today.

In this country we need co-operation, and not class war. Those who advocate a class war, and ... stir up class antagonism for political ends are a menace to the peace and prosperity of this country ...

The Liberal views with concern the activities of pressure groups of all varieties who by force of numbers or money or power or because of the key positions they hold in the economic life of the community, seek to impose their own claims on the Government without thought of the common good, and so submerge the common man in the clamour of sectional interests.

The Liberal is equally opposed to those who see the common man in the mass, and who subordinate the individual to what they believe to be the greater good of the State, and who under the several systems of collectivism would reconstruct the world without regard to human nature.

Liberalism is not mere selfish individualism. The doctrine of laisser-faire passed out of Liberal thinking 50 years ago. It is a social individualism that imposes duties as well as rights on each and on all. Personality cannot be fully realised except in a community. The Liberal idea is not a concourse of little men each concerned simply with their own advantage, but a commonwealth of self-respecting, self-directing citizens accepting their mutual responsibilities and co-operating for the general good. But this co-operation cannot be forced.

Only a free man can work with his fellows in building a good society, that society where enlightened self-interest and service go hand in hand. The conditions of the good society are liberty, property, and security, and the greatest of these is liberty.

The Liberal as the name implies, is a believer in liberty ... he would give to each individual the right to live his life in his own way provided only that he does not interfere with the rights of other men. He should be free to do as he wishes subject only to the rule of law. All law is a restraint of liberty, yet without law, liberty cannot exist. Liberty as it is worked out within a community is not a simple matter. There are at least four aspects of liberty — national, political, personal and economic ...

National liberty is the freedom we enjoy as an independent nation within the British Commonwealth, the liberty for which we fought and which we can best maintain, even at some sacrifice of our sovereign rights, under the rule of law which the United Nations Organisation is working to establish.

Political liberty, the proud heritage of British people, is best illustrated by the rights and privileges of this House, and the free elections and the secret ballot by which we its members were selected to represent the people.

Personal liberty is the freedom under the rule of law to think and act, and to speak and worship as we will ...

A fourth ... is economic liberty. No man is really free unless he possesses in a sufficient degree the material basis of liberty, so that he is free from the anxiety of how to support himself and his family.

No man can really make the most of his personality if his livelihood is insecure. But in the pursuit of economic liberty the Liberal does not reject the present economic system. Within the framework of private enterprise and competition, with collective bargaining, 'decasualisation' of labour, and schemes of profit sharing and co-partnership, this economic liberty for the common man will be achieved. Social security ... makes a considerable contribution to that economic liberty ... social security is an essential part of Liberal policy.

President Roosevelt, a very great liberal, established many measures of

Prime Minister John Marshall addresses a National Development Conference at Parliament.

social security in the United States of America, and incidentally coined the phrase which was later imported into this country. Similarly in England, Lord Beveridge ... is a Liberal He has always been a Liberal thinker ... the idea of social security was initiated in this country many years ago by a Liberal Government ... (but) in our search for social security we must beware lest we lose our economic security.

Social security can be provided under any form of government but economic security cannot survive except in a free community ... (where) the idea of economic liberty includes the rights of a man to choose the kind of work he wants to do, to change his work from time to time ... to move from one job to another ... to work for himself ... to employ men to work for him, or to be employed ... and above all the equal opportunity of acquiring the training and education to fit him for that work ...

We are well aware that liberty has dangers and temptations of its own. The man who is free to do as he likes ... will not always choose to do what is right ... Compulsion to do right not only denies the integrity of personality, it is the essence of tyranny ... The same applies to those

345

attractive watch words, 'security', 'efficiency,' and 'planned economy'. The Liberal ... believes in security, but only if it goes hand in hand with liberty. Security obtained at the expense of liberty is bought at too high a price ... efficiency by legislation, efficiency by compulsion, efficiency by dictatorship at the expense of liberty, is bought at too high a price.

The Liberal believes in planning for, planning for freedom, planning in a well-ordered community under the rule of law. Planning for a free economy, as the Liberal sees it, is planning for free enterprise to function without the evils which have attended its development ... It is planning ... to co-ordinate but not to dominate ... to remove obstacles and restrictions, to regulate ... for the best functioning of the economy ... to encourage enterprise, initiative and independence, and to give the ordinary man vested rights in his own living and the right to plan for himself.

But when planning is taken over by the State for the purpose of what is called creating a 'planned national economy', the Liberal is on the side of the individual ... in such planning individuals ... have come to be regarded not as persons but as puppets, not as free men planning their own lives, but as planned men doing what the planners think is good for them.. In a planned economy almost unlimited powers must be placed in the hands of those charged with the planning — economic powers are joined with political powers in the hands of the State.

The Liberal views such an accumulation of power with alarm. It is the breeding ground for dictators.

From what I have already said it is clear that the Liberal believes in property ... because property is connected with personality.

Property is essential both to liberty and security. For that reason Liberals have ... advocated ownership for all ... The encouragement of small businesses; the encouragement of co-partnership in large businesses; the control of land aggregation; the settlement of individual farmers on their own farms, and the establishment of every family in their own home ... We can have a property-owning democracy. That is the real answer for the increased production of wealth and for the better distribution of that wealth when produced. That is the Liberal answer.

We have liberty, property and security, but the greatest of these is liberty. True progress can only be progress towards liberty. Let us not be deceived by any sentimental belief in the inevitability of progress. No reading of history supports the view that mankind is always marching on to better things ...

Tyrannies of various kinds have arisen to take man back to servitude ...

The Liberal knows that it is not progressive but reactionary to attempt to control and make uniform by law the personal conduct and habits of men ... it is not progressive but reactionary for the State to attempt to undertake the tasks of commerce and industry ... (or) to place a higher value on efficiency and security than liberty ... in recent years we have valued liberty too lightly; we have seen it overthrown and crushed in Fascist and Communist countries alike ...

It is not surprising that Hitler was most scathing in his attacks on Liberalism ... that Karl Marx and all Communists after him have attacked Liberalism ... that Professor Laski[163] ... a major prophet of socialism (writes) 'of the final dividing line between Liberalism and socialism. There is no middle way.'

No one will deny that the party which has been the government of this country since 1935 has been motivated by humanitarian ideals, but no one who is honest will claim that they have a monopoly of those ideals. As the methods and aims of socialism are becoming clearer through experience, more and more people are beginning to realise that a great gulf separates the Liberal and the socialist.

It is a gulf both of principle and method, and I am on the side of the Liberals. I am happy to say that the principles which I have enunciated are all tenable within the party to which I ... belong. Its policy is based on those principles, and its practice, when it becomes the government, will be directed to achieving them.

After 12 years as Deputy Prime Minister and a brief spell as Prime Minister, Marshall retired from politics in 1974, receiving a knighthood. He left the national arena with the nickname 'Gentleman Jack'.

In 1973, after his defeat at the polls, British television interviewer David

---

163 *Scholar and political scientist, and chairman of the British Labour Party 1945–46.*

Frost referred to Marshall's reputation for being 'nice' and 'a gentleman', to which he replied: 'I never claimed to be a gentleman … I think it is fair to say I try not to hurt people …'

Resolution, Not Resolutions

Sir Carl Berendsen

April 20, 1948

In retrospect, Sir Carl Berendsen[164] the orator looks like a drama queen. With the authority of his political masters as the nation's spokesman on the world stage, he helped in 1947 to change the world. As Permanent Representative at the United Nations, while Ambassador in Washington, in a single speech, he struck one of the most significant blows ever by a small nation for a small nation.

In 1947, the United Kingdom was forced to give up its Mandate in Palestine. Would that Mandate be resumed by a United Nations Trusteeship? Or would Palestine be partitioned between its Arab and Jewish peoples? The decision in 1947 had been for Partition. But at the last moment, in 1948, the United States had second thoughts. With the risks of conflict so high, should the international community not maintain a Trusteeship?

In the single most powerful intervention observers can recall until Dag Hammarskjöld later faced down Nikita Krushchev, Berendsen killed off the American initiative with his address on April 20, 1948.

With a Presidential election due in six months, President Truman, influenced by the General Assembly vote, as well by the Jewish vote in

---

164 *Mr Ambassador: Memoirs of Sir Carl Berendsen (Victoria University Press), edited by Hugh Templeton, 2009.*

New York State, and the plea of his Jewish haberdasher friend and partner, then acknowledged an independent State of Israel.

World history would never be the same again.

Here are excerpts from Berendsen's speech to the United Nations:[165]

... The tragic situation leading to this meeting has laid a heavy responsibility on all members, and upon all governments, the duty, as well as the right, to set forth our views plainly. Last November we admitted the problem was difficult and intractable, the cumulative result of many events in the past, and in particular the Balfour Declaration in 1917. That like most international documents is open to various constructions ...

The United Kingdom was given the Mandate for Palestine with the approval of many nations now present. They have administered the mandate with high motives and some degree of success. They have tried to reconcile the irreconcilable, but neither Jew nor Arab has been prepared to compromise. There has been periodic bloodshed, involving on many occasions the two contesting sides, and also the British.

The British have had a thankless job and at last they have decided they can no longer bear alone the odium of an international task, while others are free to criticise without accepting responsibility.

After mature and anxious consideration in November 1947 the Assembly decided ... by a two thirds majority, that the best available course was partition with economic union. An imposing list of States supported that plan. How many indeed still hold those views? Of course no State favouring partition with economic union thought the solution to be perfect.

The New Zealand Government believes that partition with economic union offers the best solution. I believe the Assembly has decided to do the right thing, but in the wrong way.

In November I pointed out that the partition plan was good but that if the Assembly assumed the right to divide the State, it should also assume the duty of implementing the plan in a peaceful and orderly manner.

---

165 *Further Consideration of the Question of the Future Government of Palestine — Opening of the General Debate, Second Special session of the General Assembly First Committee, April 20, 1948.*

Sir Carl Berendsen: the voice of New Zealand at the UN

I was anxious as to the success of the plan if there were no provisions for enforcement.

The Assembly preferred to gamble on the issue and has lost, but the losses are being paid by the people in Palestine, mainly by the Jews and Arabs, but also by the British.

The Assembly's disgrace is that it had not faced inevitable facts. Many naively professed to believe that enforcement was unnecessary, despite the seriousness of the Arab warnings and pleas. It is hard to understand how anyone could have thought a peaceful solution was possible, since the problem admitted of no perfect solution. Nevertheless the plan could have been effective if proper steps had been taken.

Other representatives last year appeared to think that, although force was needed, it had been provided for from two sources. There were to be both Arab and Jewish militias which were to keep order; and moreover, the Security Council would ensure enforcement. The former concept again was very inadequate; and as for the latter we need only consider the existing situation. Out of that error of judgment we have the present situation, where murder and outrage are rampant.

The risk is that the General Assembly will lose the public confidence upon which its authority depends ... Unless the Assembly offers steady and consistent leadership it will lose its following, and confusion and dismay will ensure. This does not mean policies should remain immutable when circumstances change.

But if partition with economic union was right in November, the New Zealand delegation believes it is right today. The circumstances have not changed since the matter was so carefully considered and debated in November. The only new factor in this case is a series of murders and outrages on both sides. Neither the Jewish nor the Arab action can be defended or explained. Both should be strongly censured. Both called for repression by lawful force. Whether the actions were alleged to be for or against partition, outrages remained outrages.

Nothing, or at least very little, has been done ... to further the November decision or take counter measures against the known opposition. Yet it is now alleged that partition has become impossible because of a series of outrages. These acts should have been foreseen ... they are no excuse for abandoning the Assembly's decision. The Assembly will be taking a very grave responsibility if it allows its resolution to be stultified by illegal violence. As to the force required to implement partition, it will not be greater than that needed to impose a Trusteeship. If members will accept a share of duty in order to implement trusteeship, they should equally do so to implement the decision of last November.

The New Zealand policy for the present Assembly is to enforce its decision on partition, undeterred by violence. The plan is the best available under the circumstances. We should give earnest thought before any abandonment of principle because of outrages which have been foreseen. Otherwise we will strike a tragic blow against the United Nations. We should not capitulate to threats and violence. We cannot maintain order in the world by words alone.

New Zealand will continue to urge the enforcement of partition. Of course, we will examine any proposals which can achieve a just and reasonable truce, and would indeed welcome them warmly.

Palestine is a test case for the future of the United Nations.

What is required is not resolutions, but resolution. Nations should not add to the irresponsibility of our November decision for partition without provision for enforcement, the further and perhaps final irresponsibility of surrender to illegal force.

Berendsen made many brilliant speeches. He was an orator with a sense of history. As a young soldier in England he had heard a fine orator in Herbert Asquith. In his prime, he lived with the oratory of wartime leaders Churchill and Roosevelt. His own speeches at San Francisco were the highlight of the Peace Treaty ceremonies. His words on Japan moved his audience, as it still does any reader with the slightest perception of the pity and tragedy of war, the triumph of victory, and the beneficence of a just rather than a Carthaginian Peace.

Berendsen's speech on the Anzus Pact captured in particular the sharp edge of his small country's concern for co–operation in the ongoing search for peace and security in the Pacific world. The oratory is compelling:

We in New Zealand are not of those who ask ... We are not of those who

353

demand ... We are not of those who are content ...

The power comes from the heart and mind of a brilliant mandarin, a lifetime servant of the State who had striven throughout that life of service for the 'co–operation of all right–thinking peoples.' In the classical sense, we may conclude this 'good man was indeed born to serve others.'

At the signing of the Anzus Pact and the Treaty of Peace with Japan, Berendsen said:[166]

> *I sign this treaty on behalf of my country ... with a firm confidence of real and lasting achievement. We in New Zealand are not of those who ask what we are not prepared to give, we are not of those who demand help which we are not prepared to accord; we are not of those who are content to leave to others burdens which we ourselves should assume.*
>
> *In our short history we have always been ready to give what we have been prepared to ask. Man for man we have played and are playing our full — sometimes in legitimate pride, we think more than our full part in those great struggles of our time which have called for the co–operation of all right thinking peoples.*
>
> *And the pact we sign today is one of co–operation, a joint offer and assurance of aid, real and immediate should aid be needed. In this treaty the three signatories accept the same, a common duty. It is not a guarantee of the security of New Zealand by the United States and Australia, of Australia by the United States and New Zealand, of the United States by Australia and New Zealand. It is a common undertaking to regard a danger to one as a danger to all, a common assumption of a formal duty — the same identical duty — by each of the three parties. It is a reaffirmation ... that these three countries, which have fought together in two great wars, have established a true and lasting comradeship and goodwill, and a common trust and confidence ...*
>
> *Each of the parties has proved not only its fidelity to its pledged word but its ability and its determination, if and when the dread need arises, to turn from acts to words, and to prove, by its courage and its resolution,*

---

166 *Mr Ambassador: Memoirs of Sir Carl Berendsen (Victoria University Press), edited by Hugh Templeton, 2009, page 291.*

its ability to fight, when fight it must, to preserve its liberty and its way of life. In this treaty the three parties serve notice, clear and unequivocal, that, in the words of the treaty itself 'no potential aggressor could be under any illusion that any of them stand alone in the Pacific area.'

The treaty therefore rests upon the solid basis of common interests and ideals, upon the regard and affection of the respective peoples, upon their common desire for peace and upon their common determination to resist aggression. It reflects also the inescapable facts of geography on the one hand and on the other the especial perils to which the Pacific may be exposed in the course of this world wide conflict between liberty and slavery with which the whole of mankind is today oppressed.

And the reassurance which this treaty affords us enables us to approach with an easier mind and a fuller confidence, the task that lies before us next week, the completion of a peace treaty with Japan, a treaty of generosity, of forbearance, of reconciliation and of renewed hope for the future.

Nor is the treaty isolationist in its nature. We in New Zealand have no reason to fear any suggestion, malevolent or ignorant, of selfish or isolationist intentions. Our history — the history of two world wars and of New Zealand's armed and active participation all over the world in those causes which we have believed to be just — is the answer.

We believe, and our acts and our policies have implemented that belief, that a true democracy, must be willing to serve wherever democracy needs to be defended.

And accordingly the treaty does not restrict itself to its parties alone; it contemplates close and constant consultation with others of like interests or in like peril. By creating an area of stability in the Pacific, this treaty must be expected to reduce world tensions and thus to provide a reinforcement of, and a contribution to, the general system of international security which is today slowly — but we hope surely — being erected.

By providing directly a strong measure of defence against attack in the Pacific it does at the same time, in so doing, make it possible for its parties to play their part elsewhere; because the problem that the free world is facing today is a global problem — it is merely the manifestations of that problem which may from time to time appear to be local.

And finally the treaty has no effect whatsoever unless and until one of its parties is attacked. It is purely and solely a measure of self–protection ... It is defensive in purpose and in effect, a threat to no one ... a reassurance, an affirmation, an undertaking that in case of need none of its parties will stand alone ...

The notice that is served today upon any evil–doer might indeed have the effect of eliminating for all time that very aggression which alone can bring this treaty into practical application. There lies our hope — and our belief ...

From this and every other point of view the treaty is clearly, demonstrably and entirely in conformity with the aims and the principles of the United Nations ...

Today, we sign this Treaty, which offers such great hope to all of us, here in the Praesidio, a centre of great historical significance, the repository of a wealth of memories and traditions today we make a new tradition, create a new memory, of something which, if God pleases, we will find to be good and prove to be enduring.

Here at the Golden Gate we sign a beneficent pact which I believe, may itself open a golden portal to the peace, prosperity and happiness of the Pacific, and the future that lies before us.

'No Surrender'

Sidney Holland

July 11, 1951

Sidney Holland was 'a shrewd politician, and man of action, who led from the front,'[167] a buoyant, strong leader, and tough, demanding Prime Minister. Astute if not intellectual — he seldom read a book — he was a 'natural' vigorous genial speaker who liked to feed off interjections.[168]

In 1940, with Keith Holyoake out of Parliament, Holland had seized the leadership of the National Party. Based in Christchurch, he had melded National's rural and urban wings into a powerful nationwide party with a tight, disciplined parliamentary caucus. Eager, and confident in himself and his inner cabinet, including his strong–willed Minister of Labour, Bill Sullivan,[169] Holland as Prime Minister dominated Parliament and established an effective Cabinet Secretariat.[170] His major failure in leadership was in not replacing the Second Chamber his administration

167 J.R. Marshall speech for 50th Anniversary National Party.
168 A Coming Man. S.G. Holland 1940–1949 Nina Templeton (Thesis, Otago University).
169 Marcia Spencer, The incoming tide: Sir William Sullivan and the 1951 waterfront dispute (M. Spencer), 1998.
170 One American observer noted that Holland seemed 'temperamentally closer to the average American Rotarian than an average upper class Briton', p 101, Malcolm McKinnon Independence and Foreign Policy.

Sidney Holland (1893–1961)

abolished on taking office.[171]

In the 1940s the Labour Government had suffered at the hands of militant trade unions. As early as 1947, Sullivan had written to Holland 'some day these wreckers will have to be dealt with.'

Used to exercising industrial muscle, the most militant, of them, the Waterfront Union, relished combat with the new National Government. Strategic circumstances had, however, changed. Soon after the 1949 election of the first National Government, the Cold War, in June 1950, had turned hot. With New Zealand involved in the Korean War, a conflict that threatened our food exporting economy, the wharfies spoiled for a fight as the export season built up, and made the mistake of challenging the sovereign State to battle.

In February 1951, the Holland Government, at Sullivan's insistence, took up the challenge.

---

171 *Constitutional Reform Committee 1952, including National MP lawyers like R.M. Algie(final chair) J.R. Marshall and J.R Hanan, recommended a Senate of 32 party–appointed senators to review — but also to initiate — legislation, and consider petitions, local bills and delegated legislation.*

On February 21, Holland announced live on radio:[172]

Yesterday, Tuesday, at noon, I called the representatives of the watersiders to my room. And I issued them what would be interpreted as being an ultimatum and said that the government would be loath to take any extreme action, but we felt that, if conditions of emergency did exist, that we would require the powers of such a proclamation to deal with the situation.

Now we didn't take the action that some people would expect of us, and that is to declare a state of emergency there and then. We disclosed to the watersiders themselves knowledge of our intention and said unless work is resumed — normal work throughout New Zealand, is resumed on the wharves tomorrow — that's today now, Wednesday, then a proclamation of emergency will be declared.

Cabinet invoked the Public Safety Conservation Act put in place during the Depression. This the union bosses may have forgotten, but not the officials of the Department of Labour. Only after the 151–day battle on the wharves had been won did Sullivan as Minister of Labour introduce legislation on July 11, 1951, to validate the State of Emergency under which the country had been operating.

Walter Nash, the new Leader of the Opposition, was caught astride his 'neither for nor against' statement, a trap that Holland in a powerful, feisty speech appealing to the people, sprang.

The 1951 snap election showed the extent to which the public had got sick of years of union blackmail and strikes. Holland himself simply claimed the debate as one of the most significant of the Session.

In retrospect, his speech was a significant moment in our history. The violence attending the 1913 strike had been much in his mind. His experience as a Special Constable stood him, he claimed 'in good stead as to how a general strike should not be handled.' Ministers and officials had to work out within its peculiar context methods for an exceptional battlefield. Their good fortune was the existence of emergency legislation

---

172 *'PM Holland declares state of emergency, 1951', URL: http://www.nzhistory.net.nz/media/ sound/sidney–holland–declares–state–of–emergency, (Ministry for Culture and Heritage). Audio of this speech is available.*

that let the government mount a rules–based campaign under the law.

Holland went to the House on July 11, 1951, to set out his plan for dealing with the waterfront workers:[173]

> *Sir, this is perhaps one of the most important debates we shall have ... It deals with the fundamental basis of democratic government in New Zealand.*
>
> *... We ask Parliament to approve of the Government's action in declaring a State of Emergency ... in making regulations ... (in) administration of the situation arising out of the strike ...*
>
> *In February, this country received a challenge. A challenge was thrown down; the security of our country was at stake. All Communists were behind the challenge. I do not say all those who were in the challenge were, but all Communists were behind that challenge.*
>
> *War was declared on this country of ours, and the government of the day faced an unprecedented situation. To fail would have meant the end of constitutional government.*
>
> *To have failed would have been a victory for direct action, for victimisation, for terrorism ... for Communism ... to fail, we felt, would be a betrayal of the people. That is our view. We stand in our places in Parliament to say so.*
>
> *The Government, not experienced in the handling of crises such as this, gave the most careful and thoughtful consideration to the problems and the questions of planning.*
>
> *There were two or three things we decided and determined ... there would no capitulation; there would be no surrender; there would be no appeasement.*
>
> *We looked around for some example we might follow in other countries or in this. We found in no country a set of rules for the management of the situation we were confronted with, that would suit the situation here in the way that we wanted to handle it. So we worked out plans ourselves to introduce something new in the management of our industrial crisis.*
>
> *We were determined to have no more of the 1913 method of managing*

---

173 *Industrial Dispute: State of Emergency, New Zealand Parliamentary Debates (Hansard), Volume 294, page 260.*

it in which special police or special constables were sworn in, batons were used freely and free labour was employed to break down the resistance of the people who were on strike. We employed new methods ... of dealing with militant strikers ... by the gazetting of regulations under the Public Safety Conservation Act. That has been the authority for the handling of the strike until this moment. Without that Act and those regulations we could not have administered the country's affairs during this time of crisis, and we could never have got the country back to work with our honour intact.

We then decided ... to keep supplies of goods flowing to the people ... there was no reason why the people of Britain should go without food, or the people of our country should go short of essential food and supplies ...

And we determined ... there would be no picketing on this strike ... We said there would be no picketing, and there has been virtually no picketing. We said there would be no intimidation. There has been a lot of intimidation, but a lot less than there would have been had we not been firm and remained in control. We made up our minds that the rule of law must survive. We made up our minds that we were going to govern ... I can stand in my place tonight and say that this Government has governed.

We then searched the law to see what powers we had, and we found that the Act that enabled us to administer the affairs of the country properly was the Public Safety Conservation Act, which gave power to gazette regulations to deal with the situation ... regulations which admittedly are very far reaching ...

In deciding on the nature of the regulations ... we felt we had to take only the powers that the public would support us on, and throughout the handling of the strike we have tried to carry the public with us by informing them of the basis of the regulations we have used, and the necessity for them. It is true ... we had no specific mandate to employ these methods.

The crisis that faced us was without precedent. We had not told the electors in 1949 that we would do what we have done, because we had not then made up our minds. What we did say was that if there was trouble the Government would ... discipline the people who broke the laws, and discipline those who defied constitutional government ...

We have passed through a very anxious time. Ours was not an easy task ... I have occupied a good deal of my sleeping time thinking of how we could best service this lovely country of ours; how we could respond to the requirements of the people; and how we could honour the pledges we had given them, and how we could prove worthy of the respect of those who expected action — who expected results from their democratically elected government.

I am a Britisher through and through, and I am proud of it. I am proud of the British way of life. I am proud of the British rule of law. I shall ... always strive to preserve the British way of life.

Winning the strike is not everything. It is a lot; it is important, but it is not the last word. The methods employed to administer the affairs of a country, during a period of crisis such as this, are important, and it is right and proper that members opposite ... can and do express their views ... It is their right and their duty to call attention to the fact that extreme methods ... have been employed ...

The question is this: 'Have the methods we employed been supported by the public?' I believe they have ... We on these benches say that they have; those on the benches opposite say they have not ... I say ... that unless all we have done has the approval of the public ... we have no right to be on these benches ... Nevertheless, I believe that we have the overwhelming support of the people ...

I am taking advantage of my place in Parliament here tonight to inform the public in the hope that the public will be impressed by what I say, just as the leader of the Opposition and other members opposite hope ... that they will find favour with the public ... That is the idea of broadcasting Parliament.

Our methods are new, but I think I can say that they have been effective. Democracy has been preserved; I am proud to say that.

The pattern that we have adopted lays down the pattern of the future management of industrial trouble of this type and magnitude ... we have made a valuable contribution to the industrial peace and the progress of our country.

I believe that a result of this strike we shall have harmony for some years to come.

It is worthwhile, from a Government point of view, to examine some of the regulations ... the only difficulty people have found themselves in has been when they have attempted to incite other people to join in and spread the trouble so as to make the Government's task and the country's problems greater still. No honourable person who wanted to go about his life in the ordinary manner has been inconvenienced to the slightest degree by the application of the regulations.

One of the regulations provides that if anyone procures, encourages or assists in the spread of the strike for incitement, he commits an offence. Who will complain about that? It is an unlawful strike.

We took power to freeze union funds. That was a big step to take — to interfere with anyone's rights. However I believe that power was necessary to ensure that the strike did not spread, to ensure that people were not starved, and to ensure that goods and services essential to the well being of the people were kept flowing ...

Then we also took power ... to suspend awards while they were in operation ... (and) power to refuse the registration of unions ...

We took power to employ the servicemen on the wharves ...

We took power ... to prohibit people going onto the wharves ...

We took power to prevent picketing. No member opposite would object to that ...

We found these regulations in fine form, for they were in the pigeonholes when we took office ... We had very few alterations to make ...

We took power to stop processions ...

Also we gave the police power of entry ...The Minister of Labour gave an amazing exposure of the methods employed by these people ... that sort of thing ought to be stopped ...

I accept responsibility for taking that sort of power ... our moderation in the administering of the powers we had has been a large contributing factor to our success. We hope we are at the end of this business, but we desire to justify what we have done ...

Many charges have been hurled at us from the other side of the House ... The Leader of the Opposition has had most to say ... Naturally members

363

of the Government take grave notice of the charges leveled against us.

We have been doing what we think to be our best for our country. We have been trying to do our plain duty towards those who entrusted us with the responsibility of Government. We have done what we considered to be fair and just. We have tried to protect loyal citizens from being attacked by these people, by enemies of our land, and the enemies of our Empire, who would if they could overthrow us.

And for our pains the Leader of the Opposition had these things to say: 'The Emergency regulations were the most iniquitous ever written into the laws of the country. They abrogated all human rights.'

I want to remind the House that the Leader of the Opposition is a very important person. For some time I was Leader of the Opposition, and I tried to occupy that position with dignity. I have no doubt that the right honourable gentleman who is leader of the opposition at the present time is trying to do the same. A heavy responsibility rests upon his shoulders in the language he uses an in the statements he makes.

Occupying the position he does, and having been a deputy Prime Minister and being a Privy Councillor, when he makes charges of that kind it is up to the Government to take notice of them. He said 'Freedom of assembly was gone; freedom of speech was gone; the sanctity of private correspondence was swept away.'

He came to me with the Deputy Leader of the Opposition and made complaints about his telephone being tapped. The Deputy Leader of the Opposition has been round the country telling people that mail has been opened ...

The idea is to smear us; to say to the people the Government is interfering with private correspondence ...

There has not been one letter opened. There has not been one telephone tapped.

The leader of the Opposition has also stated ... 'The Government was continually intimidating the people.' He said: 'The Government had authorised raids on trade union secretaries' offices.' ... 'This is Fascism; the Government has introduced regulations which menace every freedom.' These are grave charges ... He said the regulations were the closest approach to a dictatorship that New Zealand had ever known

... That is a charge of Nazism ... Could any one level a graver charge than that against a political opponent, or a party, or a Government? The member for Sydenham said just now, 'This is exactly how Nazi Germany started' ...

A former Minister ... said the regulations were a threat to democracy ... the regulations were outside the law and had cost the Government the people's confidence. Well that is his view ...

I have retailed as fairly as I can ... the series of charges leveled against this Government. I say that they are not capable of proof, and that if they could be proved, this Government should be swept from the Treasury benches. I would have no right to stand this place while those charges are there, even if the regulations were removed. We are taking them off as far as we can ...

Grave charges have been made ... In a desire to see whether we are right or the Opposition is right, whether our claim that we have the support of the country is correct, or whether the Opposition is right when it says we have forfeited our right to the confidence of the people and it should take our place, the Government has decided, after the most careful thought and consideration, that as soon as it is practicable I will advise his Excellency the Governor General that he dissolve this Parliament so that the Government's administration can be submitted to the judgment of the people themselves.

Members: 'Hear, hear.'

I believe that this is the proper course for us to take in view of the charges leveled against us, and in view of the importance of the decisions we have taken. The people of New Zealand are the governors of New Zealand. They have entrusted us with the responsibility of government. I believe we have discharged our trust. The Opposition say we have failed and deserve no confidence. I say the people are our real rulers and tonight I stand in my place in Parliament, proud to be a member of a Government and Administration that took up the challenge and stood its ground firmly and squarely — a Government that knew no appeasement, no surrender, and no betrayal. We have been faithful to our trust.

On 30th November 1949, this Government dedicated itself to the service of the people. We have been tested and not been found wanting. I shall face the people of New Zealand, who entrusted me with the responsibility that I proudly carry today, with confidence. Whatever happens I will gladly and cheerfully accept the decision of the voters. We will go to our constituents to give an account of our stewardship, and our friends opposite will do the same.

The proper course is to allow the real rulers of New Zealand to express in secret ballot at the ballot box their judgment on the administration of the Government ...

So it is with a great sense of pride that I stand here tonight, surrounded by my colleagues, prepared to go, not at the last minute, but at the moment we are challenged, to lay before the people our administration, and to give an account of our stewardship, so that British democracy will survive, and so that people will have the opportunity of hearing the case argued from both sides.

Let us do the proper and best thing in democratic government and that is to ensure that government of the people, for the people, and by the people shall not perish from the earth.

In perspective, the battle for the waterfront in 1951 provides a remarkable example of parliamentary governance in crisis. Holland and his cabinet, prodded by Sullivan accepted, like Harry Truman, that the buck stopped with the executive but that the Executive had to secure the approval of Parliament, and ultimately the people. Intelligent critics[174], noting Parliament's lost monitor of a Second Chamber, did complain the emergency regulations impaired the freedom of the Press, but Holland's vindicatory speech gives the lie to his oxymoronic labeling as 'a totalitarian', just as our first–past–the–post ballot provided decisive confirmation of the virtues of parliamentary governance.

---

174 *Charles Brasch, September 1951, p442 Landfall Country (1947–61) by Charles Brasch.*

'Too Nervous'

Sir Edmund Hillary

February 11, 1954

Whenever the nation has been polled to name their favourite New Zealander, Sir Edmund Hillary has almost always been an easy winner. Humble and straightforward, he epitomised the stereotypical Kiwi male who prefers action to words.

Having conquered the world's highest mountain peak on May 29, 1953, and with impeccable timing — for the young Queen Elizabeth was to be coronated three days later — the lanky beekeeper from Tuakau[175] became an instant and global celebrity.

Within weeks of returning from Mount Everest, he was being asked to make speeches, and to conduct lectures in Europe and North America, usually in tow with fellow members of the expedition.

But newspaper reports of the day describe a taciturn New Zealander, shy and bashful and certainly unused to speaking in public.

On February 11, 1954, Hillary, sherpa Tensing Norkay and expedition leader Sir John Hunt were invited to Washington to be honoured by the National Geographic Society. President Dwight D. Eisenhower would give them medals in the White House.

---

175 *Shaun Barnett. 'Hillary, Edmund Percival — Early life', from the Dictionary of New Zealand Biography. Te Ara — the Encyclopedia of New Zealand.*

367

Edmund Hillary speaks to a crowd in 1958 after returning from the South Pole.

Soon after the party arrived at the Oval Office, the event started to go awry. [176]

President Eisenhower entered and clearly had no idea who his visitors were. Once reminded, he took them into the White House Conference Room filled with film crews and journalists. After introductory remarks, the President turned to Sir John Hunt, extended his hand and said: 'Sir Edmund …'

The embarrassed New Zealander leant forward and whispered into Eisenhower's ear: 'Sir John Hunt.'

The President recovered: 'Er, Sir John, may I tell you that it is a great privilege …'

Then it was Hillary's turn.

After receiving his medal, he was asked to step up to the microphone to say a few words. The world's most famous New Zealander was getting the

---

176 *Mark C. Jenkins, National Geographic Archives, 2003.*

chance to speak to the world from possibly the most prestigious venue in the United States.

Hillary laughed, said nothing and backed away from the microphone.

'No talking?' the President asked.

Silence and a shrug from the Kiwi.

Later, Sir Ed was asked by reporters why he had said nothing.

He replied: 'I was too nervous.'[177]

In those early years after Everest, Sir Ed compensated for his lack of desire for public speaking by taking part in shared lectures, and by writing about his experiences in newspapers, magazines and books.

In later years, he became more comfortable as a speaker — a combination, perhaps, of practice and acceptance that people were always going to want to hear whatever he had to say.

For a man of few words, he will still be remembered for the five he chose to share with his friend George Lowe when he completed his descent of Everest:

We knocked the bastard off.

---

177 *Australian Associated Press, February 11, 1954.*

End of the Empire

T.L. Macdonald

November 21, 1956

The British Empire ended not with a bang but with the fizzle of the Suez Crisis. Sick, ill–tempered British Prime Minister Anthony Eden challenged an Egyptian army officer seizing control of the key to the old Empire, the Suez Canal. Because he was British, and they knew him, New Zealand followed faithfully in Eden's footsteps.

Prime Minister Sidney Holland and his ministers, including his Minister of External Affairs, T.L. (Thomas Lachlan) Macdonald,[178] were second generation New Zealanders. Both had fought in the Great War. The British Empire William Massey had lauded in 1918 was for them a living reality. Few understood India's independence in 1947 had ended Britain's status, confirmed in the withdrawal from the Palestine Mandate in 1948, as an Imperial power.

Macdonald's speech to the General Assembly out of the hand and eye of one of the brilliant young mandarins of the new Department of External Affairs, Tom Larkin, is one of the most elegant and thoughtful dissertations of any New Zealand Minister, at home or abroad.

Of notable dignity and courtesy, our Minister of External Affairs came

---

178 *Malcolm Templeton. 'Macdonald, Thomas Lachlan — Biography', from the Dictionary of New Zealand Biography. Te Ara — the Encyclopedia of New Zealand.*

across as a man of complete integrity. He spoke in a strong, firm deep voice, confident in himself and his advisers, well–briefed and in command of a subject of extraordinary complexity.

The comparison is, of course, between Berendsen's fiery speech in 1947— insisting that it was the right thing to do to proceed with the partition of Palestine — and Macdonald's defensive clinch on the Suez debacle which Berendsen notably condemned as the wrong thing to do. Macdonald's speech stands, indeed, as a superb defensive exegesis, unlikely to be improved upon, however long historians find value in New Zealand's role in the international community. It stands on the high point of 'co–operation' in the search for peace, security and progress, called for in the UN Charter 'in an interdependent world'.

The speech rests on several notable pillars. Macdonald picks up on the authority New Zealand earned by the sacrifices of 2 NZEF in the dramatic Mid East theatre in World War Two that he sees as confirmed by the Soviet Union, as the Cold War intensified, stymying international co–operation in maintaining peace and security. He then recognises the leap forward under Dag Hammarskjöld in briefly turning the UN into an effective institution for keeping the peace. He then makes the case, if the co–operation on which the UN Charter is based is to prove meaningful, to follow the rule of law rather than force in settling international disputes.

On a sticky wicket, Macdonald's was a compelling performance delivered long before the Secretary of State, John Foster Dulles, complained to its perpetrators at the too abrupt cessation, at his President's behest, of the Anglo French invasion.

Macdonald's speech to the UN General Assembly on November 21, 1956:[179]

Mr President, the concern of New Zealand with the maintenance of peace in the Pacific area is a direct one. However, history has given us tragic proof of the importance of the Middle East to our security and communications.

Twice in recent times New Zealanders have been called upon to

---

179 *UN General Assembly Official Records, Session II 1956–57, Volume 1, pages 212–216 November 21, 1956.*

372

stake their lives and resources in its defence against aggression. Eighty thousand of our soldiers out of a population of less than two million fought in the Middle East in the second world war for the victory which made possible the founding of the Organisation.

What has happened in the Middle East in recent weeks is of the greatest importance to us.

New Zealand's attitude towards Anglo–French intervention in the recent fighting between Egypt and Israel has already been made clear. From the outset it has had full confidence in the intentions underlying the action taken with France by the United Kingdom.

There have been other times when the United Kingdom, virtually alone, has acted in the world's interest, against odds even weightier than the weight of adverse opinion. Time will show, we believe, that in this case too, action was taken in the general interest rather than in pursuit of narrow ends ...

... We consider it a gain that the extent of Soviet penetration in the Middle East, the magnitude of its supply of arms in the areas, and the malevolence of its intentions should have been unmistakably exposed ...

... It is a gain that this situation should have provided the stimulus for the creation of a United Nation Force, perhaps the first step towards investing the United Nations with the practical means to make its decisions effective.

And it is a gain that it should at least have brought home that it is time — and it is perhaps the last opportunity — for this organisation to stop backing away from the hard realities and difficulties in the Middle East.

For make no mistake — this organisation has backed away.

It is true that the responsibility for a lasting settlement of Middle East problems depends, in the long run, on the countries of the area. But there is much that the United Nations can do and might already have done.

In 1948 the Palestine Conciliation Commission was appointed to assist negotiations between Israel and the Arab States.

No debate on the work of the Conciliation Commission has been held in the Assembly since the abortive discussions of 1952. With the exception of the refugee question ... no aspect of the Palestine situation (despite its

T.L. Macdonald (1898–1980)

steady deterioration) has been discussed here until the last fortnight. And this over a period of years in which the inability of the Security Council to act constructively and impartially has become increasingly evident.

In 1951 the Security Council passed a resolution stating the restrictions placed by Egypt on shipping to and from Israel were an abuse of the right of visit, search and seizure and calling on Egypt to cease such restrictions. This resolution, though at once rejected by Egypt, was not followed up until New Zealand presented another resolution on the matter in 1954. This was at once subject to a Soviet veto.

That veto was the second 'protective veto' cast by the Soviet Union — protective in the sense that whatever the merits of the case, it was intended to thwart any Security Council action which was unfavourably regarded by the Arab States. Since then the only resolutions which the Security Council has been capable of adopting have been those containing censure of Israel.

Certainly in the past fortnight there has been no disinclination on the part of the majority in the Security Council or the General Assembly to deal with the situation created by the Israeli attack on Egypt and the Anglo–French intention. Certainly too there has been no failure on the part of the General Assembly to respond to the admirable and imaginative proposal of the Minister of External Affairs of Canada for the creation of a United Nations Emergency Force.

I well understand that the Assembly's consideration of the Middle East problem has been restricted by the need, concurrently, to examine the problem of Hungary. And I am aware that while the two American resolutions relating to long term aspects of the Palestine problem were shelved by the Emergency Assembly, there is provision and opportunity at this Assembly for consideration of the basic elements of the whole Palestine problem.

Nevertheless I am not alone, I think, in detecting already a reluctance in some quarters to extend our work from the study of the effects to the study of causes, and to accept the responsibility from which we have retreated in recent years.

It was with this in mind that the NZ representative, Sir Leslie Munro, proposed on 1 November that the whole problem of Arab Israeli relations should be fully and effectively considered at the present Assembly.

In respect of the Suez Canal, the question of Egyptian interference and restrictions on Israeli shipping has been absorbed in the more serious possibility that similar restrictions and interference may, to suit the interests of Egypt and at the will of Egypt, be leveled against any user of the Canal.

Similarly, the question of a peace settlement between Israel and the Arab States has been coloured and transformed by developments of the past seven years. In consideration of a final settlement account must now be taken of the diminishing relevance to existing conditions of certain provisions of the Assembly resolutions of 1947 and 1948; Israel's successful consolidation of the statehood conferred on her by the Assembly and the clear evidence of her determination to maintain it; the declared intention of Colonel Nasser to destroy Israel and the apparent willingness of the Soviet Union to assist that objective; the manifest inadequacy as permanent frontiers of the armistice lines agreed upon in 1949; the continued existence of the refugees in conditions of wretchedness, and the disinclination of either side, Arab or Israeli, to make the political decisions which would assist the alleviation of their suffering, the mergence of an imperative need for unified development of the water resources of the Jordan Valley; the record of Security Council decisions with relation to Suez Canal traffic, frontier incidents, and projects on the river Jordan; and finally, Israel's recent attack on Egypt.

My Government has always taken the view that by its decision in favour of the creation of Israel, this Assembly assumed obligations in regard to the future development of relations between Israel and her Arab neighbours.

It is now time, we think, to draw the proper lessons from the history of this organisation's association with the Palestine situation. Surely one of those lessons is that the absence of open warfare is no assurance of peace.

The primary obligation of the United Nations is to see that peace — a just peace — is preserved. It is not enough for this purpose to hold the ring, to examine and to discuss recurring abuses of armistice agreements. The organisation must be resolute and determined in its search for a permanent solution.

In the view of my delegation, the Assembly should now frame recommendations on the Palestine problem and should at the same time decide what obligations it is prepared to assume in order to give them meaning. It is obvious that the situation which will prevail when the United Nations has a force in the Middle East capable of taking over from the forces of the United Kingdom and France will not be static but dynamic. It is obvious too that unless steps are taken to make the situation better it will get worse.

Clearly the ultimate responsibility in this situation rests, and must rest with the States concerned. The Arab states, we believe, must accept Israel; whatever her transgressions, Israel is a state, a member of this Assembly, virtually a creation of this Assembly, whose extinction this Assembly, cannot and, I believe, will not tolerate. But if there is an obligation on the Arab states to accept Israel, there is an equal and perhaps greater obligation on Israel to make herself acceptable to the Arab states.

There are immediate steps which it would be both generous and wise for Israel to take. At the time there is special need for restraint and generosity in the administration of the Gaza strip. And beyond that I have particularly in mind arrangements for the payment of compensation and an undertaking, within the framework of an overall settlement, to re-admit a significant number of refugees.

It is in assisting reconciliation of the two sides, inducing them to meet together and negotiate, that my delegation believes the Assembly can play its most important part. We are accordingly in agreement with the purpose of the two American draft resolutions submitted here on 3 November.

We favour a serious and immediate effort by the Assembly to formulate proposals on the basis of which a lasting reconciliation might be achieved. Greater powers and lesser powers, those directly concerned and those who are not — we must all be prepared to accommodate our interests to the purpose and our view to the realities of the situation.

I join in the tributes which have been paid to the devotion to duty of the Secretary General. In a series of protracted crises, he has had to remove himself austerely from all national considerations and has had to endeavour to guide sovereign states towards peace and harmony.

Few men at this time bear a heavier load of both the cares and the hopes of the world.

Mr President, this is an interdependent world and it is a world of change. In the thoughtful introduction to his annual report the Secretary General said: 'We live in a period of fundamental and rapid changes in the relationship of nations and peoples having differing cultures and social systems. The new age that is emerging is an age of promise. It could also be one of disaster. We are seeking to cope with world issues of great difficulty but equally of high challenge.'

The Secretary General concludes this passage of his introduction: 'The hope of finding peaceful, just and constructive solutions of these issues rests upon our ability to foster the growth of understanding, co-operation and mutual accommodation of interests among all nations.'

May I emphasise the words 'understanding, co-operation and mutual accommodation.' It is easy in a world of change to dwell primarily on the necessity to accept change. Indeed the changes in the last ten years have few, if any, precedents in human history. New, independent states have risen to take their place in the United Nations and, under the inspiration of liberal ideals, economic and social co-operation for the welfare of the individual has taken dramatic steps forwards. These changes we welcome and support. But we must not mistake anarchy for progress, any more than we must confuse progress with the hollow misrepresentation of fundamental democratic principles.

Colonel Nasser's nationalisation of the Universal Suez Canal Company is a significant example of such confusion. I have no intention here of entering into a discussion of the legal merits of that action, although I believe them to be slender. The special significance of Colonel Nasser's action was, however, that it rejected the concept of an interdependent world. Indeed it flew in the face of wise advice given by Colonel Nasser's predecessor General Neguib. In his book published a year or two ago, General Neguib wrote:

'Today we are at last in a position to reclaim the national sovereignty of which we have so long been deprived. But if we were to assert it successfully, we must conform to cosmopolitan standards of behaviour. Otherwise we may find ourselves in an unequal conflict with the world powers whose strategic interests are involved in the Suez Canal ...'

Invoking the national interests of Egypt, Colonel Nasser seized a utility in which for 90 years the principle of impartial international service had received the highest form of expression. His action was a breach of those relations of confidence and trust which alone can provide the basis of economic and social advancement everywhere. Its import for the underdeveloped countries is clear. Anarchy, not progress, will result from the summary destruction or confiscation of all that the Western world has contributed in skills, facilities and knowledge to the economic and social and cultural progress of nations which have recently achieved political independence.

If we are to avoid anarchy, if we are to achieve a peaceful, ordered progress to wards the objectives of human welfare which are now within mankind's capacity, conditions of confidence and trust must be cultivated. This imposes heavy responsibilities on all the members of the United Nations in the pursuit of what they deem to be their national rights and interests. If a legal right is claimed but disputed then it is desirable that confirmation be sought from the highest international tribunal, the International Court of Justice. If the right is confirmed or unchallenged, there may still be other interests to be recognised and certain standards of international conduct to be observed in the exercise of the right. If the matter comes before this organisation, it behoves all of us to weigh carefully the expression of our views.

About the Authors

Hugh Templeton, QSO, AO, is a former New Zealand diplomat, politician and author with a particular interest in his nation's history. Having studied history at Otago University and as a Rhodes Scholar at Oxford University, he served with the Department of External Affairs in London, Wellington and Western Samoa before entering Parliament. He held various Cabinet roles in the National Government 1975–1984, including Minister of Revenue, Minister for Trade and Industry and Minister of Broadcasting. He played a key role in the establishment of the Australia–New Zealand Closer Economic Relations agreement, for which he received an Honorary Officer of the Order of Australia award in 2009. He is the author of *All Honourable Men: Inside the Muldoon Cabinet 1975–1984* (Auckland University Press), and *The Problematical Journey: The Templetons of Southland*. He also edited *Mr Ambassador: the Memoirs of Sir Carl Bernendsen* (Victoria University Press).

ABOUT THE AUTHORS

Ian Templeton, twin of Hugh, CNZM, OBE, is the doyen of New Zealand political reporting, having covered Parliament for more than half a century.

Having completed double degrees in English and economics at Otago University, he became a newspaper journalist and in 1968, co–founded the weekly political newsletter, *Trans Tasman* (for which he remains its senior editor).

He has written several books on New Zealand politics, including co–authoring *Election '69: An Independent Survey of the New Zealand Political Scene* and *In the Balance: Election '72*. In May 2011, he was awarded an honorary doctorate by Massey University. He has been awarded the Cowan Memorial Prize and a Qantas lifetime achievement award for his contribution to journalism. He is a life member of the parliamentary press gallery.

Josh Easby is a publisher, writer, editor and former executive who has worked for media companies in New Zealand and internationally. An award–winning journalist with the *Auckland Star*, where he was news editor, he has managed newspaper and radio companies and currently runs his own independent book publishing business. He is the deputy chair of Radio New Zealand. He has written or edited many non–fiction books including titles on sport, music and business.

381

Acknowledgements

We are grateful to the following sources of images reproduced in this publication:

Page 10 (Samuel Marsden); page 22 (Tamati Wake Nene); page 27 (John Robert Godley); page 45 (Renata Kawepo); page 50 (Thomas FitzGerald); page 59 (Rewi Maniapoto); page 100 (King Tawhiao); page 119 (Kate Sheppard); page 138 (Minnie Dean). Source: Wikipedia Commons.

Page 351 (Carl Berendsen). Source: United Nations.

Page 113 (Rev. Rutherford Waddell). Source: Archives Research Centre, Presbyterian Church of Aotearoa New Zealand).

The following images are reproduced courtesy of the Alexander Turnbull Library:

Page 34: Wivell, Abraham 1786-1849. Wivell, Abraham 1786-1849:Edward Gibbon Wakefield, Esq. Engraved by B Holl from a drawing by A Wivell, 1823. London, 1826. Ref: A-042-023. Alexander Turnbull Library, Wellington, New Zealand. http://natlib.govt.nz/ records/22334692.

Page 80: Morris, John Richard (Jnr), 1854-1919. Sir Julius Vogel. Youngman bequest: Portrait of Sir Julius Vogel and a photograph of the Osterley (ship). Ref: PAColl-0439-1. Alexander Turnbull Library, Wellington, New Zealand. http://natlib.govt.nz/records/23112841.

Page 91: Alais, William Wolfe: Sir George Grey (engraving from a photograph, ca 1861). Ref: NON-ATL-0004. Alexander Turnbull Library, Wellington, New Zealand. http://natlib.govt. nz/records/22914243.

Page 100: Artist unknown: Te Whiti. Nelson, 1883. Ward, John P: Wanderings with the Maori prophets Te Whiti and Tohu ... from their arrival in Christchurch in April 1882 until their return to Parihaka in March 1882. Nelson, Bond, Finney & Co., 1883. Ref: PUBL-0113-01. Alexander Turnbull Library, Wellington, New Zealand. http://natlib.govt.nz/records/23110535.

Page 124: John McKenzie. Ref: 1/1-006726-G. Alexander Turnbull Library, Wellington, New Zealand. http://natlib.govt.nz/records/22829385.

Page 133: Portrait of William Pember Reeves. Ref: 1/2-031782-F. Alexander Turnbull Library, Wellington, New Zealand. http://natlib.govt.nz/records/23208478.

Page 154: Richard John Seddon. Seddon family: Photographs relating to Premier Richard John Seddon and his family. Ref: 1/2-047794-F. Alexander Turnbull Library, Wellington, New Zealand. http://natlib.govt.nz/records/22667872

Page 160: James Carroll. General Assembly Library:Parliamentary portraits. Ref: 35mm-00136-d-F. Alexander Turnbull Library, Wellington, New Zealand. http://natlib.govt.nz/ records/22742338.

Page 164: Sir Maui Wiremu Pomare. S P Andrew Ltd: Portrait negatives. Ref: 1/1-

ACKNOWLEDGEMENTS

019098-F. Alexander Turnbull Library, Wellington, New Zealand. http://natlib.govt.nz/records/23010076.

Page 178: Sir Joseph George Ward. Schmidt, Herman John, 1872-1959:Portrait and landscape negatives, Auckland district. Ref: 1/1-001806-G. Alexander Turnbull Library, Wellington, New Zealand. http://natlib.govt.nz/records/22871604.

Page 184: Politicians and a crowd, outside Parliament Buildings, upon the declaration of war with Germany. Smith, Sydney Charles, 1888-1972: Photographs of New Zealand. Ref: 1/2-045239-G. Alexander Turnbull Library, Wellington, New Zealand. http://natlib.govt.nz/records/22472392.

Page 187: Robert Semple addressing workers in Auckland. Ref: 1/2-044237-F. Alexander Turnbull Library, Wellington, New Zealand. http://natlib.govt.nz/records/22574345.

Page 192: Francis Henry Dillon Bell. New Zealand Free Lance: Photographic prints and negatives. Ref: PAColl-5469-012. Alexander Turnbull Library, Wellington, New Zealand. http://natlib.govt.nz/records/23106663.

Page 203: William Ferguson Massey. Schmidt, Herman John, 1872-1959: Portrait and landscape negatives, Auckland district. Ref: 1/1-001538-F. Alexander Turnbull Library, Wellington, New Zealand. http://natlib.govt.nz/records/22773582.

Page 213: John Alfred Alexander Lee, Labour Under-Secretary, giving a speech (Orakei, Auckland?). Whites Aviation Ltd: Photographs. Ref: WA-67319-G. Alexander Turnbull Library, Wellington, New Zealand. http://natlib.govt.nz/records/22857067.

Page 218: S P Andrew Ltd. S P Andrew Ltd: Photograph of Frank Milner. Ref: PAColl-8998. Alexander Turnbull Library, Wellington, New Zealand. http://natlib.govt.nz/records/22666853.

Page 227: Elizabeth Reid McCombs. Gustafson, Barry:Photographs, negatives and albums used in Barry Gustafson's biography of Michael Joseph Savage, and other photographs originally belonging to P C Webb and Sidney George Holland. Ref: 1/2-150372-F. Alexander Turnbull Library, Wellington, New Zealand. http://natlib.govt.nz/records/23136870.

Page 233: Joseph Gordon Coates. New Zealand. Department of Internal Affairs. War History Branch: Photographs relating to World War 1914-1918, World War 1939-1945, occupation of Japan, Korean War, and Malayan Emergency. Ref: 1/2-036287-F. Alexander Turnbull Library, Wellington, New Zealand. http://natlib.govt.nz/records/23042052.

Page 245: Lord Bledisloe. Crown Studios Ltd:Negatives and prints. Ref: 10x8-2186-F. Alexander Turnbull Library, Wellington, New Zealand. http://natlib.govt.nz/records/22820677.

Page 255: Michael Joseph Savage on the campaign trail. Ref: 1/2-051739-F. Alexander Turnbull Library, Wellington, New Zealand. http://natlib.govt.nz/records/22317948.

Page 262: Tahupotiki Wiremu Ratana. Blundell, W G:Lantern slides. Ref: PA11-058-04. Alexander Turnbull Library, Wellington, New Zealand. http://natlib.govt.nz/records/23049464.

Page 267: Walter Nash. New Zealand. Department of Internal Affairs. War History Branch: Photographs relating to World War 1914-1918, World War 1939-1945, occupation of Japan, Korean War, and Malayan Emergency. Ref: 1/2-036300-F. Alexander Turnbull Library, Wellington, New Zealand. http://natlib.govt.nz/records/22898065.

Page 276: William Downie Stewart, London, England. Original photographic prints and postcards from file print collection, Box 15. Ref: PAColl-7081-59. Alexander Turnbull Library, Wellington, New Zealand. http://natlib.govt.nz/records/22326843.

Page 284: Ernest Rutherford. Tourist and Publicity. Ref: 1/2-035078-F. Alexander Turnbull Library, Wellington, New Zealand. http://natlib.govt.nz/records/23218542.

Page 289: Carl August Berendsen. S P Andrew Ltd:Portrait negatives. Ref: 1/2-043579-F. Alexander Turnbull Library, Wellington, New Zealand. http://natlib.govt.nz/records/22852335.

Page 297: Apirana Turupa Ngata. Ref: 1/4-021044-F. Alexander Turnbull Library, Wellington, New Zealand. http://natlib.govt.nz/records/23254047.

Page 302: Apirana Ngata speaking outside Ngati Raukawa meeting house, Otaki. New Zealand Free Lance: Photographic prints and negatives. Ref: 1/2-058067-F. Alexander Turnbull Library, Wellington, New Zealand. http://natlib.govt.nz/records/22674940.

Page 309: Michael Joseph Savage. Ref: 1/2-053946-F. Alexander Turnbull Library, Wellington, New Zealand. http://natlib.govt.nz/records/23084754.

Page 312: Edward Puttick. New Zealand. Department of Internal Affairs. War History Branch:Photographs relating to World War 1914-1918, World War 1939-1945, occupation of Japan, Korean War, and Malayan Emergency. Ref: PAColl-5547-015. Alexander Turnbull Library, Wellington, New Zealand. http://natlib.govt.nz/records/22904346.

Page 322: General Auchinleck decorating Lieutenant Colonel Howard Karl Kippenberger with the DSO. New Zealand. Department of Internal Affairs. War History Branch:Photographs relating to World War 1914-1918, World War 1939-1945, occupation of Japan, Korean War, and Malayan Emergency. Ref: DA-02166-F. Alexander Turnbull Library, Wellington, New Zealand. http://natlib.govt.nz/records/22899092.

Page 324: Creator unknown: Photograph of Peter Fraser reading before microphone. Ref: PAColl-8211. Alexander Turnbull Library, Wellington, New Zealand. http://natlib.govt.nz/records/23183308.

Page 338: Portrait of Charles Hazlitt Upham, VC and Bar. New Zealand. Department of Internal Affairs. War History Branch:Photographs relating to World War 1914-1918, World War 1939-1945, occupation of Japan, Korean War, and Malayan Emergency. Ref: DA-06981. Alexander Turnbull Library, Wellington, New Zealand. http://natlib.govt.nz/records/22594286.

Page 345: Prime Minister John Marshall opens the second National Development Conference, Parliament, Wellington, New Zealand. Further negatives of the Evening Post newspaper. Ref: EP/1972/1340-F. Alexander Turnbull Library, Wellington, New Zealand. http://natlib.govt.nz/records/23250317.

Page 358: Prime Minister Mr Holland. Negatives of the Evening Post newspaper. Ref: 114/346/10-G. Alexander Turnbull Library, Wellington, New Zealand. http://natlib.govt.nz/records/22912933.

Page 368: Edmund Hillary giving speech. Crown Studios Ltd:Negatives and prints. Ref: 1/4-108274-F. Alexander Turnbull Library, Wellington, New Zealand. http://natlib.govt.nz/records/22706268.

Page 374: Thomas Lachlan MacDonald. Negatives of the Evening Post newspaper. Ref: 114/210/13/3-F. Alexander Turnbull Library, Wellington, New Zealand. http://natlib.govt.nz/records/23224580.